Managing Ancient Monuments:
An Integrated Approach

Managing Ancient Monuments:
An Integrated Approach

Edited by
André Q. Berry and Ian W. Brown

Gwasanaeth Archaeoleg Clwyd Archaeology Service

forms part of the Heritage Group within the Department of Development and
Tourism, Clwyd County Council.

In association with:

association of County Archaeological Officers

ACAO COUNTRYSIDE CONSERVATION AND MANAGEMENT SUB-COMMITTEE
The aims and objectives of the sub-committee are the identification of good practice in archaeology and
countryside conservation management and the dissemination of such information to ACAO members
and others; the promotion and provision of training in techniques of sites and landscapes management;
encouragement to farmers and statutory bodies in the development of their roles as integrated land
managers; and increasing public awareness of the inter-relationship of archaeology and the countryside
through interpretation, presentation and other appropriate measures.

Designed and typeset by *Design*+**PRINT** Clwyd County Council

Published by Clwyd Archaeology Service, Clwyd County Council, Department of Development and Tourism, Shire Hall, Mold. Clwyd. CH7 6NB.

ISBN 0 900121 99 8

Front cover:

Flint Castle, Clwyd (N.G.R. SJ 247 733), Scheduled Ancient Monument F3 in the guardianship of Cadw: Welsh Historic Monuments. Looking north north west, with the Dee estuary (Site of Special Scientific Interest, Ramsar site and Special Protection Area) in the background.

© Copyright Clwyd-Powys Archaeological Trust. Ref. 87-C-91.

Contents

Foreword by the Chairman of Clwyd County Council   VII

Rhagair y Cadeirydd   VIII

List of Contributors   IX

Introduction:

Integrated Environmental Resource Management and the Conservation of the
Archaeological Heritage - Ian W. Brown.   XI

Data for Nature Conservation in Statutory and Voluntary
Heritage Agencies - Paul T. Harding.   I

The Sum of all its Parts: An Overview of the Politics of Integrated
Management in England - Graham Fairclough.   17

Integrated Management Plans: Historic Scotland's Experience -
Lesley Macinnes and Katherine Ader.   29

The National Trust's Approach to Integrated Conservation Management -
David Thackray, Rob Jarman and Jo Burgon.   37

The Countryside Stewardship Scheme: Testing the Way Forward for
Integrated Countryside Management - Maddy Jago.   49

The Nature Conservation Importance of Standing Remains -
John Thompson.   61

Conservation of Bats in the Management of Ancient Monuments -
A.M. Hutson.   71

Caer Drewyn: Hillfort and "Boulder Field" Habitat -
André Q. Berry and Brian W. Fox.   79

Langcliffe Quarry: A Balancing Act - Robert White.   87

Forestry Management and Archaeology - Graham Lee.   97

"Hen Caerwys": A Deserted Medieval Settlement Under Woodland -
André Q. Berry.   105

Heathland and Grassland Management for Conservation -
Robin J. Pakeman.   113

Lordenshaws: A Management Agreement for an Historic Landscape -
Paul Frodsham, Andrew Miller and Albert Weir.   123

Wetlands - Integration for Habitat Conservation, Ecology,
Sustainable Exploitation and Archaeology: An Overview -
Dr. Margaret Cox.   129

Integrated Management of Archaeology in Coastal Waters -
Ben Ferrari.   135

Salt Marsh Loss to Managed Retreat in Essex: An Integrated Approach
to the Archaeological Management of a Changing Coastline -
P.J. Gilman, D.G. Buckley and S. Wallis.   143

Archaeology and Coastal Zone Management -
Antony Firth.   155

The Role of the *Protection of Wrecks Act 1973* in Integrated Management
of the Marine Archaeological Heritage: A Personal View -
Ian Oxley.   169

Assessment, Stabilisation and Management of an Environmentally
Threatened Seventeenth Century Shipwreck off Duart Point, Mull -
Colin J.M. Martin.   181

Who's Who in the Environment? -
The Environment Council.   191

Chairman's Foreword

Since the work of W.G. Hoskins and Oliver Rackham there has been an increasing awareness of the role of human influence in the form and development of the landscape and, more recently, of the importance of our archaeological heritage in providing habitats for wildlife - from shipwrecks as artificial reefs for marine life to the crevices in masonry monuments as roost sites for bats.

Clwyd County Council's commitment to an integrated approach to the management of the countryside and ancient monuments was recognised through the appointment of an environmentalist to work alongside our archaeologists in managing and promoting the cultural heritage. Such an approach, we hope, has resulted in the more balanced management of our monuments and has certainly seen increasing public enthusiasm and support for archaeology.

Clwyd, of course, is not alone in having the vision to realise the importance of an integrated approach to management of the cultural heritage and this volume reflects the range of such work being undertaken by many organisations across the UK. It is based on the proceedings of a seminar of the same name held at Birmingham University in September 1993 and organised by Clwyd Archaeology Service in association with the ACAO Countryside Conservation and Management Sub-Committee. The volume explores the many facets of integrated management both terrestrial and maritime, from the limits of our territorial waters to the built heritage.

As with the companion volume "Erosion on Archaeological Earthworks: Its Prevention, Control and Repair" I am sure that this volume will make a valued contribution to the conservation of our archaeological heritage, particularly in promoting the inter-relationship of the many disciplines that comprise our historic landscape.

Peter G.A. Walker JP
Chairman, Clwyd County Council

Rhagair y Cadeirydd

Yn sgil gweithiau llenyddol W.G. Hoskins ac Oliver Rackham mae'r ymwybyddiaeth o'r ffaith fod dyn yn gallu dylanwadu ar ffurf a datblygiad ein tirwedd wedi cynyddu fwyfwy, ac yn ddiweddar hefyd mae pobol wedi dod yn fwy ymwybydol o bwysigrwydd ein hetifeddiath archaeolegol fel mannau sy'n cynnig cynefin i'n bywyd gwyllt - hynny yw, o longddrylliadau, sy'n gallu creu riff artiffisial er mwyn i greaduriaid y môr wneud ou cartref ynddyn nhw, i holltau mewn cofadeiladau cerrig sy'n troi'n fannau clwydo i ystlumod.

Daeth ymroddiad Cyngor Sir Clwyd i'r syniad o reoli cefn gwlad a henebion ar-y-cyd i'r amlwg pan benodwyd amgylchfydwr i weithio law-yn-llaw â'n harchaeolegwyr i reoli ac i hyrwyddo'r etifeddiaeth diwylliannol. Mae hynny, gobeithiwn, wedi arwain at reolaeth mwy cytbwys o'n cofadeiladau ac yn sicr mae wedi creu brwdfrydedd a chefnogaeth cyhoeddus tuag at archaeoleg.

Nid gan Clwyd yn unig, wrth gwrs, mae'r weledigaeth i sylweddoli pwysigrwydd rheolaeth integredig o'n hetifeddiaeth diwylliannol, ac mae'r gyfrol hon yn dangos ystod eang y gwaith sy'n cael ei wneud gan nifer o drefniadaethau ar draws y Deyrnas Unedig. Mae'r gweithgarwch hwn yn tarddu o seminar, oedd yn dwyn yr un enw, ac a gynhaliwyd ym Mhrifysgol Birmingham ym Medi 1993; Gwasanaeth Archaeolegol Clwyd a'i drefnodd mewn cyd-weithrediad ag Is-Bwyllgor Cadwraeth a Rheolaeth Cefn Gwlad yr ACAO. Mae'r gyfrol hon felly yn archwilio'r gwahanol agweddau ar reolaeth integredig, hynny yw, ar y ddaear a than y môr, o ffiniau pellaf ein dyfroedd tiriogaethol hyd at ein hadeiladau treftadol.

Rwy'n sicr y bydd y gyfrol hon, fel y llal fu'n trafod "Erydiad ar Wrthgloddiau: Sut i'w Atal, ei Reoli a'i Atgyweirio", yn gwneud cyfraniad gwerthfawr i'r gwaith o warchod ein hetifeddiaeth archaeolegol, ac yn enwedig yn y gwaith o hyrwyddo cyd-weithio rhwng y gwahanol ddisgyblaethau sy'n gofalu am ein tirwedd hanesyddol.

Peter G.A. Walker JP
Cadeirydd, Cyngor Sir Clwyd.

List of Contributors:

Katherine Ader   Northern Ecological Services, Clifton, Dinnet, Aboyne. Aberdeen. AB34 5JY.

André Q. Berry   Clwyd Archaeology Service, Department of Development and Tourism, Shire Hall, Mold. Clwyd. CH7 6NB.

Ian W. Brown   Clwyd Archaeology Service, Department of Development and Tourism, Shire Hall, Mold. Clwyd. CH7 6NB.

D.G. Buckley   Planning Department, Essex County Council, County Hall, Chelmsford. Essex. CM1 1LF.

Jo Burgon   The National Trust, 33 Sheep Street, Cirencester. Gloucestershire. GL7 1QW.

Dr. Margaret Cox   Department of Conservation Sciences, Bournemouth University, Dorset House, Talbot Campus, Fern Barrow, Poole. Dorset. BH12 5BB.

Graham Fairclough   English Heritage, 23 Savile Row, London. W1X 1AB.

Ben Ferrari   Royal Commission on the Historical Monuments of England, National Monuments Record Centre, Kemble Drive, Swindon. SN2 2GZ.

Antony Firth   Department of Archaeology, University of Southampton, Southampton. SO9 5NH.

Paul Frodsham   Northumberland National Park Headquarters, Eastburn, South Park, Hexham. Northumberland. NE46 1BS.

P.J. Gilman   Planning Department, Essex County Council, County Hall, Chelmsford. Essex. CM1 1LF.

Paul T. Harding   Environmental Information Centre, Institute of Terrestrial Ecology, Monks Wood, Abbots Ripton, Huntingdon. Cambridgeshire. PE17 2LS.

A.M. Hutson   The Bat Conservation Trust, The London Ecology Centre, 45 Shelton Street, London. WC2H 9HJ.

Maddy Jago   Countryside Commission, South West Regional Office, Bridge House, Sion Place, Clifton Down, Bristol. BS8 4AS.

Rob Jarman   The National Trust, 33 Sheep Street, Cirencester. Gloucestershire. GL7 1QW.

Graham Lee   North York Moors National Park, The Old Vicarage, Bondgate, Helmsley, York. YO6 5BP.

Lesley Macinnes   Historic Scotland, Longmore House, Salisbury Place, Edinburgh. EH9 1SH.

Colin J.M. Martin   Scottish Institute of Maritime Studies, University of St. Andrews, Fife. KY16 9AJ.

Andrew Miller   Northumberland National Park Headquarters, Eastburn, South Park, Hexham. Northumberland. NE46 1BS.

Ian Oxley   Archaeological Diving Unit, Scottish Institute of Maritime Studies, University of St. Andrews, Fife. KY16 9AJ.

Robin J. Pakeman   Institute of Terrestrial Ecology, Monks Wood, Abbots Ripton, Huntingdon. Cambridgeshire. PE17 2LS.

David Thackray   The National Trust, 33 Sheep Street, Cirencester. Gloucestershire. GL7 1QW.

John Thompson   Shotton Cottage, Godings Lane, Harmer Hill, Shrewsbury. Shropshire. SY4 3HB.

S. Wallis   Planning Department, Dorset County Council, County Hall, Dorchester. Dorset. DT1 1XJ.

Albert Weir   Northumberland National Park Headquarters, Eastburn, South Park, Hexham. Northumberland. NE46 1BS.

Robert White   Yorkshire Dales National Park, Yorebridge House, Bainbridge, Leyburn. North Yorkshire. DL8 3BP.

X

Integrated Environmental Resource Management and the Conservation of the Archaeological Heritage

Ian W. Brown

County Heritage Officer, Clwyd County Council

The relationship between environmental and archaeological resource management is close. Historic sites frequently form significant components of the landscape and are important for their wildlife or geological interest. Likewise, the concept of the "historic landscape" is now recognised as being capable of wider environmental management. The management of the historic resource comprises the integration of what may be conflicting land-use demands (archaeology, access, wildlife and agriculture for example) influenced by society's values and financial constraints.

The human population is expanding and more and more demands for living space, food production, development, transport provision and recreational needs are being placed on a finite amount of land. Usher (1973) defines "biological conservation", as *"essentially concerned with the interaction between man and the environment"*. Thus the *"fulfilment of conservation objectives for a biological resource requires the resource's management in perpetuity on the basis of a sustained production of the resource.... and a, sustained demand on the resource or environment by man"*.

In producing this definition and, as he states, broadly equating conservation *per se* with biological management, it is recognised that "management" can take many forms; it may involve controlled "neglect" or direct human interference. The essential feature, however, is that there should be "sustention in perpetuity" and that an ecosystem should not be altered to such an extent that biological production is eliminated. Thus over-exploitation or under-exploitation should be eliminated for any management practice if that natural resource is to be conserved.

This definition is useful when considering the management of the historic resource in that the sustenance of the productivity of the overlying biological structure can not only serve as a protector of the underlying archaeology, but is also crucial for the maintenance of historic sites and landscapes alike. Thus, over-exploitation of an ecosystem, for example by heavy recreation pressure or overgrazing, or under-exploitation resulting in an increase in shrubs or woody species, for example on limestone grassland, can drastically alter the landscape and result in degradation of the archaeology.

Of course nothing is clearcut, and it is sometimes argued that in the pursuit of "archaeological correctness" the sustainability of biological resources can be ignored. Cox (this volume) refers to problems on wetland sites, and the proposals forwarded in the late 1980s to clearfell limestone woodland of significant landscape and ecological importance to expose the Iron Age hillfort of Castell Cawr at Abergele, Clwyd (N.G.R. SH 936 767), provide ample evidence of failure to provide holistic solutions to management problems.

Pakeman (this volume) outlines the loss of heathland, grassland and moorland in Britain, predominantly to agriculture and forestry, the dramatic declines stated having resulted in loss of habitat and species diversity and substantial alteration to the landscape. Caused mainly by the concentration of national Government policy, assisted by EU funded incentive schemes, on increased food production, such environmental degradation has seen a

Plate 1. The interior of Castell Dinas Brân, overlooking Llangollen and the Dee valley.

corresponding degradation and loss of the historic resource (Wathern et al., 1987; Brown, 1994). Despite moves toward decreases in agricultural production incentives through ESA, Set-aside and other schemes such as Countryside Stewardship as outlined by Jago (this volume), important wildlife habitats and historic landscape features such as hedgerows, continue to be lost to a rapid extent. As Lee describes (this volume), although early forest plantings before the use of deep ploughing paradoxically conserved rather than destroyed archaeological sites, modern forestry operations can and do cause significant damage. The conservation of the archaeological heritage is, therefore, intimately associated with the conservation of the natural resource. As Harding (this volume) discusses, however, up to date information on the natural resource is essential if both are to be conserved.

It follows, therefore, that resource management in its widest form will entail the consideration of a wide variety of factors and a wide variety of disciplines will become involved. Thus, as Frodsham, Miller and Weir discuss (this volume) an "integrated" approach to conservation where archaeology, ecology, landscape, land-use and public access are all

considered together as part of a single complex, is vital to the development of management prescriptions for both historic sites and landscapes. This point is further emphasised (this volume) by Macinnes and Ader in relation to Historic Scotland's experience and by Thackray, Jarman and Burgon in discussion of the approach adopted by The National Trust. Archaeological conservation should not be seen as an end in itself but as part of a wider holistic view of the environment. It is in the use of this concept that perhaps the most acceptable and enduring means of conserving archaeological sites and landscapes lies.

Not all archaeology however is manifest below ground, and as Thompson outlines (this volume) ruined historic structures, from megalith to castle to industrial site, can provide a wide variety of ecological habitat and great species diversity. Thus the stone ramparts of Caer Drewyn hillfort in Clwyd provide an important habitat for species of lichen (Berry and Fox, this volume). Likewise, archaeological sites are often important for rare fauna and Hutson details the importance of standing masonry to the 14 species of bat resident in the UK (this volume).

The approach being adopted in Clwyd to the long-term management of Castell Dinas Brân, near Llangollen (N.G.R. SJ 223 431; Berry, 1992; Plate 1) is an example of an integrated approach to resource management referred to above.

Owned and administered by Clwyd County Council, Castell Dinas Brân is located at the eastern end of the Dee valley and lies at the summit of a prominent hill rising to 270m. The total land holding of scheduled area is 3.7ha. The medieval castle, built by the Welsh lords of Powys Fadog in the 13th century, appears to stand in the north western corner of a much older fortification, that of an Iron Age hillfort, the defensive bank skirting the precipitous slopes of the hill. Terrace-like features within the interior may possibly be the remains of hut emplacements. The castle has remained in a ruinous condition since AD1277.

Apart from the monuments, the hill is important from an ecological, landscape and recreational point of view. The hilltop upon which Dinas Brân stands is a geological SSSI, comprising calcareous shales and siltstones of a type uncommon in the region. Due to the calcareous nature of the bedrock, the hill supports a diverse flora characterised by lime-loving species such as small scabious (*Scabiosa columbaria*), thyme (*Thymus drucei*) and harebell (*Campanula rotundifolia*). It is also notable for supporting a number of uncommon species which occur more frequently on the nearby Eglwyseg Rocks. The hill dominates the town of Llangollen and, located only 1.5km from the town centre, forms a significant although not intensively used informal recreation site.

The broad framework for long-term management and investigation of the site, involving specialists drawn from the fields of archaeology, ecology, land and recreation management has the following aims:

• To investigate the archaeology of Dinas Brân and its environs including the surrounding upland fringe;

• To interpret the archaeology, landscape, wildlife and geology of Dinas Brân and its environs to the general public, particularly as an educational resource;

• To explore the potential for excavation at Dinas Brân with the objective of enhanced public understanding and display.

In the wider landscape context:

• To investigate the archaeological potential of the Dee floodplain and its hinterland;

• To implement field survey of the upland fringe;

• To investigate and conserve ecological and geological habitats and exposures and species present;

• To develop a network of recreational routes and visitor access points to key identified landscape components.

Dinas Brân is not, however, being viewed in isolation. It is very much a component part of the historic landscape comprising the Dee valley, Eglwyseg Rocks and flanking upland areas of the Llantysilio Range. Its investigation, management and interpretation should endeavour to set the site within its contemporary historic landscape context, as far as is possible, and should embrace the conservation and recreational use of the valleys corridor, Berwyn fringe and upland area as a whole as well as integrating with similar investigations at Caer Drewyn hillfort at the confluence of the Dee and Edeirnion valleys, some 15km distant.

In recent years there has been a substantial increase in interest in maritime, freshwater and coastal zone archaeology. This consists not only of the archaeology of specific vessels and wreck sites but also of ports and installations, trade and seafaring, communities and communications and the palaeoarchaeological record.

As in the consideration of terrestrial sites and landscapes, it is to the concept of integrated management solutions between the natural and archaeological resource, as outlined by Firth (this volume), that attention must be focused if both are to be conserved; both being threatened by natural and human-made developmental pressures, as described by Gilman, Buckley and Wallis (this volume) on the Essex coast. In comparison with terrestrial environments, however, little is known about the management of the underwater archaeological heritage, nor indeed about the management of underwater ecosystems in general and the ways in which archaeological remains interact with them (Oxley, this volume). It follows, therefore, that integrated systems of management for both underwater wrecks and for wider protected zones is made that much more difficult to achieve. This is further complicated by the fact that, unless they are specifically protected, underwater sites in UK waters can be quite legally disturbed or destroyed, compounded by the fact that the extent of the resource is itself by no means clear.

As a starting point, however, there are parallel aims between archaeological and nature conservation interests. Ferrari (this volume) outlines the problems associated with fishing interests and marine and archaeological conservation, indicating that forms of protected designated zones could form a basis for integrated management. Oxley details encouraging developments in this context in the Lundy Marine Nature Reserve in the Bristol Channel whilst, in the consideration of the archaeological investigation of wreck sites, Martin (this volume) discusses the necessity of an understanding of the environment of the seabed and *"mechanisms for destruction, dispersal, integration and stabilisation"* before the observed remains can be interpreted in archaeological terms.

Clearly therefore, in both the terrestrial and maritime environments, there are areas of common interest between the various disciplines and such common ground necessitates interdisciplinary, integrated solutions to management.

The papers presented in this volume, written by eminent practitioners in their own fields, present these areas of common interest as a means of widening debate in what is essentially a new approach to archaeological study.

● References

Berry, A.Q. (1992) Integrating Archaeology and the Countryside: Clwyd County Council's Approach to Archaeological Sites Management in, Macinnes, L. and Wickham-Jones, C.R. (eds) *All Natural Things: Archaeology and the Green Debate*. Oxford: Oxbow Monograph 21. 155-160.

Brown, I.W. (1994) Archaeological Site Management and Erosion Control: The Environmental Context in, Berry, A.Q. and Brown, I.W. (eds) *Erosion on Archaeological Earthworks: Its Prevention, Control and Repair.* Mold: Clwyd County Council. XI-XIII.

Usher, M.B. (1973) *Biological Management and Conservation*. London: Chapman and Hall.

Wathern, P., Young, S.N., Brown, I.W. and Roberts, D.A. (1987) Upland Policy and Archaeological Resources in North Wales. *Land Use Policy*, 4. 342-346.

Data for Nature Conservation in Statutory and Voluntary Heritage Agencies

Paul T. Harding

Biological Records Centre, Institute of Terrestrial Ecology

● Introduction

Nature conservation includes the protection and study of the present day and recent past flora and fauna, the geology and the geomorphology of the landscape. In Britain, nature conservation is undertaken by four statutory agencies: English Nature (EN), the Countryside Council for Wales (CCW), Scottish Natural Heritage (SNH) and the Joint Nature Conservation Committee (JNCC) which were set up in the *Environmental Protection Act 1990*. Local authorities also have statutory responsibilities for nature conservation as a result of legislation (DoE, 1994). There is a strong voluntary nature conservation movement, focused on the Wildlife Trusts and the Royal Society for the Protection of Birds (RSPB), and on the National Trust (NT) and the National Trust for Scotland (NTS).

It is not unexpected that some sites which have been recognised as being of importance for archaeology and other human-made heritage are also of importance for nature conservation, and *vice versa*. Absence of disturbance, due to traditional types of land use, or the designation of sites for natural or archaeological heritage, have served to protect both types of interest at many sites. This inter-relationship of interests has been reviewed recently by, for example, authors in Lambrick (1985) and Macinnes and

Wickham-Jones (1992), and Macinnes (1993).

Similarly, areas used for military purposes, such as practical training areas, have inadvertently protected many archaeological and natural history features for at least the last 50 years (for example, see Morgan Evans, 1992).

The need for information on the nature conservation value of such heritage and military sites is basic to the success of safeguarding both aspects. It is all too simple for experts in their respective fields to assume that the other type of expert has access to comprehensive information on the features of interest at sites. This is not the case - Scheduled Ancient Monuments (SAMs) and Sites of Special Scientific Interest (SSSI) are based on the best information available at the time; often this information is incomplete, out of date or inaccessible.

Scheduled sites encompass what were believed to be the best examples of their respective types at the time, but additional areas exist outside these sites. Put simplistically, the landscape is a continuum of nature in which are some recognised highspots - the "wider countryside" where nature exists in a largely unprotected state, with the scheduled sites where some measure of protection is afforded through national and local legislative processes. However, the existing systems to protect heritage and nature (e.g. SAMs and SSSIs) are not without problems. For example, the study and protection of Holocene (post-glacial) "geological" features, such as peat bogs, and their unique record of the development of our wildlife, landscape and land use, continues to fall in the gaps between orthodox nature conservation, geology and environmental archaeology (Buckland, Eversham and Dinnin, 1994).

Thus, the archaeological/human-made heritage agencies, which have statutory or charter obligations to protect nature, are faced with several problems to which the availability of information on nature is

International Treaties and Legislation

1. *Ramsar Convention on Wetlands of International Importance Especially as Waterfowl Habitat 1971*

2. *The Convention on International Trade in Endangered Species of Wild Fauna and Flora 1975 (CITES)*

3. *Berne Convention on the Conservation of European Wildlife and Natural Habitats 1979*

4. *Bonn Convention on the Conservation of Migratory Species of Wild Animals 1979*

5. EC Council Directive 79/409 on the *Conservation of Wild Birds 1979*

6. EC Council Directive 92/43 on the *Conservation of Natural Habitats and of Wild Fauna and Flora 1992*

7. *Rio Convention on Biological Diversity 1992*

National Statutes and Circulars

1. *National Trust Act 1907* (NT only)

2. *National Trust for Scotland Order Confirmation Acts 1935 and 1938* (NTS only)

3. *National Parks and Access to the Countryside Act 1949*

4. *Protection of Birds Act 1954-1967*

5. *Countryside Act 1968*

6. *Nature Conservancy Council Act 1973*

7. *Badger Act 1973*

8. *Wild Creatures and Plants Act 1975*

9. Circular 108/77 DoE *Nature Conservation and Planning*

10. *Wildlife and Countryside Act 1981*

11. *Wildlife and Countryside (Amending) Act 1985*

12. *Countryside (Scotland) Act 1987*

13. Circular 27/87 DoE *Nature Conservation*

14. *Environmental Protection Act 1990*

15. Planning Policy Guidance 9: Nature Conservation 1994

Table 1. Legislation relevant to the nature conservation responsibilities of heritage agencies.

central. This paper describes these problems, examines how they are being addressed by six agencies and makes some recommendations about how the problems may be overcome.

● The Need for Information on Nature Conservation

As landowners or land managers, the archaeological/human-made heritage agencies, English Heritage (EH), Historic Scotland (HS) and Cadw: Welsh Historic Monuments, have statutory obligations under the *Countryside (Scotland) Act 1987, Countryside Act 1968* and the *Wildlife and Countryside Act 1981* (WCA) to safeguard and protect wildlife and features of geological importance at the sites in their care. In a similar way, the National Trust (NT), the National Trust for Scotland (NTS) and the Ministry of Defence (MOD) have responsibilities to protect both the archaeological and natural history features of sites in their care. All these agencies are subject to a range of legislation relevant to nature conservation (Table 1) and all take account of nature conservation in the management of sites in their care. Some sites are subject to statutory protection as Sites of Special Scientific Interest, scheduled under WCA. At these and other sites, species protected under Schedules 1, 5 and 8 of WCA, or species and habitats protected under international legislation or conventions, may be present.

The needs for information on nature conservation may be expressed as four basic objectives, which are common to all six agencies:

● 1 To fulfil statutory obligations;

● 2 To advise on key features of importance for nature conservation, such as protected and threatened species;

● 3 To advise on site use and management;

● 4 To promote the interest and enjoyment of the public, where appropriate.

It should be noted that EH, HS and Cadw have overall objectives, regarding nature conservation, which are similar to each other. The two national trusts also have similar overall objectives and their respective charters include explicit reference to the conservation of nature. The Conservation Office of the MOD was set up to support the MOD policy to pursue active conservation measures on its land, in so far as these are compatible with operational and other requirements of the Services.

None of these agencies operate in exactly similar circumstances: for example, even the constraints of the Countryside Acts and WCA affect HS, Cadw and MOD differently from EH, because they are agencies of the Crown and therefore cannot be prosecuted under those Acts.

● Review of the Heritage Agencies

A review, commissioned by EH, of the collection, management and use of data for nature conservation in heritage agencies, national trusts and the Ministry of Defence was undertaken in January to March 1993 (Harding, 1993).

The objectives of the review were:

● To describe the methods used by EH to collect and store information relating to nature conservation, and to assess the current practices in relation to the perceived needs for data within EH as a whole;

● To similarly describe methods and practices in five other national agencies for which nature conservation is only part of their responsibilities or for which nature conservation is an ancillary responsibility;

● To report to EH the findings from the five agencies and to relate the findings to the

needs of EH, identifying examples of good practice.

Each agency was visited on at least one occasion, to interview relevant staff and examine materials and processes used to provide the agencies with information related to nature conservation at sites in their care.

● English Heritage

A Nature Conservation Adviser (NCA) was seconded from EN in April 1990 to work within the Landscape Branch, part of the Technical Services Group of EH. Although now retired, the Adviser is retained as a consultant to EH. In December 1992, EH and EN introduced a joint Statement of Intent to promote greater liaison between the two organisations (see *English Nature* issues 5 and 10, and EH's *Conservation Bulletin* issue 19).

Botanical surveys of Historic Properties, of which there are some 400, have been commissioned from acknowledged specialists. The two-stage surveys draw on existing sources of data and include site visits to assess the importance of sites. The better or more promising sites are surveyed in more detail. In addition, surveys of other groups have been commissioned where appropriate (for example of lichens on walls or of bats). Preliminary and detailed botanical surveys have been completed in the South West Region of EH, and surveys are underway in the South East Region. The NCA carries out some surveys and advisory work himself: most of the advisory work concerns the development of ground maintenance contracts or the preparation of management plans.

Experimental management procedures are being carried out at some sites and detailed records of these trials, and the methods and materials used, are kept on the file for the relevant site. Botanical monitoring related to site management is being carried out at some properties using random quadrats or randomised mini-quadrats within 10m x 10m permanent quadrats.

In addition to the properties in the direct care of EH there are some 13,000 SAMs and 200 registered Historic Parks and Gardens. No attempt has been made to systematically survey these, but the NCA gives advice and has made a study of the relationship between nature conservation and the landscape management of parklands.

All data are managed in paper form and are largely site based. Site files for each property contain records and notes on wildlife/geology and nature conservation issues, together with general correspondence. These files are held "centrally" in at least three locations (EH Registry, Landscape Branch and NCA), but all files do not necessarily contain the same information. Site files are also held at the appropriate regional offices. Survey reports are held by the NCA, the Landscape Branch and the relevant regional office of EH.

The central advisory capacity of the NCA and Landscape Branch is mainly responsive. Comprehensive information is needed at this central level, for example in the preparation of management plans. Regional and site staff are kept informed of matters relating to nature conservation at sites and, in conjunction with EN, the NCA holds several training courses to give EH staff (across disciplines and grades) a better appreciation of nature conservation. However, most dissemination of information depends on personal contact and direct liaison. The NCA has also contributed articles on nature conservation to issues of EH's *Conservation Bulletin* and the *English Heritage Magazine*.

● Cadw: Welsh Historic Monuments

The four Inspectors of Ancient Monuments (IAMs) are based at Cadw headquarters in Cardiff, each covering all types of properties and monuments in his/her region. There are some 130 properties in care throughout Wales, with additional scheduled monuments in the care of other agencies. Cadw does not have in-house ecological expertise and obtains its ecological

information and advice through expert consultation. Although Cadw collaborates with CCW (and formerly with NCC), there is little overlap between Cadw properties in care and SSSIs, although designated properties abut, as at Carreg-Cennen Castle (N.G.R. SN 667 191).

In Clwyd, the post of Archaeological Sites Management Officer, funded jointly by Cadw, CCW and Clwyd County Council, was set up in 1990 with responsibility to promote the inter-relationship of archaeology and countryside in the County (Berry, 1992).

The initial phase of ecological surveys has been directed to sites where active repair and management of the property is being undertaken. The Dyfed Wildlife Trust (DWT) was commissioned for one year, beginning in August 1992, to compile information on the ecological interest and species occurring at three properties: Wiston Castle (N.G.R. SN 023 181), Haverfordwest Priory (N.G.R. SM 957 152) and Lamphey Palace (N.G.R. SN 018 009). The work included site surveys by relevant specialists and the collation of existing information from sources available to DWT. Priority was given to data on ferns and lichens (especially on walls), ground flora, bats and invertebrates. The results, as written site reports, with map based summaries, highlight particular features of interest and propose suitable management. Further commissioned surveys were undertaken in Dyfed during 1993. Biological information on other properties has been acquired from several sources, for example on bat roosts at Carew Castle (SN 044 037) from the Pembrokeshire Coast National Park ecologist.

All information from surveys is, or will be, held on paper files at Cadw HQ. The survey data collated by DWT is not intended to be held on a database at Cadw. The data collated by DWT, with support from Cadw, will remain the property of DWT.

● Historic Scotland

Historic Scotland has retained ecological consultants, Northern Ecological Services (NES) to carry out a survey of the ecological interest of its properties in care. There are some 330 such properties, for which HS has overall responsibility for site management. This work has been carried out over three years (April 1991 to March 1994) with a research grant from the Scottish Office. In addition, there are over 5000 scheduled monuments which are not being covered by the biological survey, but which are visited and reported on at intervals, normally of between every two and four years, by one of the ten regionally-based HS wardens.

The survey by NES has given priority to general biotope descriptions and listing the species of vascular plants present, based, where possible, on existing sources of information and on brief site visits. Some zoological information was collected where appropriate.

The NES survey followed a five stage procedure:

● 1 Compile data from SNH via the appropriate regional or area offices (Scottish Wildlife Trust [SWT] and local records centres were not consulted);

● 2 Assess the botanical data collated by BSBI on behalf of HS in the late 1980s (where available);

● 3 Visit the site and conduct a Phase 1 Habitat Survey (plus target notes) (see England Field Unit, 1990), including preparation of standard coloured habitat maps. Compile lists of notable and characteristic vascular plants, and any other flora and fauna observed;

● 4 Confirm any problematic plant identifications and consult local BSBI vice-county recorders and published floras;

● 5 Consult local bat and bird specialists where appropriate.

Site reports have been prepared for individual sites, following a standard pattern. Ecologically more important sites are usually dealt with in greatest detail, especially regarding site management. These reports are intended to be read and understood by non-biologists, such as HS architects and area superintendents, as well as ecologists, and include detailed maps locating biotopes and vegetation types, features of particular interest and areas described in the sections on site management. Management recommendations in the NES reports are being included in site management specifications for maintenance contractors, with effect from 1994.

At some sites, long-term changes in management have been proposed which would need monitoring and review over a period of 5, 10 or more years. The reports also describe the potential for developing interpretation of the wildlife interest of the site and, as part of their contract, NES have begun preparation of interpretative material for six properties.

Independent of the survey by NES, a consortium of HS, SNH, SWT and the Royal Household, with a specially recruited Project Officer, has prepared a draft management plan for the 260 hectare Holyrood Royal Park (N.G.R. NT 27 SE).

All the information collected or collated by NES is held in paper form, including notebooks and maps. Although HS maintains a database on its monuments, mainly of information relating to the land holding, a computerised database has not been developed or employed to handle data from the NES survey, but the reports are held as word processor files.

Copies of the NES survey reports are kept in at least two locations within HS, and as paper copies and word processor files by NES. The reports on individual properties in care are disseminated to HS works staff as appropriate. HS hold the copyright of the data collected on its behalf by NES, although some data are secondary and may be the copyright of other agencies (such as

SNH). A programme for interpretation of the wildlife interest of properties is being developed by HS, building on the work of the survey.

● National Trust

The National Trust began biological surveys of its properties in about 1975 and its own Biological Survey Team (BST) was formed in 1979. In 1992 the BST consisted of five permanent full-time surveyors and one technical support post, plus three part-time volunteers and access to managerial and support staff. The work of the BST is augmented by the Chief Adviser on Nature Conservation and his three specialist Advisers who contribute to the overall resource of information on properties as part of their duties. Regional surveyors have been appointed in the Lake District and North Wales. There is also a Regional Nature Conservation Adviser for Northern Ireland. Their roles overlap with those of both the BST and the Advisers and they join the BST, when it is in the region, and supply data to the team and the Advisers.

The BST surveys NT properties (both owned and leased) in England, Wales and Northern Ireland. Not all properties are surveyed by the BST: those which are managed by conservation agencies usually are omitted and areas of intensively used agricultural land are not surveyed in detail. There is a rolling programme to survey properties and when the first phase of survey was completed in 1989, some 80%, by area, of properties had been covered.

Since 1989 the BST has been returning to the regions covered in the early years of the survey, to update surveys and management recommendations, and to survey for the first time those sites which have been acquired since the initial round (approximately 20% of properties). The rolling programme of surveys occupies approximately 80% of the work of the BST with 8 to 12 weeks (May to August) each year being spent in the field by the whole team. Any one property is usually visited only once and therefore cannot be

surveyed in great detail, but normally several of the BST take part in each visit. Surveys identify features of interest and provide a resource of information for the specialist advisers and regional staff. The BST identifies and proposes the management requirements necessary to maintain and enhance the nature conservation interest of properties.

The basic survey normally provides, for each site:

● A Phase 1 Habitat Survey summary of biotopes and land use including information on species composition of vegetation, on any notable species and on vegetation structure;

● Maps of vegetation types and communities, and of areas of particular interest;

● Lists of species noted, with emphasis on plants, invertebrates and birds (NB these are not comprehensive species inventories);

● Evaluations of features of importance;

● Management guidelines.

The survey of zoological groups is based on assessing the most important biotopes at a site, concentrating effort on those and on the particular groups likely to include species of significance, for example indicators or rarities. Data on freshwater organisms is not as complete as for terrestrial flora and fauna. Because the Trust owns very little land below low water mark, it holds few data on marine wildlife. Information on features of geological/geomorphological interest and soils is derived mainly from secondary sources.

During the period spent on site survey in the region, the BST seek data from local sources, such as local records centres, county wildlife trusts, local specialist groups, the regional offices of the statutory conservation agencies and property staff. Data collected by the Advisers during site visits are usually placed on site files which are then accessed by the BST when the property is surveyed, as part of the general background data-gathering prior to survey.

The BST consists of experienced specialists and most validation of data is carried out by members of the team, with support where necessary from the Advisers. Data from local sources usually are taken at face value although some unusual records will be queried with the originators.

The results of the field surveys, including specimens for identification collected in the summer months, together with any other collated information, are worked through to written reports during the remainder of the year. The site reports are compiled by members of the BST, usually one botanist and one zoologist.

Notes compiled during site visits, subsequent identifications and any material from other sources are normally held in unique paper files at the Cirencester office. These records go back to 1977 and, in some cases, even earlier. Copies of the BST survey reports and associated maps are held at Cirencester, at the appropriate regional office and at the property itself. Data are exchanged with many organisations, including the statutory conservation agencies.

Reports prepared from 1989 onwards have been produced using word processed text and the original text files are held at Cirencester. Databases for selected groups (rare plants, birds, bats and habitats) have been compiled using the PARADOX database management system. A pilot study to develop information technology within the Trust has been conducted and development of the use of Geographical Information Systems (GIS) in the NT is under active consideration.

● National Trust for Scotland

NTS has employed an ecologist since 1989 and most of the Ranger staff carry out some recording of wildlife. An ecological survey began formally in 1991 to cover over 50 properties which are open to the public. Several of these properties are managed in partnership with other agencies. Properties covered in the ecological survey contain significant areas of land, mainly semi-natural areas, woodland and farmland, but also include a few which are mainly gardens. A set of Ecological Survey Guidance Notes describe the survey and the format of site files in detail. The Notes also include examples of the recording forms and *pro formas* used.

The results of the survey are being compiled as Ecological Survey Files for each site, containing all available ecological information about the site. Most of the information gathered by the survey relates to biotopes and land use (Phase I Habitat Survey), vascular plant species and plant communities. Information on fauna is more patchy, with that for birds and bats being the most readily available. Most of the data collection is by NTS staff, with a little information from outside sources. Almost no data come from volunteers. The results of surveys by the NCC Uplands Survey Team, covering all upland SSSIs in the care of NTS, have been made available by SNH. Data validation is based on the experience and judgement of the ecologist. In 1992, two specialists were contracted to provide information on the *Lepidoptera* and lichens at some sites. Recording by Ranger staff provides information which updates the ecological survey (e.g. additional species and observations on the effects of management) and is to be trawled in annually from each site to update the site file.

The format of the ecological survey records, as site files, is such that they should be available and intelligible to non-specialist users, particularly for management planning. In their present form they are very accessible. Although text for the site files is word processed, there is, at present, no intention to hold survey records in a database or map-based information in a GIS.

Table 2. Ecological survey strategies in six agencies

●●● High priority for information gathering

●● Medium priority for information gathering

● Some information gathered

	EH	HS	Cadw	NT	NTS	MOD
Define site type	●●	●●	●●	●●	●●	●
Existing data:						
In-house sources	●	●		●●	●●	●
National sources	●●●	●●		●	●	●
Local sources	●●●	●●	●●●	●●	●	●●
Phase 1	●	●●●	●	●●	●●●	●
NVC communities	●●	●		●		●
Plant species lists	●●	●	●●●	●●●	●●	●●●
Cryptogams lists	●	●	●	●	●	●
Birds	●	●	●●	●●	●	●●
Bats	●●●	●●●	●●●	●	●	●●
Amphibia	●	●	●	●	●	●
Other vertebrates	●	●	●	●	●	●
Lepidoptera	●		●	●●	●●	●●
Odonata	●		●	●●	●	●●
Other invertebrates	●		●	●●	●	●●

The site files and results of the ecological survey provide an information resource to advise regional staff, who are ultimately responsible for decisions on the management of properties. A full set of site files is held by the NTS ecologist and a copy of the full file is held at the relevant site (if staffed). Regional offices usually hold selected parts of files for sites which are staffed, but hold full files for those sites which are not staffed. Information on SSSIs is exchanged with SNH on an informal basis.

● Ministry of Defence (DLS 12) Conservation Office

The MOD Conservation Office (MOD CO) forms part of the Defence Lands Service. It co-ordinates and provides advice on the conservation of wildlife, geological features, Scheduled Ancient Monuments and features of archaeological interest on sites administered or used by the Ministry of Defence in the UK (and on sovereign bases overseas). Details of the MOD CO and its role are contained in Chapter 5 of the Joint Services Publication 362 and its work is reviewed in the house journal *Sanctuary*. It is staffed by the Conservation Officer, the Assistant Conservation Officer and two clerical support staff, with two or three undergraduate students on one-year industrial placements.

Priority is given to sites recognised as being of high value for wildlife, particularly areas on MOD land designated as SSSI in Britain or ASSI in Northern Ireland. At such sites, conservation groups are established where suitable expertise is available. A conservation group (or at least a focal point of contact on the site) is mandatory where there is a SSSI/ASSI on MOD land. There are some 200 groups, of which about 160 were considered to be active in 1993. The composition of groups normally includes Service personnel at the site, representatives of relevant statutory and voluntary organisations and local specialists.

Conservation groups provide an interface between the MOD use of the site and the interests of nature conservation and archaeology. An important part of their work is the collection of biological survey information about the site. The scope of these surveys and the resultant site dossiers depends on the local expertise available. Birds, deer and vascular plants are normally covered at all sites.

Site dossiers are compiled at the Conservation Office from information supplied by or obtained through the conservation group for the site. Some 90 dossiers have been compiled, with additional site files for other sites where the volume of data available does not yet warrant a dossier.

Data may be in a variety of forms, but most site dossiers contain summarised information on species and habitats - often as lists of species for a whole site of many hundred hectares. Dossiers contain references to primary sources of information (e.g. surveys by conservation agencies) not held in the dossier.

The site dossiers, in paper form, are held at the relevant site and at MOD CO where data for some dossiers also are held as word processor files (but not as a database). Copies of dossiers also are held by representatives of the statutory conservation agencies where they serve on conservation groups. A pilot project to include some nature conservation (and archaeological) information on Salisbury Plain, Wiltshire in a GIS has been set up by the MOD at Salisbury.

With the disposal of selected MOD properties, a summary of the ecological interest of the site is provided, with the purchase documentation, to the potential purchasers. A copy of the site dossier is normally supplied to the eventual purchaser, but is not retained by MOD after disposal of the site.

● Summary of Practices in Ecological Survey

Table 2 summarises the range of strategies adopted by the six agencies. The survey

topics used in Table 2 are those described in the following section (Priorities for Data Relating to Nature Conservation). All the agencies work to some form of guidelines, however informal, but EH and NTS have produced guidance notes for those undertaking surveys on their behalf.

The survey strategies of HS and NTS are well focused, but are probably unable to respond adequately to the full range of potential applications within the agency. Mainly for reasons of getting the best usable results for the funds available, the survey strategy of EH places emphasis on vegetation. Given this limitation, the EH strategy has the potential to fulfil most of the range of potential applications, but certainly not all. However, the financial resources allocated by EH for surveys are smaller than for all the other agencies except Cadw.

EH, HS and Cadw have concentrated their survey efforts on those sites for which they are solely or mainly responsible for the management. As a result, the majority of scheduled monuments, landscape parks and gardens, which are managed by others, have not been covered in the present rounds of survey and assessment by these agencies.

None of the agencies have undertaken monitoring or audit of the effects of site management as a major priority. However, NT is re-surveying properties after an interval of some 10 years and also is considering the need for better audit of the management of its properties. EH is monitoring the results of habitat restoration at some sites.

● Priorities for Data Relating to Nature Conservation

The existing practices, relating to nature conservation, of the six agencies have been developed pragmatically over varying periods of time. The following section places these practices in a prioritised sequence, which should be considered in the development of future policies on surveys and the management of data.

● Ecological surveys

● Define the property type

For an ecological survey to be initiated, some knowledge of the property is essential so that a list of priorities for survey may be drawn up. For example, the priorities for a property with large areas of open space, such as grassland, parkland and water-bodies, will be different from those for a property which is mainly built environment and mown grass. Information of this type would normally be held on agency files, so that this level of investigation should be a desk exercise, carried out in-house.

● Examine existing data

Existing ecological information about the property and its immediate environs should be sought and examined. The main targets could include the following:

● Statutory conservation agencies. The three national headquarters and regional offices and sub-offices. The Joint Nature Conservation Committee including the Species Conservation and Vertebrates Branches;

● Ministry of Defence, Conservation Office - if on MOD land;

● National Park Authority - if in National Park;

● Ministry of Agriculture Fisheries and Food - if in an Environmentally Sensitive Area;

● Biological Records Centre (Institute of Terrestrial Ecology);

● Local wildlife trust;

● Local biological/environmental information/records centre

● Local specialists (e.g. BSBI vice-county recorders, bird, bat and badger groups,

Butterfly Conservation branches, local natural history societies).

Although these sources may hold a wide variety of data, priority should be given to compiling a list of metadata (for example a list of the datasets which are known to, or which may cover the property). In addition, the following datasets should be extracted in full if available:

Protected and Red Data list species;

Nationally scarce and "notable" species;

Recognised "indicator" species (e.g. ancient woodland plants, epiphytes and saproxylic *Coleoptera*).

Depending on the success of this phase of data gathering, commissioned surveys at a range of levels will be necessary.

● Commission surveys

● Biotope and plant community surveys

The entry level for surveys must be to characterise the basic biotopes present. For this the Phase 1 Habitat Survey methodology is now well established (England Field Unit, Nature Conservancy Council, 1990) and the Target Note system is particularly useful. Much of the information from a Phase 1 Habitat Survey is map-based and therefore is in a form which could be digitised for incorporation into a GIS.

More detailed surveys of semi-natural vegetation should use the National Vegetation Classification (where available) (Rodwell, 1991 onwards), but the NVC does not include highly modified vegetation types such as agricultural and derelict land and urban habitats, which may be of importance for some wildlife.

● Botanical qualitative and quantitative surveys

Simple species lists for a whole property are of limited use, other than to highlight that some species of particular interest may be present. Lists of some plant species, especially characteristic species, will arise from the target notes in a Phase 1 Habitat Survey, but these should be augmented to cover ecological, archaeological, structural or topographical features of interest. Species lists for particular features strengthen the case for conservation management of those features. For example, walls and buildings may be important for lichens and large old trees and dead wood may be important for lichens and fungi.

Populations of important species should be measured, using the most appropriate methods for the circumstances. Such measurements should be repeatable and preferably should form part of a planned monitoring programme.

● Vertebrate surveys

Although vertebrates form only a small part of our fauna, in the public perception they are of great importance. In the cases of bats and of rare breeding birds there may be real need for concern to safeguard species at some sites, and where water-bodies are present, amphibia may be important. Priority should be given to surveys of:

● Birds - breeding and roosting sites, feeding grounds;

● Bats - breeding and roosting sites;

● Reptiles and amphibians - especially breeding sites;

● Other vertebrates - especially breeding sites and protected or rare species.

● Invertebrate surveys

Invertebrates offer a challenge to the conservationist and land manager. Many species are significantly more sensitive to the effects of management than most vascular plants. Unfortunately, the taxonomic expertise necessary to identify reliably most invertebrates is scarce. For this purely logistical reason, invertebrates are often not an important feature in the

assessment of sites for wildlife. Generalised guidelines for the management of sites for invertebrates are given by Kirby (1992). However, some invertebrate groups are sufficiently well known for surveys be considered. Such groups include:

● *Lepidoptera* (butterflies and moths) - where possible with evidence of breeding;

● *Odonata* (dragonflies) - where possible with evidence of breeding;

● Other macro-invertebrates, (prioritised according to the biotopes available).

● Monitor the effects of management

Surveys and the collection of data relating to nature conservation are driven mainly by statutory requirements and in many cases result in the active management of properties to take account of wildlife. Relatively little consideration seems to have been given by agencies to monitoring the effects of this management. Similar criticism may be levelled at most statutory and voluntary conservation agencies, and they are beginning to address the need to assess the effectiveness and value for money of management procedures. The work of the nature conservation agencies may provide opportunities for the heritage agencies to collaborate and gain experiences on site management, as has already begun with EH and EN (*English Nature*, issue 10).

● Geology, Geomorphology and Soils

All six agencies considered that protection of geological and geomorphological features was part of nature conservation, but none undertook separate surveys of such features, except in the case of SSSIs with geological interest. The management of such features and soils involves considerations different from those for wildlife. In particular, famous exposures may be subject to over-exploitation for rock or mineral samples or for fossils. Large rock faces may provide opportunities for rock climbing which may come into conflict with conservation interests.

Access to existing data is often difficult, but there is a growing resource of information on locally important geological features at some local records centres, mainly through the National Scheme for Geological Site Documentation and the *Regionally Important Geological/Geomorphological Sites Project* (RIGS).

● Data Management

● Use of databases and GIS

The most unexpected aspect of the review of agencies in 1993 was the absence of long term data management policies, for data relating to nature conservation, at all the agencies covered. None of the agencies managed large volumes of data from ecological surveys using computerised databases. NT has a number of small databases for rare and protected species, but they have only limited applications. Most of the agencies indicated that they were considering the use of databases.

There is a GIS capability within EH, but this has not yet been investigated in the context of spatially referenced ecological data. NT and MOD have begun to investigate the use of GIS, but only as pilot studies which do not, as yet, involve ecological survey data.

It is inevitable that use of databases, and probably GIS, will become a priority for agencies in the foreseeable future. Before commitments are made, it is essential that each agency examines its throughput of data, for example by logical data modelling and systems analysis. The potential commitment of resources to database and GIS management is considerable and needs to be considered in relation to the predicted supply and use of data.

● Archiving information

All the agencies hold at least two complete copies of ecological survey reports, etc, in separate locations. In addition, full or partial copies may be held at other locations. However, none of the agencies had a clear archiving policy, other than through a departmental registry where it existed (but it should be noted that departmental registries are not permanent archives).

In the absence of computerised databases, it is essential that paper copies of data are safeguarded against accidental loss (for example "borrowing" of files), fire, flood and the natural decay of ink and paper. Photographic records are vulnerable to the same hazards.

● Data Dissemination

● Dissemination within agencies

The levels to which information derived from ecological surveys is disseminated within agencies are generally similar, dependent on the hierarchical structure of the organisation, but with little documented structure. In all cases, information disseminated within agencies was as paper (reports, files, lists and maps).

● Dissemination to outside agencies

None of the agencies reviewed had defined policies on the release of data. Most agencies suggested that they would expect to provide copies or summaries of nature conservation data to the relevant statutory conservation agency, especially for SSSIs. The release of data to other potential users (other than for nature conservation and research) had scarcely been considered by agencies. Most agencies took the view that "a need to know" would have to be established by the prospective user and some charge might be made for use for commercial purposes.

The growing demand for environmental information and recent legislation on access to information are likely to result in increasing demands, from outside organisations, for nature conservation data held by heritage agencies. If only for these reasons, it would be in their own best interests for the heritage agencies to develop formal policies on access to data.

Conclusions

The starting point for this paper was a review, undertaken early in 1993 for EH, of the acquisition, management and use of data for nature conservation in five national heritage agencies and the Ministry of Defence (Harding, 1993). My original commission was to advise EH on how other agencies, with similar commitments and objectives to their own, dealt with these issues. In the case of the three statutory heritage agencies (EH, HS and Cadw), work on nature conservation is necessarily ancillary to their primary work - safeguarding archaeological and human-made heritage. For NT, NTS and MOD, this form of heritage has equal standing with natural heritage.

My findings from the review indicate that much well-intentioned work is being undertaken, but that, not unexpectedly, resources are scarce and therefore what can be achieved is limited. At the top of the range, NT currently devotes at least £100,000 *per annum* to nature conservation surveys and possibly a similar sum to advice, when all support services and overheads are included. For this type of expenditure the NT has carried out surveys at most of its properties over the last decade. Cadw has only recently begun to commission ecological surveys, with funding of a few thousand pounds.

Whatever resources are available to agencies, it is essential that they should define what they are trying to achieve and how the results of data collection will be carried through to applications and then to auditing their use. For this reason, it may be useful to set out five recommendations to be considered by heritage agencies when considering or reconsidering their policies on data collection and management for nature conservation.

Recommendations

Define the objectives of data collection and management.

There are four priority objectives for agencies to undertake surveys and to manage the resultant data:

- 1 To fulfil statutory obligations to protect nature under Acts of Parliament and international laws and conventions;

- 2 To achieve cost effective site management, which is sympathetic to nature conservation, whilst protecting the archaeological/historical interest of properties;

- 3 To develop the greater public enjoyment of properties, including educational use;

- 4 To monitor and audit the effectiveness of the first three objectives.

Prioritise nature conservation surveys

These priorities are discussed earlier. Agencies should have definite statements of survey policies and priorities which would provide structure to present and projected work. EH, HS and Cadw, are conducting ecological surveys and assessments of only those sites for which they are solely or mainly responsible for the management. As a result, the majority of scheduled monuments, landscape parks and gardens (those which are managed by others) are effectively excluded from these agencies' commitments to nature conservation. In England alone this amounts to more than 13,000 sites. In this situation, there is a real danger that irreversible damage may be done to the nature conservation interests of scheduled monuments, due to a lack of basic ecological information and the means of interpreting and disseminating that information.

● Conserve geological features

Whilst accepting that geological conservation sometimes conflicts with the protection of historic sites, it is clear that most of the agencies reviewed regard geological conservation as of secondary importance to wildlife conservation.

Reliable, up to date, site based geological information is often inaccessible, but local and national registers of geological and geomorphological sites are being developed. These registers will, in future, provide a baseline of information on known sites of importance.

● Develop data management policies

Policies should be directed by the extent of data required at the relevant levels in the organisation. A thorough appraisal of existing and required data pathways within the organisation, and also to and from the organisation, should be undertaken as part of the processes of defining objectives and priorities. In the near future, the use of relational databases and GIS must surely be essential for data to be used effectively.

Facilities for archiving the results of surveys should be provided.

● Liaise with others

The review has shown that each of the agencies reviewed has developed its own strategies to address ecological and geological surveys and resultant data management. Some wheels have been re-invented and some aspects have been avoided because of the apparent inherent difficulties.

There is scope for useful exchange of practical information and experience between the six agencies, and for input from the statutory nature conservation agencies (Joint Nature Conservation Committee, English Nature, Scottish Natural Heritage and the Countryside Council for Wales), the voluntary nature conservation agencies The Wildlife Trusts and the Royal

Society for the Protection of Birds). Biological recording networks already exist, for example through the Biological Records Centre of the Institute of Terrestrial Ecology and the British Trust for Ornithology. A national system for integration of the large volumes of biological survey data held by these and many other agencies is being promulgated by the Co-ordinating Commission for Biological Recording, with support from the Department of the Environment, the Joint Nature Conservation Committee and the Natural Environment Research Council.

● A Counsel of Perfection?

As a biologist concerned with the acquisition, management and use of data for research and nature conservation, I hope that I have not been too "biocentric" in my approach to this topic. Nature conservation is at best only part of the responsibilities of the heritage agencies being considered. However, if hard won resources are to be devoted by the agencies to nature conservation, it is essential that they are used to best effect. I have attempted to describe the strengths and weaknesses of the present situation and to propose some ways forward. With the possible exception of the National Trust, the existing resources of data, currently held in paper forms, are so large that they inhibit considering the computerisation of most of the existing data. A move to relational databases and GIS will inevitably lead to greater use of data, but this should not be at the expense of the collection of new data, about additional sites, to update existing information and, above all, to audit the effectiveness of management measures.

● Acknowledgements

I am grateful to John Thompson, the Nature Conservation Adviser to English Heritage, for initiating the review in 1993 and for his encouragement and advice regarding this paper. It is also a pleasure to acknowledge the following for their help with the review: Rick Turner (Cadw), Duncan Macniven, Lesley Macinnes and Gordon Barclay (Historic Scotland), Kathy Ader (Northern Ecological Services), John Harvey and Keith Alexander (National Trust), James Fenton (National Trust for Scotland) and James Baker and Amanda Waddingham (Ministry of Defence). I am also grateful to Charles Copp, Tom Grant, Stephen Sutton and Barry Wyatt for their help in various ways.

● References

Berry, A.Q. (1992) Integrating Archaeology and the Countryside: Clwyd County Council's Approach to Archaeological Sites Management in, Macinnes, L. and Wickham-Jones C.R. (eds) *All Natural Things: Archaeology and the Green Debate* Oxford: Oxbow Books. 155-160.

Department of the Environment 1994. Planning Policy Guidance: Nature Conservation, PPG 9 London: HMSO.

Buckland, P.C., Eversham, B.C. and Dinnin, M.H. (1994) Conserving the Holocene Record: A Change for Geomorphology, Archaeology and Biological Conservation in, O'Halloran, D., Green, C., Harley, M., Stanley, M. and Knill, J. (eds) *Geological and Landscape Conservation*. London: The Geological Society. 201-204.

Nature Conservancy Council (1990) *Handbook for Phase 1 Habitat Survey - A Technique for Environmental Audit.* Peterborough: Nature Conservancy Council. England Field Unit.

Harding, P.T. (1993) *The Acquisition, Management and Use of Data for Nature Conservation in English Heritage and Similar National Agencies.* Unpublished contract report to English Heritage. Huntingdon: Institute of Terrestrial Ecology.

Kirby. P.(1992) *Habitat Management for Invertebrates: A Practical Handbook.* Sandy: Royal Society for the Protection of Birds.

Lambrick, G. (ed) (1985) *Archaeology and Nature Conservation.* Oxford: Oxford University Department of External Studies.

Macinnes, L. (1993) Archaeology as Land Use in, Hunter, J. and Ralston, I. (eds) *Archaeological Resource Management in the UK - An Introduction.* Stroud: Alan Sutton. 243-255.

Macinnes, L. and Wickham-Jones, C.R. (eds) (1992) *All Natural Things: Archaeology and the Green Debate.* Oxford: Oxbow Books.

Morgan Evans, D. (1992) The Paradox of Salisbury Plain in, Macinnes, L. and Wickham-Jones, C.R. (eds) *All Natural Things: Archaeology and the Green Debate.* Oxford: Oxbow Books. 176-179.

Rodwell, J.S. (ed) (1991) *British Plant Communities,* Vol.1: *Woodlands and Scrub,* Vol.2: *Mires and Heather,* Vol.3: *Grasslands and Montane Communities.* Cambridge: Cambridge University Press.

The Sum of all its Parts: An Overview of the Politics of Integrated Management in England

Graham Fairclough

English Heritage

● Ideas

Archaeology's "loss of innocence", mourned by some and celebrated by others, was not merely the discovery that archaeological "facts" are not always what they seem, or that not everything can be taken at positivist or empirical face-value. It relates also to the realisation that archaeology does not exist in isolation from other disciplines or values. We accept that there are alternative views and interpretations of the past, and we must equally accept that "our" monuments are at the same time someone else's ecological site or habitat. We are always ready to tell other conservationists that the whole landscape is an historic artefact, but we are not always quite so ready to accept that it is also a natural environment, nor that its scenic and associative values can be equally important to the community at large. All the terms which describe the countryside should be taken simply as shorthand for the different value systems by which we perceive and identify our environment. Some of these value systems, which may be equally valid, are not oriented towards conservation at all, but are concerned first (for example) with valuing the landscape as an economic resource. Any serious project for integrated management should start, explicitly or not, from a position which accepts this, and it is of course the starting point of this collection of papers.

Many languages can be used to express the indivisibility of the landscape, from the simple claim that "everything connects" to more complicated space-driven or holistic constructs. One current approach, useful if only because it commands the attention and perhaps the resources of Government and other policy-makers, is through the rhetoric of the post-Rio concern for Biodiversity and Sustainable Development; both concepts operate very significantly on the basis of integration (DoE, 1994a and b). They recognise that the countryside is an environmental whole, that it is the sum of all its parts; they recognise too that it is vulnerable, and that its survival depends on careful demand management, and that land-use planning should be informed by a combined approach to value, understanding and appreciation. The idea of biodiversity in particular accepts that landscape is human habitat as much as it is natural habitat; and that people, in the past and still today, are the prime regulators of biodiversity.

The UK Action Plan identifies biodiversity as not just a natural phenomenon but a human construct. It defines three basic factors which determine biodiversity, and only two of these (soil and climate) are "natural" factors, and even then not wholly unmodified by human activity. The third factor is people and their actions: that is the role of human history itself, and particularly the archaeology of the countryside. Conversely human activity in the past should also be seen as part of the natural world, even while at the same time regulating it - the biodiversity arguments thus help both poles of environmental conservation. For present purposes, however, biodiversity is just another word for cultural landscape, as the UK Action Plan itself implicitly recognises.

In this increasingly broad approach, sustainability too plays a part, as a cradle or crucible for integration. Countryside management and the planning system is its active tool and landscape assessment and SMRs form a basis for its interactive, interpretative data-base. Some of this is beginning to influence real work on the ground, from Stewardship (see Jago - this volume) and even within the Ministry of Agriculture, Fisheries and Food (MAFF), in National Parks and some local authority farm schemes, and within increasing numbers of development plans (English Heritage et al, 1993).

Institutional structures or policies do not currently reflect the theory of integration to any great extent, however. There are three statutory conservation agencies in England - English Heritage, English Nature and the Countryside Commission. In addition, not covered in this paper, the National Rivers Authority has significant conservation duties, whilst the Rural Development Commission, it could be argued, ought to have them. Each has mainly separate functions, and although there are trends towards much closer collaboration (English Heritage's contribution to this will be the subject of most of this paper), the process still needs to be taken much further. Collaboration at present thus tends to be strategic rather than site-oriented, but it is fuelled by the Government's commitment to sustainable development and biodiversity. Even at Government level though, at least in England, there is also a split, again into three although on different lines - Department of National Heritage (DNH) with its heritage remit, Department of the Environment (DoE) with its countryside concerns sitting alongside quite different planning and rural development interests, and MAFF with its own interesting blend of agricultural and environmental ambitions.

Local authorities, notably National Parks, have been more successful in pursuing integration on the ground, both at individual sites like Lordenshaws (see Frodsham - this volume) and through one-stop-shop schemes like those in the North York Moors or Peak Parks. Groups in the voluntary sectors (Royal Society for the Protection of Birds [RSPB], Campaign for the Protection of Rural England [CPRE], county wildlife trusts, Council for British

Archaeology [CBA], etc) have separate sectoral interests, but many have proved very capable of achieving integration at site level, and some have done so also at strategic level (RSPB through sustainability and Environmental Assessment for example, and CPRE in all directions).

Finally, it is worth pausing to wonder whether those who farm and manage the landscape even notice these sub-divisions in the first place, rather than simply regarding land as land whatever its perceived conservation value. There is less need perhaps to argue for an integration of approach than to demonstrate to farmers the value of comprehensive ways of seeing and appreciating the landscape which include historic and archaeological dimensions. How to do this could form a separate book, however, and is not the subject of the present paper.

At site level, the interaction of archaeological and nature conservation interests is obvious and multiple. Examples include the good survival of some types of archaeology in valued semi-natural habitats which have acted as archaeological reserves (especially in damaged landscapes such as earthworks in woodlands in intensive arable areas), or the coincidence, because of past historic processes, of well-preserved earlier-abandoned archaeological sites with more marginal or inaccessible land which has encouraged the evolution of biodiverse habitats; this includes human creations ranging from the Norfolk Broads to abandoned moats and fishponds, or the nature conservation value of "monuments" (e.g. lichen on ruined structures or stone circles, or the value of parkland trees for beetles and other invertebrates).

Nature conservation values, more broadly, can be indicators of the health, survival and completeness of historical landscape systems; and conversely archaeological sites and their condition are clear indicators for the environmental health of the natural countryside. But underlying all this is the general point that the English landscape, and therefore its habitats and wildlife, is a largely human artefact. From the macro level of the existence and distribution of moorland and heath, to the detailed level of protected natural or historic sites offering protective refuges for the other interests, there is clearly a symbiotic relationship.

At a slightly different level, the historic landscape is not only the end result of centuries of historic and natural processes, but it is "topped-off", or some would say actually created, by present-day appreciations and perception. It has been argued that landscapes do not exist unless perceived by somebody ("the walk creates the landscape", at least in the artist Richard Long's work [Shanks, 1993]), or via the medium of formal presentation (for instance a Heritage Coast guided walk [Heritage Coast Forum, 1994]). Such current and new perceptions are important, but there are also past, historic, perceptions to be recognised, because the view of what is natural or "proper" in the landscape has changed through time, and has affected both so-called "conscious" landscape design decisions as well as land-use and farming choices. This includes current perspectives (for example appropriate uses for redundant farm buildings) on what the countryside is to be used for, not least on the set-aside issue, the role of farmers, and the relative priorities to be given to "consumers" of the countryside. There is also the semiotics of the words "nature" and "culture", and the point at which they come full-circle as "national culture" - those values which "naturally" belong to a particular society, culture (in Childean archaeological terms) or **nation**.

The concept of landscape is central to this debate on integrated management. Whether it is described as historic or not, the wider view which landscape simultaneously both demands and offers can encourage an holistic approach. Landscape is the sum of all its parts; its ecological aspects are already being mapped and

characterised as carefully as its scenic and visual attributes have been for several years (Countryside Commission, 1993), and there are the beginnings of a similar concern to understand the historical dimension of the landscape just as thoroughly (Countryside Commission, 1994a). Historic landscape has many levels, from the national vista of work such as the Countryside Commission's New Map project, in future the Countryside Character Programme (Countryside Commission, 1994b) or the Monument Protection Programme's (MPP) mapping and classification work (eg of Medieval settlement pattern), to the regional and local scales of, for example, county landscape assessments or site and farm survey grant. The term "historic landscape" could be seen as a metaphor, referring to the idea that the whole landscape is made by human activity; it carries within its meaning an appreciation of the physical manifestation of the interaction of people and the environment through time; it can also point to its role as a forum, or context, for discourse, to unite environmental, conservation and socio-economic concerns. It is therefore, as an idea, the best vehicle for the integration which is the subject of the papers in this book.

The idea of historic landscape plays its part in several ways, for example by allowing management at all scales and with easy connection to sustainable development (State of Environment reports via landscape assessments) and biodiversity (its history and causes), or by establishing frameworks for taking account of both natural and historic values. It can also go far towards encouraging public awareness, and accessibility (on all levels) to the landscape. Finally, it helps us to break free from the strait-jacket of selective protection by designation, and to give due weight to regional diversity and local character and distinctiveness as well as to national importance. Historic landscape (and landscape in general) is in this view the theoretical or philosophical equivalent of whole farm management plans.

● Actions

The bulk of the remainder of this paper discusses some of the mainly strategic initiatives by which English Heritage is currently pursuing integration (and encouraging it in others) at a national level in England. Other papers in this book give more detailed site case-studies. For convenience the present discussion is set against the existing organisational background, describing work with English Nature first and with the Countryside Commission second. There are of course disadvantages of focusing in this way on the work of only the two national agencies because it perpetuates the non-integrated divisions which this book seeks to dissolve, and it ignores a lot of good work in this direction by many other bodies, not least ACAO itself, central for example to the historic facets of Countryside Stewardship; and the CBA, which was instrumental for example in prompting the English Heritage/English Nature Statement of intent in the first place. Whilst the full merger between English Nature and the Countryside Commission which was considered by DoE during 1994 is at present unlikely to take place, both agencies are fully committed to developing closer working at policy and project level; the following overview of English Heritage's links with both agencies should soon therefore be overtaken by events.

● English Nature

English Heritage's work with English Nature has a formal basis, established when the Chairmen of the two agencies signed in December 1992 a *Statement of Intent for the Conservation of the Natural and Archaeological Environment*. It is periodically reviewed. An earlier statement had been prepared by NCC and all three national archaeological agencies on the mainland, in part at the CBA's suggestion during parliamentary debate.

The joint Statement highlights the inter-relationship of archaeology and nature conservation, and each agency's concern for the other's interests. It identifies the need for exchange of information, for the agencies' respective interests to be taken into account when directly managing land, and for mutual liaison and integration. Detailed issues include the need for improved data-transfer, greater liaison and partnership at operational level down to and including individual cases such as SSSI and English Heritage Historic Property management plans, and proposals for improvement of staff awareness. The important roles of local authorities and voluntary bodies, such as CBA, are also highlighted in the Statement.

A more detailed Action Plan is drawn up to support the Statement. The Action Plan for the first year of the Statement's operation included English Nature's Campaign for a Living Coast (managed retreat and estuary management plan, for example), lowland peat, pilot data transfer, secondment and training. This Action Plan was reviewed at a formal meeting of the two agencies in December 1993 at Old Winchester Hill, Hampshire, and subsequently revised for 1994, to add for example, Natural Areas and Historic Landscapes, Lowland Heath, Parkland, earth sciences and bat conservation.

The Statement and its Action Plan is essentially a strategic document. At one important level it acts as a focus for wider liaison, which takes place on local initiative as often as at national instigation. A number of specific projects have also arisen from it directly however. A similar approach is now being taken to build on existing work by National Park archaeologists: a Statement of Intent has been prepared by English Heritage/Cadw and the National Parks, with the Countryside Commission as co-signatories, to promote the conservation by the Parks of their cultural heritage.

The following is a brief account of some of the current or new initiatives revolving at national level around the English Heritage/English Nature Statement.

• Staff awareness

Central to the whole purpose of the partnership is a concern with staff training and understanding. Several training courses have been held for English Heritage staff on nature conservation issues, for instance on grassland ecology in Wiltshire, and reciprocal courses are planned for 1994 for English Nature staff. English Heritage has benefited for three years from the secondment of an NCC regional officer, John Thompson (see Thompson - this volume) to identify, for example, the nature conservation interests of English Heritage's Historic Properties and to help establish appropriate management plans; this work has contributed to the success of the training course programme and is continuing on a consultancy basis. Its value to English Heritage has been recognised by the decision to recruit an ecologist in English Heritage. In the opposite direction, an English Heritage Field Monument Warden, Eileen Moss, worked in 1993-94 on a part-time secondment to the English Nature local office at Lyndhurst. She identified issues of common interest, assisted in the preparation of a number of English Nature site management plans, developed methods for English Nature staff to insert archaeological information from SMRs into SSSI and National Nature Reserve management records, and drew up basic guidelines for English Nature local staff on the treatment of archaeology within nature conservation. The local and personal partnerships which arise even from such local short-term secondments have a lasting value, and their lessons can be exported to the practices of other local teams, or into national practice - English Nature's system for producing site management statements is currently being examined for the scope to incorporate archaeological consideration.

• Earth sciences

Mutual interests have been underlined in a number of fields as a result of the Statement. For example, the correlations between archaeology and earth sciences have long been recognised, even before Boxgrove, but they have been little explored at a wide level. Early steps to raise awareness have been to prepare reciprocal articles on this commonality of interest, first in English Heritage's *Conservation Bulletin* and later in English Nature's magazine *Earth Heritage*. Other work has involved discussion of the potential conflicts between earth science conservation philosophy (which sometimes requires that exposures are left open, or even "cleaned up" or cut-back because emphasis is put, in archaeological terms, on the "exploitative" stage of the management cycle) and the mainstream archaeological concern for preservation *in situ*, preferably below ground and undisturbed. English Heritage membership of the Geological Society's Conservation Committee is also a useful forum to take forward some of these debates.

• Bats

Another arena for potential conflict between archaeology and nature conservation is that of bat roosts within historic buildings, notably churches (see Hutson - this volume). Whilst bats need protection, they can nonetheless cause damage to wall paintings and other fittings in churches. The issues are not straightforward to resolve and the Statement of Intent has given a framework for a research project devised and managed by the EH AM Laboratory to quantify the precise scale of the problem - what size of bat population can be tolerated, can capacity thresholds (for bats and buildings) be established, whether the impact of bats varies from species to species, which may help us to define new practical solutions - in other words, a micro-scale application of the sustainability principles of capacity and threshold, in which the receptors (the assets) are also the impacts (threats)!

• The coast

A major English Nature concern at present is with the potential for managed coastal retreat in the face of rising sea levels, particularly on the eastern coast of southern Britain. Rising sea level itself can obviously threaten archaeological features, but management solutions to the problem can also be damaging. Increasing understanding of the complex dynamics of coastal processes for example, and recognition that "hard" engineering solutions to coastal protection can have very detrimental environmental impacts (for example by drowning saltmarsh squeezed between sea and sea wall), has led to a shift towards trying to manage the coast with the flow of natural processes, rather than against it. Theoretical techniques are also being developed and tested to allow saltmarshes to migrate through breaches in existing sea walls towards newly constructed defences further inland; archaeological sites in these areas of course cannot migrate and our problems are of a different sort. It may be preferable, for example, to allow coastal erosion at some points in order to ensure that sediments are available for re-deposition elsewhere on the coast to prevent inundation, but how would we choose between preventing loss of, say, a cliff-edge promontory fort or intertidal structures? These issues involve many other difficult problems of economics, politics and land-ownership, and of course it is a strategy which has archaeological implications. English Nature (with MAFF, which has primary coastal flood defence responsibility) is running a pilot scheme in Essex to monitor the effect of managed retreat, and this could provide an opportunity for studying some of the implications and solutions. The archaeological implications are manifold - removal, in whole or in part, of historic sea walls, possible erosion of archaeological deposits by marine incursion, including changes to the intertidal zone, destruction of sites by establishment of new creek systems, and burial of earthworks below marine silts and saltmarsh. Conversely, however, there may be sites where managed retreat offers the chance to maintain appropriate water-levels on wetland sites. There should also of course

be a concern for the potential loss of distinctive types of coastal historic landscape, not least the archaeology of land reclamation itself.

● Natural Areas

Finally, mention needs to be made of English Nature's Natural Areas programme, which is intended to provide a national strategic policy framework for most of its work over the next decade or so. It divides England into 92 terrestrial and 24 maritime zones, called "Natural Areas", on the basis mainly of 19th and 20th century floras; the patterns of land-use, habitat and geology; and, of the local knowledge of English Nature regional teams. Each Natural Area possesses a distinctive ecological mix closely determined by geology and topography. Many are recognisably historic zones as well, however, which is a further instance of cultural underpinnings to biodiversity. It should be possible for each Area to identify broadly-defined "cultural affinities" which distinguish it from other Areas: the specific ancient enclosed fields and managed woodlands of the Chilterns, for example, and the distinctive prehistoric and medieval landscape systems of Bodmin or Dartmoor; or the intensive agricultural use of the Northumberland Coastal Plain, with its legacy of Improvement-age field systems and model farmsteads preserving fragmentary survivals of earlier landscape.

Definition of these cultural affinities throughout the country would be a very fruitful task, providing a way of measuring at regional scale the coincidence and inter-relationship of archaeology and ecology. It could also further our appreciation of archaeology's regional diversity, and provide a framework for more detailed local study and analysis, whether of archaeological sites and patterning or (as a set of study areas, and perhaps a set of preliminary research agendas) for historic landscape. English Nature is using Natural Areas to prioritise its work, by setting appropriate broad objectives for each Area. In due course these priorities may come to influence a great deal of agri-environmental policy and landscape enhancement, and it is important that the place of archaeology in Natural Areas is not overlooked.

The Natural Areas project mirrors the growing concern of archaeologists for landscape-scale study and conservation. Both to some extent represent the same evolution of thought - the widening of archaeological interest in monuments (or sites) to their setting and context, and now to the wider inter-related system which we term historic landscape; and nature conservation's move from species protection, to habitat conservation, and now to a growing concern for the whole countryside and to landscape ecology (Selman, 1994). Both disciplines recognise that protection of small "reserves" is often uneconomic and by itself philosophically flawed, and is in the longer-term unsustainable and limited in its success. A greater concern for the whole landscape, even in a broad-brush way, for instance encouraging sympathetic land-use on a whole-farm or a regional basis, eg Environmentally Sensitive Areas (ESAs), is likely to protect sites more effectively by creating a more supportive setting.

● Countryside Commission

Many of these broader issues are also central to English Heritage's recent joint work with the Countryside Commission, notably our shared concern for the whole environment rather than for selected areas or reserves and our recognition that the concept of landscape offers an overall philosophy for integration, agricultural change and development planning. There is also a shared interest in the principles of sustainable development as an appropriate frame of reference for the whole landscape conservation project. Most of the English Heritage/Countryside Commission work has taken place within the context of my own part-time one year secondment to the Commission.

Recent liaison has taken several forms. We prepare and publish joint (indeed tripartite,

with English Nature) planning guidance (English Heritage *et al* 1993, 1994) We have both advised MAFF, for example on the selection of the third and fourth tranches of ESAs and the definition of prescriptions. At the same time, we have attempted to strengthen the environmental dimensions of the Common Agricultural Policy as it moves towards a slightly more coherent package of agri-environment schemes, such as greater cross-compliance on livestock headage payments, or focusing longer-term set-aside onto land of archaeological sensitivity, or the new public access provisions, for which archaeological/historical sites are a prime criterion.

● Countryside Stewardship

Most important in this sphere, however, at least in recent years, has been the Countryside Stewardship scheme which the Countryside Commission is managing for a five year pilot period (1991-96) on behalf of DoE and in association with English Heritage and English Nature. Recent English Heritage involvement has taken several directions. At national level, improved guidelines for Stewardship staff for the archaeological objectives of the scheme have been drawn up by English Heritage, and disseminated through regional training courses involving County Archaeological Officers and Field Monument Wardens. The guidelines cover identification and selection of archaeology as well as advice on positive management and potentially damaging work. They also establish the second main direction of English Heritage involvement in Stewardship, the drawing-up and monitoring of detailed notification and consultation procedures designed to give archaeologists a greater opportunity to draw lasting benefit from Stewardship schemes.

With the increasing success of Stewardship in improving the management and condition of archaeological sites, these benefits are many and varied at local level. The programme has seen scrub-clearance on the Cambridgeshire Dykes; the withdrawal from the plough of some Oxfordshire hillfort interiors; extensive returns to pasture in some areas of the Wiltshire Downs; the restoration of the setting and landscape relationship to other earthworks of Wansdyke; the protection in Stewardship of a number of areas of Northamptonshire ridge and furrow; the conservation and reinstatement of Cornish field-wall patterns and much-needed assistance at Laxton with the maintenance of the open field system, and so on. Such schemes are time-consuming to achieve, and require a significant degree of archaeological input at county level, but they need to become a greater priority for archaeologists of all types.

● Historic landscape

The central element of English Heritage's work with the Countryside Commission, however, revolves around landscape issues. The Commission's view of landscape is holistic - that landscape must be seen as the sum of all its parts, historic and archaeological as much as scenic or ecological (Countryside Commission, 1993). Similarly, "natural beauty", its statutory concern, is recognised as a shorthand for the landscape as a whole, including full recognition of cultural heritage (Countryside Commission, 1994). It is, indeed, a Commission objective that the statutory definition of natural beauty is modernised to reflect this.

The Commission is also fully wedded to the concept of active conservation and of integration (English Heritage et al, 1993). The landscape cannot be fixed, and it cannot be left untouched as a museum or reserve: it has reached its present forms predominantly as a result of human interaction with nature, principally by means of traditional, long-term management practices. Where possible, these practices need to be sustained (as at Laxton, with its Stewardship agreement). Where past practices are lost beyond recall it is necessary either to find alternative practices

which produce a similar effect or to help the creation of new landscapes which keep whatever is necessary from the past, adding to it in ways which prolong, or are in sympathy with, past directions.

This concern with helping to shape the whole future landscape lies at the root of the need for archaeological conservation to integrate with landscape conservation. Landscape conservation, and notably the techniques of landscape assessment which the Commission has developed and promoted, is also one of the most promising opportunities for enlarging and disseminating an archaeological appreciation of the landscape, its historic dimensions and its archaeology.

English Heritage has therefore worked closely with the Countryside Commission to broaden the Commission's work on historic landscape. Views from the Past, a policy statement emerging from the secondment, was issued by the Commission in 1994, initially as a consultation draft, to set out the Commission's concern for the historic dimension of the landscape (Countryside Commission, 1994a). It introduced the concept of twin perceptions, of "past" and "present" historic landscapes, of the multi-variate ways in which archaeology and the past can be read in the landscape, and of the wealth of components and elements (from archaeology to managed moorland, field walls to palaeoenvironmental deposits, farm building to trackways, etc) which constitute the historic dimension. It also emphasised the complexity of the historic landscape, the primary importance of historic process and causation (the reasons why our landscape looks as it does, understanding of which must be a pre-requisite for conservation or landscape change), and the need for better methods of identifying, analysing and describing historic landscape. This is most effectively achieved as part of the landscape assessment procedure (Countryside Commission, 1993), by a concern with characterisation of the whole of the landscape, rather than by ascribing value-laden appreciation of quality to highlighted parts only, and by a greater emphasis on "character areas" than on typologies.

Many landscape assessments have now been carried out, principally at district, county and AONB level. The best (a few) take some account of archaeology and historic landscape, but the majority are essentially assessments of scenic value, accompanied by simple historical narratives or a mention of the major and most obvious archaeological monuments. New methodologies need to be developed before landscape assessment fully embraces historic landscape character, and local authorities may be best-placed to do this. The Commission itself, in collaboration with English Heritage, has carried out research as part of a landscape assessment of Bodmin, and later for a county-wide project in Cornwall, and the results of work by the Cornwall Archaeological Unit are very promising. Preparation of guidance on historic landscape character assessment is in hand to build on such work as a supplement to the Commission's existing *Landscape Assessment Guidance* (1993).

• Countryside Character Programme

Parallel to this, of course, is English Heritage's own research on historic landscape (Fairclough *et al,* forthcoming). Both approaches are designed to complement each other in the short-term, although in future it may be possible to merge them together. More significantly, they are designed also as steps towards national regional-scale mapping. In parallel with English Nature's Natural Areas, the Countryside Commission is preparing an analysis of England's landscape, the Countryside Character Programme, which will divide the country into "regional character areas" on the basis of landscape character (geology, topography, ecological associations, etc). The exercise was piloted successfully in the south-west in 1992-93 (Countryside Commission, 1994b) under the working title of *"New Map of England"*. At national level it is hoped that it will use a

number of variables relating to the historic landscape. These "cultural variables" include for example, the visual contribution of archaeological sites to the landscape, the regional pattern of settlement types and of field system diversity and form, and industrial archaeology. The regional character areas will therefore grow out of the historic as much as the scenic or ecological dimension. Equally important, techniques of historic landscape assessment will be able to focus in more detail on the archaeology of the landscape within these compatible and homogeneous zones when more detailed description is carried out. It should also be possible to lay the New Map alongside some of the outputs of the Monuments at Risk Survey (MARS) project or of landscape work in the MPP.

These two mapping exercises, the New Map and Natural Areas, are not being pursued in isolation. The aim, in c.1996-97, is to produce a common map with associated assessments and objectives. This has the working title of Regional Character Map, and a working group has been formed (drawn from English Heritage as well as English Nature and Countryside Commission, and including DoE), to steer the various elements of this procedure in a parallel direction.

This type of exercise might seem at first glance far removed from the detailed case studies of integration presented elsewhere in this book. Site-specific work cannot exist in a vacuum however - philosophical frameworks (biodiversity and sustainability for example), procedural systems (the English Nature/English Heritage Statement of Intent, the new English Heritage/CC/National Parks Statement) and national strategies and priorities based on global understanding are also necessary. Integrated management, like conservation itself, is sometimes as much about politics as about action on the ground, and after all Archaeology (and its practice) is a form of social politics!

● Conclusions

At the risk of repetition, it might be worthwhile in conclusion to draw out some of the main points in the foregoing discussion.

There are various ways of defining the desirability of integrated management. "Management" needs to be used as a broad term, taking in the planning system and national conservation strategy as well as site-specific monument management. Nature conservation has moved away from rare species conservation to a greater concern for habitat conservation, and on to the maintenance (and in some cases the re-creation) of the traditional and sustainable land-use systems which in the first place created biodiversity of habitat and species. English Heritage, and archaeology more generally has been striving to do the same for some years (Darvill, 1987), but there is still occasionally acceptance that we should be content to preserve sites within a largely hostile setting. Projects like the ESAs, and the slowly changing balance of environmental concerns in agricultural policy, hold out however greater optimism that we may be able to conserve sites not solely by directly managing them but also by engineering the wider socio-economic conditions of the countryside which their survival requires. Conserve, enhance and modify the landscape in suitable ways and perhaps the sites may start to take care of themselves, or at least have better prospects for survival.

This is why integrated management cannot only be concerned with hands-on site management, and why sustainable development is potentially very important (English Heritage et al 1993, and forthcoming). It is also why we need a conceptual approach to historic landscape which offers more than designation, and why it is worthwhile to put greater effort into schemes like Stewardship and the agri-environmental programme even if they do not produce immediate "hard" gains of the type that we have tended to regard as

essential (eg erosion repair, localised stock reductions, small-scale withdrawals from the plough, new archaeological survey data).

There is sometimes also a second need to take a few steps back from individual sites in order to appreciate the context of an individual management project. The results of surveys such as those which generate the Institute of Terrestrial Ecology land cover and habitat classification, or DoE's Countryside Survey 1990 and its Key Habitats project, or of MARS, and broad New Map-type assessments, are no less useful data because they are on a sample base and cannot be fed straight into site management plans. They allow us to explore archaeological management and protection problems, to assess need and identify directions for future management and integration, and to establish strategic directions. We need to find a balance, for example, between the full repair of individual monuments at a detailed level and other more extensive and less detailed work with nature conservation colleagues which might be less concerned with localised erosion repair but which might more widely and directly shape the future appearance and therefore the survival of archaeology in the countryside. Strategic survey, whether nationally or at local authority level through landscape assessment and countryside strategies, is an essential stepping-stone to full integration and to landscape-oriented approaches; and perhaps one to which the archaeological community should direct a greater proportion of its resources and attention.

A primary vehicle for integration is the whole farm management plan. This offers scope for reconciling potentially conflicting interests (whole should mean all conservation sectors as well as the whole farm territorially) and for establishing the sort of overall management within which the need for "harder" and more specific site management and protection may well diminish. They can also attract a greater level of conservation-friendly resources to a farm. They are not new, as several papers in this collection testify, having been pioneered for example in some counties and in National Parks, and within the ESA system, but they are becoming more common and are increasingly at the core of Stewardship now that it is fully combined with the Hedgerow Incentive Scheme. At a county level, Countryside Strategies can act as multiple farm plans, with many of the same advantages, although again they tend to be an area of work where archaeological concerns have not made themselves heard.

There is a further level of integration which is worth exploring here. Integration, ie taking a "whole" approach, should also mean that the full range of value, significance and importance is addressed, local as well as national, just as much as the whole range of conservation interests. In whole farm management terms, or in integrated management, it is not always practical or effective to settle for management of only the few nationally important sites, or to suggest to local communities that only these are important. They may require particular concern in some cases, but not necessarily always, but the maintenance and enhancement of local character itself should also be regarded as a matter of national importance. Relatively humble features such as field walls and unlisted barns, cultivation terraces or trackways, contribute to local distinctiveness and to local historic landscape character, and therefore to any desire to create an appropriate setting and milieu for sites. This transcends the individual importance of any one site.

Finally, moves towards greater integration ought to encompass the whole range of how we value and appreciate the past. Archaeologists usually measure importance by a site's potential for (more or less) academic information, but it can legitimately be measured in other ways. There is clearly nature conservation value, but many other values exist - for example amenity value, local values, the powerful affective values of perception, a site's role in fostering local identity and self-identity, accessibility (even if

the uses to which access is put may not always be our choice). All this applies particularly at a landscape scale. It may be proper, for example, to exclude much, perhaps most, ridge and furrow from the Schedule, and to focus instead on those areas which by virtue of representativeness, relation to settlement etc, have greatest evidential value in archaeological terms, but it may not be so proper in the context of broader local (as well as national) landscape management to exclude evidential value of less academic, less formal, less unique and more popular forms. This again returns us to the importance of historic landscapes as an idea or as a metaphor for people's self-identity, awareness of their origins and for their sense of belonging, as much today as at any time in the past- in other words, now as then, a landscape and a cultural heritage which derives from the integration of heritage with nature. Such an approach also opens up a new set of potential partners and allies, and of community and public support for archaeology and a new platform for conservation archaeology.

● References

Countryside Commission. (1993) *Landscape Assessment Guidance.* CCP423.

Countryside Commission. (1994a) *Views From the Past - Historic Landscape Character in the English Countryside.*

Countryside Commission (1994b) *The New Map of England - A Celebration of the South West Landscape.* CCP444.

Coupe, M. and Fairclough, G. J. (1991) Protection for the Historic and Natural Landscape. *Landscape Design* 201, June 1991. 24-30.

Darvill, T. (1987) *Ancient Monuments in the Countryside.* London: Historic Buildings and Monuments Commission for England.

DoE. (1994 a) *UK Action Plan for Biodiversity.* London: HMSO (Cmd. 2428)

DoE. (1994 b) *Sustainable Development - the UK Strategy*. London: HMSO (Cmd. 2426)

English Heritage, Countryside Commission and English Nature. (1993) *Conservation Issues in Strategic Plans*. CCP420.

English Heritage, Countryside Commission and English Nature. (forthcoming) *Conservation in Local Plans*

Fairclough, G. J. (1994) *Landscapes From the Past - Only Human Nature* in, Selman, P. (ed) 1994.

Fairclough, G.J., Lambrick, G. and McNab, A. (eds) (forthcoming) English Heritage Historic Landscape Project.

Glasser, N. (1994) Earth Science Conservation and Archaeology. *Conservation Bulletin*, Issue 22, March 1994. English Heritage.

Heritage Coast Forum (1994) A Walk on the Wild Side by Tim Collins. *Heritage Coast - The Bulletin of the Heritage Coast Forum*, Issue 11, February 1994.

Owen-John, H. (forthcoming) Archaeology and Earth Sciences. *Earth Heritage*. English Nature.

Selman, P. (ed) (1994) *The Ecology and Management of Cultural Landscapes*, Proceedings of the International Association of Landscape Ecologists (UK Branch) (IALE[UK]) 1993 Conference "Cultural Landscapes" in the Journal of the Department of Countryside and Landscape, Cheltenham & Gloucester College of Higher Education; *Landscape Issues*, 11, No.1.

Shanks, M. (1993) *Experiencing the Past - on the Character of Archaeology*. London: Routledge. 141-3.

Integrated Management Plans: Historic Scotland's Experience

Lesley Macinnes and Katherine Ader

Principal Inspector of Ancient Monuments, Historic Scotland and Principal, Northern Ecological Services

● Introduction

In the sphere of cultural heritage conservation, management planning is essential both to secure the comprehensive management of individual monuments and to integrate different aspects of management on any one site or area. This paper will consider some different types of management plans relevant to the work of Historic Scotland and will try to identify some common principles and requirements for successful plans.

The range of Historic Scotland's work demands an involvement with a fairly wide range of management plans serving a variety of purposes. The first part of this paper briefly reviews Historic Scotland's own management plans for properties directly in its care; and other land management plans, such as monument management agreements and agricultural conservation plans. It will then consider whether any general conclusions can be drawn.

The second part of this paper discusses in more detail Historic Scotland's recently completed three year project to identify and manage nature conservation features at properties in its care.

● Historic Scotland's Management Plans

The preparation of comprehensive management plans for individual properties is at a relatively early stage. The recognised elements of such plans, which cover a period of some five years and are monitored regularly, are:

● A detailed description of the monument, based on written records and enhanced by the expertise and experience of relevant staff, covering principally its archaeological, historical, architectural and natural heritage evidence, as well as the conservation history;

● The management objectives for the property, encompassing all relevant aspects, principally conservation, interpretation, presentation and marketing. As some of these may be fairly long-term, it is often necessary to distinguish between short-, medium- and long-term objectives;

● Proposed management actions, both for conservation of the property and to provide services for visitors, and the balance between these elements.

This ideal is inevitably difficult to achieve in practice in the face of constant pressures on resources and time. For example, the task of completing the descriptive inventory can be lengthy, whereas initiating management actions may be more pressing in the shorter-term, and therefore take initial priority. Nevertheless, inclusion of all elements is ultimately essential if these plans are to fulfil their full potential for the long-term management of monuments.

An audit of the nature conservation value of properties in care has recently been completed on behalf of Historic Scotland by Northern Ecological Services. The results are gradually being incorporated into the management of individual properties, leading to the integrated management and, in the best cases, interpretation of archaeological, historical and natural heritage interests. This project is described in detail in the second part of this paper.

In recent years, Historic Scotland has become increasingly involved with other organisations in individual partnership projects. Such projects generally try to integrate aspects of the cultural and natural heritage and can involve a wide range of bodies; key examples are in the Kilmartin Glen, Argyll (N.G.R. NR 89 NW), and at the Royal Park of Holyrood in Edinburgh (N.G.R. NT 27 SE). Such inter-disciplinary and inter-agency projects demand an integrated approach to management, and their essential components are:

● The identification of resources, encompassing the cultural and the natural heritage, interpretation, land management, and tourism and visitor management;

● The identification of the protection and management needs of each conservation element;

● The overall management objectives of the project, balancing protection, management and promotion.

To be successful, such integrated plans also need to include:

● A clear statement of the respective roles of individual bodies;

● An agreed time-scale for action;

● Actual and potential sources of funding;

● A balance between short-term action and long-term maintenance of the conservation resource.

● Land Management Plans

Land management plans can take a number of forms, covering both publicly-funded schemes and private initiatives. Some of these try to adopt an integrated, multi-objective approach. Two examples are considered here: Historic Scotland's own management grants and the Environmentally Sensitive Areas (ESA) scheme.

Historic Scotland's management grants take two forms: grants-to-owners and management agreements. The former tend to be applied to one-off programmes of

work, often relating to the consolidation of individual monuments, whilst the latter generally involve longer-term management. The essential requirements of each are:

● A description of the resource and an assessment of its value;

● Details of the proposed management actions accompanied, where necessary, by a sketch plan. Consolidation schemes may additionally require architectural specifications, but measured surveys are not normally a feature of the schemes.

Applications are discussed and agreed with Historic Scotland's Inspectorate staff, and monitored by its Monument Wardens, or Architects where the nature of the work demands this. These schemes seek to ensure that nature conservation interests are not inadvertently damaged in the management programme (through prior consultation with Scottish Natural Heritage, where appropriate) and increasingly try to enhance those interests where circumstances allow. The proposed Statement of Intent between Historic Scotland and Scottish Natural Heritage (currently in draft) will further increase the extent to which each organisation will try to take the other's interests into account in management plans and grant-aided schemes.

The Environmentally Sensitive Areas scheme is an agricultural grant scheme. It has multiple objectives, integrating nature conservation, archaeology and landscape within an agricultural context. The scheme operates for a ten year period, with a provision for annual reviews of individual plans and a more major review after five years. Its two main features are:

● 1) A basic set of compulsory protection prescriptions for each of the various conservation features. The range of features is identified on a survey map at 1:10000 scale, prepared on the basis of field observation rather than detailed survey;

• 2) Provision for positive management. This includes a number of mandatory prescriptions together with some voluntary options (including archaeology), brought together on a management map at 1:10000 scale.

The main strengths of the ESA scheme are its whole farm approach which encompasses the entire farming unit, not just conservation features; and its ability to balance different conservation objectives. The range of elements incorporated into the scheme normally requires a wide range of specialist advice, but this must be presented in clear terms which will enable the farmer to undertake the full management programme in a properly integrated way and with full understanding of the benefits this will bring. As the system is administered centrally by the agricultural department, there is a single co-ordinating point for general and specialist advice for each ESA, together with a single monitoring system. These provisions are very important in ensuring that the scheme's different elements are actively integrated in practice.

• Planning

Before drawing some common threads from the above, it is relevant to mention the planning system which also seeks to take an integrated approach to decision making. It does so through development planning, from Structure Plans through Local Plans to Environmental Assessments. In addition, there are an increasing number of Codes of Practice adopted by private companies and industry. While written codes often focus on single topics, such as archaeology or nature conservation, the major companies, such as in the electricity industry, have now adopted a greater awareness of, and more integrated approach to, the range of conservation interests. All of these try to identify the range of elements to be weighed up in the decision making process, and include in some measure:

• The identification of the resource, comprising desk-based research and sometimes limited field survey or evaluation. This usually covers nature conservation, archaeology, landscape and cultural or social issues;

• Proposed protection and mitigation measures. These may identify particular management requirements, but in many planning contexts do not usually encompass long-term maintenance.

• Principles of Integrated Management Planning

It is, of course, easier to prepare single subject management plans than those which are multi-disciplinary. However, whilst undoubtedly more time-consuming in preparation, an integrated approach to management plans can save time and money in the long run, because all elements are included and balanced from the outset, as far as is possible, rather than fitted in often unsatisfactorily at a late stage. Similarly, potential conflicts of interest can be addressed early in the planning process. Partnership projects also benefit from management plans of this sort to ensure that the aims and objectives of all the bodies involved are identified and kept in mind throughout the project.

On the basis of Historic Scotland's experience presented above, certain principles for successful integrated management plans can be drawn out:

• Identification of the scale and scope of the plan at the outset;

• Identification of all relevant parties that should be involved, and mechanisms for discussion;

• Identification of the strategic aims and physical boundaries of the plan;

• Identification of the resources, ideally combining desk-based research with some

Plate 1. The earthworks around Tantallon Castle support a wildflower-rich grassland, the species composition of which reflects the underlying influence of marling.

● Nature Conservation Management Plans for Historic Scotland Properties

Between 1991 and 1994 Northern Ecological Services were commissioned to produce nature conservation management plans for the 330 properties in care of Historic Scotland. The main aim of this exercise was to integrate nature conservation into overall site management, whilst retaining the protection of the archaeological and historic interest as the foremost management priority. The potential for the provision of information for visitors on the natural points of interest was also identified.

In each of the three years a selection of sites was covered by the study, which was divided into three distinct phases - survey, consultation and report production. However, consultation, which was found to be the key element of the project, in reality took place throughout all phases.

● Survey

As in any management study, collection of baseline information was the first step, and involved ecological surveys of all the sites and collation of existing information. The survey methodology had to allow a general assessment of nature conservation value of a site, but extensive surveys of all possible groups of flora and fauna could not be practicably carried out. The survey method used was based on an accepted survey methodology developed by the former Nature Conservancy Council, called the Phase 1 Habitat Survey. This concentrates on the different types of vegetation on a site, such as grassland, woodland, heath and wetland, classifying each according to plant species composition and management. This system provides a relatively effective way of assessing habitat quality, including its potential interest for fauna.

Many of Historic Scotland's properties are very small and support only amenity

survey, and including a map defining the area and individual elements of interest;

● Identification of the management objectives, including any specific protection measures for each element;

● Preparation of an overall management plan, including mitigation measures if appropriate.

● Identification of the time-scale of the plan, with separate short-, medium- and long-term proposals if necessary;

● Identification of responsibility for action and advice;

● Identification of actual and potential sources of funding;

● Establishment of review and monitoring procedures, with clear lines of responsibility;

● Sufficient flexibility to allow for changes in objectives;

● User-friendly, non-specialist, language.

grassland of little nature conservation value, and these sites were quickly dealt with. However, some of the large sites support habitat of some interest due to the fact that it has had little past modification or "improvement". In the case of grassland, the most widespread habitat type on Historic Scotland properties, "improvement" includes the application of fertiliser, cultivation and re-seeding. Unmodified habitat is known as "semi-natural". The geographical range of the sites, from lowland to upland Scotland and from west to east was reflected in the wide range of semi-natural habitat types recorded in the survey. These include upland moorland and bog at Staneydale Temple in Shetland (N.G.R. HU 285 502), lowland heath on the Antonine Wall in the Central Belt, ancient lowland woodland on the steep sides of the Nethan gorge below Craignethan Castle in Lanarkshire (N.G.R. NS 815 463), and reed swamp around the moated Caerlaverock Castle in Dumfriesshire (N.G.R. NY 025 656). Some of the sites of greatest interest lie within Sites of Special Scientific Interest (SSSIs).

Ecological interest was sometimes found to be directly connected to historical character. At a few of the sites, past marling of earthbanks has produced lime-rich soils supporting a grassland characteristic of limestone. This was noted, for example, at Tantallon Castle in East Lothian (N.G.R. NT 595 850; Plate 1), Hermitage Castle in the Borders (N.G.R. NY 496 961) and Auchindoun Castle in Grampian (N.G.R. NJ 348 374). Such grassland is naturally scarce in Scotland and therefore contains relatively rare plant species as well as being very species-rich. It also supports a great diversity of insects and other invertebrates, including butterflies, which are found in profusion at Tantallon.

Another ecological feature probably connected to site history is the occurrence of old garden species at a number of castles and abbeys in the east of Scotland. These include flowers which were grown in the past either as medicinal or culinary herbs,

Plate 2. Craigmillar Castle, where wild celery is found close to the site of the medieval kitchen garden.

such as green alkanet (*Pentaglottis sempervirens*), tansy (*Chrysanthemum vulgare*), mallow (*Malva* spp.), red valerian (*Centranthus ruber*), and periwinkle (*Vinca* spp.). One particular species of note is the wild celery (*Apium graveolens*) found at Craigmillar Castle on the edge of Edinburgh (N.G.R. NT 288 708; Plate 2). This plant is not thought to be a native of Scotland, and its usual habitat in the rest of the United Kingdom is in maritime grassland within the influence of salt spray. Craigmillar Castle, being some miles inland, would not seem to be a likely location for such a species, but the close proximity of the plant to the site of the medieval kitchen garden indicates its likely source. Wild celery was actually known in Scotland in Roman times, as faecal analysis at Bearsden Bath House has revealed (Dickson, Dickson and Breeze, 1979).

Ecological interest is also found on the human-made habitat of the monument walls at some of the sites. Certain species of wildflower and fern grow vigorously on lime mortar, but have become relatively scarce because of the decreased use of wall lime. One species in particular, pellitory-of-the-wall (*Parietaria diffusa*), is more or less restricted to old walls, but was found on numerous monuments in the south east and north east of the Country.

Although systematic faunal surveys were not generally carried out, attention was paid to signs of bats and barn owls (*Tyto alba*), legally protected species often found in the more intact monuments. Bats make use of wall crevices and cracks, roof eaves, spaces between tiles, cavity walls and other well-protected draught free places, for roosting and breeding. One species, the brown long-eared (*Plecotus auritus*), will also roost in roof apices. The presence of bats is most often indicated by their droppings, which appear mouse-like, but are dry and crumbly and fairly inoffensive. A number of large bat roosts were already known from Historic Scotland monuments, such as Huntingtower Castle, near Perth (N.G.R. NO 082 251), which contains one of the largest bat colonies in Scotland. However, quite a number of new roost sites were discovered, including several winter hibernation sites, which are relatively scarce in Scotland.

Barn owls, which have suffered a decline in feeding and nesting habitat in modern times with the rise of intensive agriculture and loss or conversion of old barns respectively, were also found to roost or nest in a number of the monuments.

● Consultation

The process of drawing up management recommendations had to proceed hand in hand with consultation to ensure that the proposals were acceptable on three counts.

● 1) The most important factor was whether the archaeological or historical interest would be affected by the recommended management. This was most applicable to measures to conserve bats, which often involved leaving roost holes and entrances unmortared. Clearly, conflict might arise if such mortaring was vital to the structural integrity of the monument. As much information as possible was provided on the location of roosts to ensure that

they remained undisturbed in any works where mortaring proved not to be vital. Where mortaring was deemed essential, advance planning, careful timing and full consultation with Scottish Natural Heritage were recommended, so that any impacts could be minimised.

Some habitat management measures, such as tree planting, could also affect archaeological or historical interest and again had to be carefully thought out. Similarly, the case for allowing flowers and ferns to grow on walls was discussed at length to gain a balance between the need for wall cleaning to prevent structural damage by roots and the desirability of conserving the more unusual species.

● 2) The second point for consideration was the practicality of the proposed measures, particularly for habitat management. Many nature conservation management techniques are very different from the traditional amenity and horticultural practices used to date on many Historic Scotland properties. The proposed management therefore had to be realistic in terms of the present resources at the disposal of Historic Scotland, particularly in terms of expertise and equipment. To this end, prescribed management techniques, particularly for grass cutting, were generally simpler than those that might be recommended when nature conservation is the main or sole management aim.

● 3) The final point for consideration was the acceptability of proposals in visual terms. Nature conservation management, particularly of grasslands, often results in a more "wild" appearance than that resulting from traditional amenity management techniques. With increased awareness of environmental issues, much of the public would probably now accept and even desire a less formal appearance to some of the monuments. However, in some cases the informal look can be inappropriate, especially where the monument is "set off" by lawns and planned vistas. Less formal management in these cases could give the impression to some people that the monument was being neglected, and a balance therefore had to be struck. Visual acceptability was also a concern where a particular facet of a monument might be obscured by the changed management. For example, longer sward heights can obscure the outline of earthworks, hindering their interpretation.

Consultation very often started with the site custodian at the staffed monuments during the initial site survey. As well as providing information on the fauna of the site, the custodians could explain current management regimes. The next stage involved a series of meetings with architects, inspectors, and works managers to discuss draft management proposals for the more important sites. These were useful in allowing us to explain the general principles of the management proposals and also provided an insight into what would be both possible and acceptable. The final part of the consultation process was to attend site meetings as part of the spring tour, in which the architects, inspectors and works managers visit a select number of sites to discuss future management requirements. This proved to be the most useful form of consultation, as there is no substitute for having the "real thing", whether an area of unimproved grassland or a bat roost, with which to demonstrate a point. It was also invaluable in allowing us to understand the potential difficulties our proposals might have for the people who would be implementing them.

● Report production

Two types of management reports were formulated. The least interesting and/or small sites were covered by management briefs, whilst the most interesting and/or complex sites were covered by management plans, these latter being more comprehensive than the briefs. Both report types comprised two sections, covering survey and management respectively. The Report of Survey, which was annotated to a colour habitat map, was kept as non-

technical as possible, but ecological terms could not be completely omitted. With this in mind, a summary paragraph, describing the main interest and value of the site, including any statutory designations or protected species that Historic Scotland should be aware of, was placed at the beginning of the report.

The management section was generally divided into two, with prescriptions and specifications. The prescriptions covered all the management recommendations for a site, with some discussion on the ecological background to each measure. This latter part was felt to be very important as it allowed an understanding of why prescriptions were recommended. The need for some form of interpretation to explain the changed management regime to the public was also identified in this section. This was felt to be particularly necessary where a relaxation of the mowing regime had been recommended. The prescriptions also emphasised the need for consultation with Scottish Natural Heritage over proposed changes to management in Sites of Special Scientific Interest.

The specifications covered those prescriptions that related to discrete areas on the ground and which could be precisely detailed, and were meant to aid the issue of instructions to ground staff, particularly in the drawing up of contract specifications. Not all prescriptions could be covered by specifications, usually because of their general, non-area-specific nature.

● Other outputs

As part of the same project, we also produced a nature conservation management manual for Historic Scotland staff. This was aimed at the site managers such as the architects, inspectors and works managers and was written to take account of the specific conditions involved in the management of Historic Scotland properties. As well as providing recommended management measures for given situations, it gave explanatory information on the principles of nature

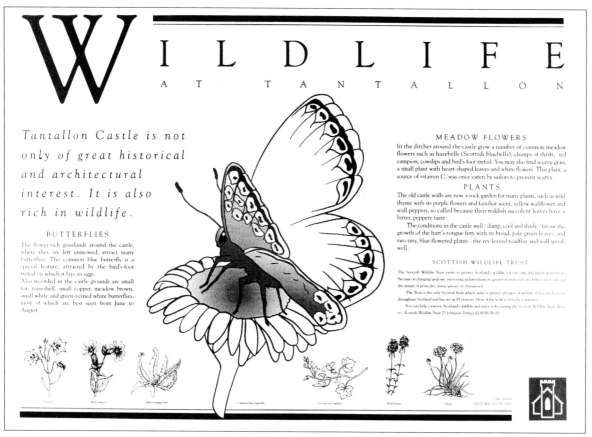

WILDLIFE
AT TANTALLON

Tantallon Castle is not only of great historical and architectural interest. It is also rich in wildlife.

BUTTERFLIES

The flower-rich grasslands around the castle, where they are left unmowed, attract many butterflies. The common blue butterfly is a special feature, attracted by the bird's-foot trefoil on which it lays its eggs.

Also recorded in the castle grounds are small tortoiseshell, small copper, meadow brown, small white and green-veined white butterflies, most of which are best seen from June to August.

MEADOW FLOWERS

In the ditches around the castle grow a number of common meadow flowers such as harebells (Scottish bluebells), clumps of thrift, red campion, cowslips and bird's-foot trefoil. You may also find scurvy-grass, a small plant with heart-shaped leaves and white flowers. This plant, a source of vitamin C, was once eaten by sailors to prevent scurvy.

PLANTS

The old castle walls are now a rock garden for many plants, such as wild thyme with its purple flowers and familiar scent, yellow wallflower and wall peppers, so called because their reddish succulent leaves have a bitter, peppery taste.

The conditions in the castle well - damp, cool and shady - favour the growth of the hart's-tongue fern with its broad, pale-green leaves, and two tiny, blue-flowered plants - the ivy-leaved toadflax and wall speed-well.

SCOTTISH WILDLIFE TRUST

The Scottish Wildlife Trust exists to protect Scotland's wildlife for our own and future generations. Because of changing land-use, increasing industrialisation, greater recreational use of the countryside and the misuse of pesticides, many species are threatened.

The Trust is the only Scottish body which seeks to protect all types of wildlife. It has reserves throughout Scotland and has set up 85 reserves. Most of the work is done by volunteers.

You can help conserve Scotland's wildlife and enjoy it by joining the Scottish Wildlife Trust. Write to: Scottish Wildlife Trust, 25 Johnston Terrace, EDINBURGH.

HISTORIC SCOTLAND

Plate 3. The information board at Tantallon Castle explains the natural history interest of the wildflower grassland.

conservation management. It was hoped that a basic understanding of the rationale for such management would assist future implementation of the management reports.

The final part of the project was the production of interpretative material for the public covering nature conservation interest at a selected number of sites, in the form of text for either information boards, such as the one which was already set up at Tantallon Castle (Plate 3), or walk leaflets.

● Conclusion

An important facet to emerge from the study was that the potential for conflict between nature conservation and historical conservation could usually be very much lessened, if not removed, by an understanding of the "twin requirements". With this in mind, an underlying aim of the project has been to try to explain why certain management is prescribed, rather than just purely producing a set of recommendations. This was also felt to be vital to the successful implementation of the management reports after the Consultant's involvement had ceased. Understanding on both sides was felt to be particularly achieved through the consultations and site visits. The project very much proved to be a "coming together of minds" between nature conservation and historical/archaeological conservation and both parties certainly benefited from the insight into the other's discipline.

● References

Dickson, J.H., Dickson, C.A. and Breeze, D.J. (1979) Flour or Bread in a Roman Military Ditch at Bearsden. *Antiquity*, 53. 47-51.

The National Trust's Approach to Integrated Conservation Management

David Thackray, Rob Jarman and Jo Burgon

Chief Archaeological Adviser, Environmental Practices Adviser and Coast and Countryside Adviser, The National Trust

● Introduction

This paper will examine briefly the range of specialisms employed within the National Trust to achieve a balance of conservation and other concerns inherent in its property management. We will briefly examine the role of surveys, including archaeological and historic landscape, vernacular buildings, nature conservation, woodlands, historic parks and gardens and environmental practices as the means of informing property managers of the special significance of their particular area of responsibility.

The implications of this mass of information for the Trust's agricultural tenants, its visitors, supporters and critics, and the communities with which it is often intimately involved, all need careful consideration. This holistic approach to property management which the Trust is working to achieve is viewed against the constant processes of change in the environment as well as in attitudes, values and perceptions. Change is part of the historical continuum, and today's developments will be tomorrow's "monuments". We have therefore adopted a very broad definition of "ancient monuments" for the purposes of this paper and have tried to express this within the context of the great diversity of the Trust's properties.

● The National Trust's Purposes

The key words of the National Trust Acts are: *"to promote...the permanent preservation...of lands and buildings...of historic interest and natural beauty...for the benefit of the nation"*. The Trust has achieved these purposes since its foundation in 1895, principally through the acquisition of land and buildings and artefacts. The current inventory of Trust property (see Appendix One) is an extraordinary indication of success. The Trust also interprets its duty "to promote" through its educational work and involvement with a wide range of other agencies, interest groups and individuals. The Trust would always seek now to extend its work beyond its property boundaries to the benefit of the wider landscape and environment.

The diversity of the National Trust's properties reflects the British countryside, remotely rural or suburban; upland or lowland; farmland and open-space; village and hamlet; anciently wooded or recent plantations; historic estates, mansions, designed landscapes and gardens; coast, estuary and river. There are also some urban properties of importance for their historic value and community opportunities.

This range inevitably includes examples of the multiplicity of statutory and non-statutory designations that apply to much of Britain. These include National Parks, Areas of Outstanding Natural Beauty (AONBs), Heritage Coasts, Listed Buildings, Conservation Areas and Scheduled Ancient Monuments (SAMs), National Nature Reserves (NNRs) and Sites of Special Scientific Interest (SSSIs), Special Protection Areas (SPAs), Special Areas of Conservation (SACs) and Environmentally Sensitive Areas (ESAs). The Trust is also involved in a number of Countryside Stewardship and Tir Cymen schemes. All of these carry particular conservation requirements and implications in terms of management expertise. A number of them recognise the importance of the historical dimension in developing their management prescriptions.

In addition to these many areas covered by one or more designations, the Trust owns substantial areas not so protected, and in these recognises the importance of understanding and preserving the particular features that are significant to the place.

Two principal objectives guide the management of such a wide range of landscapes and sites: their preservation and enhancement; and, wherever possible, the provision of public access for recreation and enjoyment. There are, and have been throughout the Trust's history, some tensions between these, yet together they must continue to underline all ensuing, detailed management objectives. The Trust is able to achieve long-term preservation through its special ability to hold properties inalienably as a result of its unique legal status (National Trust Acts). The Trust also operates a system of Covenants, whereby the owners of property undertake in a legally-binding contract with the Trust not to do certain works without the Trust's consent.

In setting the scene in this way it is obvious that the Trust must employ a whole suite of scientific, historic, aesthetic and management expertise in addressing its property management responsibilities. The disciplines involved include, *inter alia,* landscape archaeology, building history and building conservation; nature conservation and ecology; agriculture and land agency; forestry and woodland management; horticulture and garden history; access, recreation and visitor management; environmental assessment, training and education.

The management of "ancient monuments", however they are defined, is closely integrated into all these areas of activity. At this stage it would be useful to examine briefly the range of the Trust's archaeological work before going on to describe how it fits into the "management cycle". The Trust is increasingly acknowledging the importance of archaeology in providing historical information about its landscapes, sites and buildings to inform and guide detailed conservation strategies. Archaeological techniques are applied to building recording (Thackray, 1994a), park and garden surveys, the conservation of industrial sites, and landscape assessment and evaluations, as well as to the recording and conservation of field monuments. The term "ancient monument", therefore, may be taken in this context to apply equally to historic buildings, historic designed landscapes or garden features, industrial monuments, or built, historic landscape structures such as walls or hedges. Historic ecological features, including woods, heaths, grasslands, dune systems, etc are also frequently subject to archaeological analysis. Of especial importance are ecosystems which preserve historical information, such as ancient woodland soils, wetlands and peatlands, and geomorphological features.

The importance of such sites will vary, depending on rarity or ubiquity, scale, quality, robustness or fragility and age or historical depth. However, all will share some of the following values to a greater or lesser extent: scientific value, history, aesthetic quality, environmental quality, landscape value, amenity value, psychological or spiritual values.

The National Trust approaches integrated management through an assessment of the significances of a property. This is achieved by survey and research in a number of well-established formats, including archaeological and historic landscape surveys, vernacular buildings surveys, biological surveys, park and garden surveys, woodland surveys and environmental assessments.

● Archaeological and historic landscape surveys

Archaeological and historic landscape surveys have been undertaken on approximately 50% of all Trust properties to date. This process began in the 1980s, utilising a number of MSC Community Programme schemes. The Trust has now appointed archaeologists in the majority of its regions, either specifically to undertake archaeological surveys of its properties, or to manage detailed recording projects. This has generally resulted in the integration of the archaeologists into the regional management team, to a greater or lesser extent; a very valuable relationship. In addition, there is a small Head Office advisory team involved in policy development as well as the provision of property management advice. These internal services are enhanced by the use of external consultants, and a number of independent archaeological units have developed an expertise in carrying out property archaeological surveys to the Trust's format. These arrangements have enabled all the Trust's regions to have access to professional archaeological survey skills in some form or another. The survey reports are based on fieldwork and documentary research, and comprise an inventory of sites and structures with maps and plans, accompanied by an assessment of the land-use history of the property. The inventory includes conservation management recommendations for the individual sites or components of the landscape, together with recommendations for further survey and research, and the development of presentation or education opportunities.

In the Lake District, for example, these surveys have focused in additional detail on surveying and researching historic field boundaries as part of the farmed landscape, in order to determine which are of greatest historical significance, to establish priorities for retention and repair. Similarly, historic tracks and paths have been studied to aid an extensive programme of upland footpath repair and maintenance. These surveys have demonstrated the pattern of evolution, continuity and change affecting these landscapes and serve as a guide to acceptable future change and development.

The information gathered is to be held on a central database, the NT Sites and Monuments Record (SMR) at the head office at Cirencester and information will be accessed by the archaeologists in the regions. This service will be fully in operation in 1995.

● Vernacular buildings surveys

A separate, but very closely related, survey of vernacular buildings has been undertaken throughout all Trust regions. This has produced information on the structural history and importance of farmhouses, farm buildings, cottages, villages and estate houses, and some industrial buildings. Documentary research on the buildings' history complements that undertaken for the archaeological surveys and has helped to provide understanding of the social and land-use history of many hitherto unresearched areas. Both surveys have inevitably produced a number of important new discoveries which have been recognised in property management. The vernacular buildings surveys are also being held on the SMR, which will eventually be able to provide constraint maps and records for the historic environment for property managers, public affairs staff and other researchers.

● Biological surveys

A biological survey team of four ecologists has completed an initial survey of all Trust properties in England, Wales and Northern Ireland, and has recently embarked on a re-survey cycle. The team's skills include botany, zoology and geology, with particular individual specialisms.

Their survey method differs from that of the archaeologists in that they are centrally-based at Cirencester and have undertaken their survey programme as a team, systematically covering all properties in a given region during a long, summer, fieldwork season. Detailed reports are prepared following the fieldwork. Further reports result from specific site visits by the four Nature Conservation Advisers, also based at Cirencester. These latter are also considerably involved in policy development.

The biological survey reports aim to evaluate habitats, communities and species on each property in an international, national, regional and local context, in order to provide objective assessments of importance. The reports also contain ideal recommendations for management, which may be tempered by the Property Manager in the preparation of a property management plan, taking account of all other constraints on and priorities for the property. However, nature conservation requirements are generally seen as a very high priority and conflicting interests, sometimes including access and farming, have to be very carefully considered.

Conflicts with public access are usually resolved by a variety of management strategies, including zoning, the creation of sanctuaries, path and car park siting and careful wardening. In practice, high visitor pressure can be zoned to reduce impact elsewhere, whilst those areas of high impact, for example long-distance trails, such as the Pennine Way or the coastal footpaths, require more intensive maintenance. Such works are often undertaken in conjunction with other agencies, including National Park Authorities, or Heritage Coast staff. Decisions on integrated management for the enhancement of nature conservation value will apply to a greater or lesser extent on all properties, but it is worth recording that many examples of very popular sites remain of national or international importance for nature conservation. Hearn (1994: 374) cites Dovedale (N.G.R. SK 15 NW and SW), with 2 million visitors per year; Box Hill (N.G.R. TQ 15 SE), one million; Clumber Park (N.G.R. SK 67 NW), one million; Studland (N.G.R. SZ 08 NW and SW), one million; and Giant's Causeway (N.G.R. C 952 452), half a million, as examples of properties where the high quality of the wildlife value is retained, despite visitor numbers.

The close integration of nature conservation with the conservation of archaeological sites

and historic landscapes is widely recognised (Hearn, 1994: 373; Lambrick, 1985). The two disciplines share many similar aims and requirements, for example semi-natural vegetation, and long-established land-use methods with ancient habitats often the richest. The same pressures of access and agriculture apply to both. Indeed, without the knowledge of past land-use practices both disciplines would be considerably poorer; such practices include the practical, traditional skills of land-management, such as hedgelaying, stone-walling, hay-meadow or other grassland management and woodland management.

● Trees and woodlands

In a recent review of the policy and practice for the management of its trees and woods (Russell, 1992), the Trust has prepared an exemplary model for their integrated management. In this report it recognises the importance of Britain's woodlands especially semi-natural woodlands for their diverse scientific value for nature conservation and archaeology, as well as their importance for landscape protection, and public access and amenity (Russell, 1992, 11). The review also promotes the careful, restricted management of woods to retain that great diversity.

The Trust owns approximately 8,500ha of ancient woodlands and 15,000ha of plantation woodlands, much of which is now of historical value. Traditional methods of woodland management, including coppicing, pollarding and woodland grazing, and the management for timber production, have been applied throughout all of the Trust's woodlands. The understanding and evaluation of the history of woodland management for each of these woods is essential in order to maintain management systems that will respect and perpetuate the particular importance of each (Russell, 1992: 14-18). These systems will include coppicing, thinning, singling, the control of grazing and, where necessary, planting. However, diversity is also achieved by allowing natural processes to continue, including maturity and ageing, windthrow and the creation of glades, and regeneration. In this way the great variety of habitats is retained and evolves. The importance of ancient woodland in protecting undisturbed soil profiles and preserving artefacts is well understood but sometimes forgotten in practice.

This recognition of the considerable conservation values of woodlands does not preclude acknowledgement of the economic value of carefully managed timber where this is appropriate (Russell, 1992: 18). In some plantations timber production may be the principal management aim.

There are, inevitably, considerable tensions between different interests relating to the value, use and management of trees and woodlands. In the past, the economic value of the Trust's woodland was seen as of greater importance than its conservation or historic value. As a result of these recent changes of policy and practice, woodland management has become multi-disciplinary, and conservation, public access, and timber-production all have to be carefully managed together. To achieve these interests the Trust has learnt that public understanding and support are essential, especially where tree-felling is concerned, and consultation with local communities provides an opportunity to explain the conservation reasons for proposed changes in woodland management, whether they are to improve access, conserve ancient monuments, or enhance habitats.

● Park and garden surveys

Historic park and garden surveys are being undertaken to guide the conservation, rehabilitation or even restoration of designed landscapes. An Historic Park and Garden Surveyor, also based at Cirencester, undertakes or commissions many such surveys; over 70 have been achieved to date. A standard outline brief has been prepared for these, which is modified to suit individual site survey requirements. This addresses the nature conservation value, land-use history and archaeological interest of the sites, prior to the park or garden development. The subsequent history of the designed landscape is recorded in detail, with period map overlays supported by a written historical account. These generally enable the archaeological potential of the various phases of design to be assessed, and include the sites of ornamental buildings, previous garden structures, beds and parterres, ornamental water-management systems, etc.

The surveys also involve the physical recording and tagging of trees and shrubs, with information on their age, species and aesthetic function in the designed landscape recorded on a substantial database, the Woody Plant Catalogue. This record is currently being developed as a catalogue of all the Trust's plant collections in gardens, as well as of those significant features of designed landscapes.

Many later, designed parks contain residual features of their early origins as, perhaps, medieval deer-parks or warrens, including structural features such as deer-park pales or trees surviving from early, parkland wood-pasture. These are often particularly important as habitats, as well as records of the early land-use. Other parks replaced pre-existing landscapes, traces of which may survive in, for example, the form of the banks of enclosures, or ridge and furrow from medieval fields, the earthworks of removed medieval settlements or, even prehistoric sites. In a number of recent cases archaeologists have been appointed to designed landscape projects to undertake any necessary survey, recording and research arising from restoration and required to inform conservation briefs. Examples include Stowe in Buckinghamshire (N.G.R. SP 63 NE), Gibside in Tyne and Wear (N.G.R. NZ 15 NE), and Fountains Abbey and Studley Royal, Yorkshire (N.G.R. SE 26 NE).

Conflict between these various elements of conservation value has arisen in the past, largely as a result of lack of information or appropriate consultation. Damage to medieval earthworks in Wimpole Park, Cambridgeshire (N.G.R. TL 35 SW) in 1980 arose for just such a reason. The preparation of integrated archaeological and historic landscape surveys and biological surveys in conjunction with historic parks surveys should ensure that such mistakes do not occur again.

The aesthetic quality of a "tidy" landscape "created" by one of the great landscape designers is often of far less value for fauna and flora than the standing and fallen deadwood and decaying timber of a medieval wood-pasture. Hearn (1994, 373) records that a concordat was agreed in 1993, based on an integrated plan for each park, stating that ancient features should take precedence, and that deadwood should be retained. Again, integrated management is essential in order to establish priorities for the preservation of maximum value.

● Databases

Data from archaeological, nature conservation and park and garden surveys are gradually being accessioned to major databases being developed and relating to each subject area. These include the Sites and Monuments Record, the Woody Plant Catalogue, and the Nature Conservation database. Although all of these are in relatively early stages of development, or of data-entry, there is an intention to network them all in the Estates Advisers' Office in Cirencester to facilitate the process of integration, and the provision of information and constraints for property managers. This is a fundamental curatorial tool for dealing with the complexities of future management.

● Environmental Practices Review

As work on these rather more traditional areas of activity progresses, through survey and information gathering to the provision of advice for property management, the Trust is also embarking on an internal environmental audit, started in 1990, to review the whole range of Trust interests, policies and practices for their actual and

potential environmental impacts. This is now known as the Environmental Practices Review and represents a commitment from the Trust to minimise the environmental impacts arising from all its activities (Jarman, 1992).

In doing this the Trust recognises that its responsibilities are:

● To ensure that its long-term interests are not jeopardised or damaged by unavoidable human-induced environmental change;

● To promote the protection of the environment and the countryside beyond the Trust's present landholdings;

● Principally, to ensure that the Trust's own activities do not generate adverse environmental impacts.

Priority areas for changes in practices and for further evaluation have been targeted, including: energy conservation; water conservation; waste minimisation and re-use; pollution control (principally sewage and farm effluents); transport; agriculture and land management; building restoration, construction and management; and office management. Training in environmental awareness and detailed environmental management skills is fundamental to this initiative.

It is important to mention this in a discussion of integrated conservation management, as these principles will increasingly underline all Trust management for the future (Hearn, 1994: 375).

The Trust has already invested considerably in improving standards of property management for energy, sewage, farm effluent and water quality issues. Integral with this investment is the development of innovatory, environmentally-benign solutions in many related areas of management, including:

● whole farm plans;

● energy awareness training;

● water conservation initiatives;

● a risk assessment for private water supplies;

- buffer zones;

- soil conservation measures;

- peatland conservation and peat substitutes;

- sustainable tourism projects;

- "green" buildings;

- catchment management;

- promotion of non-car access to the countryside;

- renewable energy generation;

- dry compost toilet systems;

- reedbed and wetland dirty water treatment systems;

- pre-emptive waste minimisation.

Many of these will embrace the conservation of the historic environment, including "ancient monuments" as defined above. For example, the Trust is currently looking at a range of historic water-powered sites, including mills and hydro-electricity generating sites, to investigate their potential for research and development in this field through the rehabilitation of existing plant, machinery and structures, or the installation of new machinery in parallel with the old. The detailed conservation requirements of all these proposals are being assessed on a site-by-site basis. Another aspect is the pollution implications of many industrial archaeological sites on contaminated land.

Property Management Plans

Survey data from all the above sources forms an essential part of the Property Management Plan, usually drawn together by a Property Manager or Managing Agent. This document, reviewed approximately every five years, contains a synthesis of survey information with established priorities for management assessed through consultation with appropriate advisers. However, management is always a matter

of judgement. Reconciling the various interests in land is a matter of balance and significance. Some form of ranking has to be established, at least informally, so that resources can be directed at the most important sites for each interest. For example, a well-equipped farm in the eastern counties producing a high rent but containing no sites of particular archaeological or nature conservation interest would have productive agriculture as the dominant use. Conversely, an upland farm in an area of high landscape value and containing a number of SSSIs or SAMs would see agriculture as a method of maintaining the conservation interest (Thackray and Hearn, 1985). The difficulty is that few cases are clear cut and the establishment of relative significance often requires compromise.

Conservation and Agriculture

Of particular importance, therefore, is the relationship which the Property Manager or Managing Agent is able to establish with the agricultural tenants. About 45% of the Trust's landholding is occupied by farmers under agricultural tenancies or grazing licences. The main objective of the tenants will be to make a living, whilst the Trust's objectives are varied and may inhibit the farmer's ability to manage his or her business profitably. Constraints on farming imposed by conservation requirements will sometimes be recognised by a lower rent or under a management agreement, for example a Countryside Stewardship agreement with the Countryside Commission or an agreement with MAFF in ESAs. The Trust is developing similar agreements with its own tenants.

The "whole farm plan" is seen as an effective method of establishing priorities for a farm. This is a four-stage process of data collection, evaluation, site inspection and writing a farm plan.

The key to the process is the farm assessment coupled with a site inspection. It is vital that all relevant conservation interests provide information on the value of the farm, following survey, that the important disciplines are represented on the site inspection, and that priorities are agreed. It is equally important that the needs of the farm business are incorporated. It may or may not be necessary to proceed to a detailed written plan; often the process of evaluation and inspection will enable a sensible assessment of priorities to be agreed and suitable farming practices instituted. Whole farm plans have been developed for the Sherborne and Ebworth Estates in Gloucestershire and are gradually being implemented elsewhere. The successful incorporation of conservation clauses into tenancy agreements is accepted practice as new tenancies arise or as tenancy renewal provides opportunities for existing agreements. For example, the infrastructure of historic and prehistoric boundary features and sites, including late prehistoric courtyard-house settlements, is referred to specifically in the tenancy agreement for Bosigran Farm, Zennor in West Penwith, Cornwall (N.G.R. SW 425 367). Indeed, on a number of Cornish coastal properties, areas of coastal heath containing significant archaeological sites are being increasingly withdrawn from tenancies and managed in hand by careful grazing regimes, using such stock as Shetland ponies on the Lizard, or Manx sheep at Rosemergy (N.G.R. SW 415 365) and Bosigran, Zennor. These animals are able to check and reduce scrub invasion that has developed over recent decades, enhance and increase the coastal heathland value and, as a direct consequence, provide an ideal grazing medium for the sensitive archaeological features, the historic field boundaries, field-clearance features, settlement and small industrial sites that were in danger of inundation by scrub, with the subsequent threat of root damage. The reinstatement and repair of stockproof boundaries in this area also enhances the potential for carefully managed grazing regimes and has been undertaken as a direct result of archaeological surveys (Thackray and Hearn, 1985: 53). Grazing is

also being reintroduced or modified on calcareous grasslands to reduce scrub, provide the most advantageous grazing medium for both species-rich limestone habitats and for the earthworks of monuments such as Hod Hill (N.G.R. ST 857 107), or Badbury Rings (N.G.R. ST 964 030), Dorset or Dolebury Warren, Avon (N.G.R. ST 450 590).

The "whole farm plan" also enables the pollution control requirements to be properly assessed and compared with the overall objectives of management of the property. In some cases land capability and environmental sensitivity dictate that the long-term interests of the site can only be conserved by a change in the farm enterprise, rather than by investment in "end-of-pipe" pollution control technologies. The Trust is pioneering the use of Farm Plans to determine the long-term land-use of a site, to benefit soil, water, wildlife and cultural interests.

● Staffing the Countryside

The implementation of property management on the ground is the direct responsibility of the Countryside Manager or Warden, many of whom have training in nature conservation, forestry or related disciplines. The appointment of an archaeologist as warden, now Property Manager, for the Avebury area (N.G.R. SU 102 700) in 1985 established an important precedent, recognising that professional knowledge of the historic landscape or archaeology is an equally appropriate background to countryside or property management as is nature conservation. More recently (1994), an archaeologist/warden has been appointed to manage the Upper Plym Valley on Dartmoor, Devon (N.G.R. SX 56 NE and SE; SX 65 NW), with its pre-eminent complexes of prehistoric and medieval settlement and ritual sites, agriculture and industry set in a landscape important for its diversity of nature conservation values. Similar appointments are envisaged for our important historic landscapes and will provide a balance of countryside conservation skills within regional management structures which will enable the process of integration to develop yet further.

● Opportunities for Education

Environmental projects clearly have important educational value and, as with all its other conservation work, the Trust is becoming increasingly aware of opportunities to promote projects and produce information for school and adult groups. These are being developed by the Trust's Education Department working within the framework of the National Curriculum. School Guardianship schemes have developed to encourage a close relationship between individual schools and properties. In addition, the educational value of conservation work is promoted through the Trust's many active volunteering schemes, particularly the Acorn Camps. Activities range in these from habitat survey and management; to footpath and access creation and maintenance; to archaeological survey and site conservation projects. Both the educational projects and the volunteer working groups require the active involvement of property manager or warden and help to encourage a greater understanding of environmental conservation.

● Visitor Access, Tourism and the Community

The promotion of public access to Trust properties is, and always has been, one of its principal objectives. However, it will be clear from the above that there are instances where large numbers of visitors reduce, or damage that which they have come to visit, or, incidentally other features en route. Recent examples where archaeological sites have been adversely affected by visitors include the Bronze Age cairns on the summits of the Brecon Beacons, where rescue excavation was necessary to record the sites as their peat cover was lost to erosion, and as part of their consolidation; or the coastal promontory fort of Bolt Tail, South Devon (N.G.R. SX 669 396), the rampart of which is crossed by the heavily used South Devon Coastal Footpath (Thackray, 1994b: 103).

However, increasing public access is a fact of life and it becomes the responsibility of the property manager to monitor its effect on any areas of sensitivity on the property and to seek appropriate advice and carry out any necessary remedial or maintenance work. This clearly adds to the day-to-day costs of property maintenance, and, increasingly, needs to be included as a recurring item on the annual budget. The Trust has recently carried out a substantial Access Review to be published in 1995, examining in detail all forms of access to every category of property.

The role of tourism as an economic force capable of generating income to support the maintenance of historic landscapes is widely recognised (Tourism and the Environment Task Force, 1991). Tourism values the past either in its own right, or as a backdrop and setting for a whole range of outdoor pursuits or activities.

The Trust is actively seeking ways at national, regional and property levels to influence economic forces, including tourism, which can lead to detrimental changes to landscape character. In particular, the Trust is examining ways of working with the local economy which are in harmony with the landscape, including the sensitive, low-key promotion of certain properties, farm diversification schemes involving low-key tourism, finding appropriate and sensitive re-uses for redundant vernacular buildings no longer required for agriculture, or the careful design and siting of appropriate new facilities to support, or reduce the pressure on existing properties. The promotion of public transport or other non-car access to the countryside, and other sustainable tourism projects, will play increasingly important roles in future tourism and visitor management.

• Conclusion

It must be said that these processes of assessment and evaluation that the Trust is applying to its properties, are not carried out in isolation. Partnerships are essential in all these areas of activity. These include international, national and regional agencies, scientific consultation and the involvement of local communities in determining the significance of the place. The Trust is also looking increasingly beyond the boundaries of its own properties to the wider landscape to consider the impacts of development and change on the context of its properties and, indeed, the effect of its own activities on wider areas.

It must also be said that the Trust is not opposed to change, but accepts the importance of continuity, of decay and revitalisation, provided that these do not brutally affect the character and integrity of the place. The landscape needs to continue to be used both as a work-place and for visitors. The success of this depends as much on the conservation of the ubiquitous and ordinary features of the landscape as on the conservation of structures, sites and habitats of major importance.

Integrity of the landscape is not about standing still and accepting no change. Change can be manipulated by various fiscal incentives and a host of management mechanisms. This is dependant on society's willingness to accept constraints. Integrity is about a unity, a visual appreciation, a lack of "jarring", how the various elements in a landscape fit together - new and old. Integrity is about knowing the landscape's antecedents and how the new can be fashioned from a knowledge and understanding of the past.

Perhaps the "key words" for the Trust in the future interpretation of its purposes will include "precautionary approach... preventative conservation... innovation...people and sustainable lifestyles...perpetual natural resources".

• Acknowledgements

We gratefully acknowledge the help and advice given to us in the preparation of this paper by Katherine Hearn, Nature Conservation Adviser; John Young, Rural Affairs Adviser; David Russell, Chief Forestry Adviser and Philip Claris, Archaeological Adviser.

• References

Hearn, K.A. (1994) "The Natural Aspect" of the National Trust. *British Wildlife*, 5, No.6. 367-378.

Jarman, R. (1992) *The National Trust's Environmental Audit*. ECOS 13(1) 1992.

Lambrick, G. (ed) (1985) *Archaeology and Nature Conservation*. Oxford University Department for External Studies.

Russell, D. (1992) The National Trust Trees and Woodland Fund. *A Review of the Management of National Trust Trees and Woodlands*.

Thackray, D. (1994a) Major Conservation Projects: Recording Historic Buildings The National Trust's Developing Role in, Wood, J. (ed) *Buildings Archaeology Applications in Practice*. 165-182.

Thackray, D. (1994b) The Management of Monuments and Erosion Control on National Trust Properties in, Berry, A.Q. and Brown, I.W. (eds) *Erosion on Archaeological Earthworks: Its Prevention, Control and Repair*. Mold: Clwyd County Council. 103-110.

Thackray, D. and Hearn, K.A. (1985) Archaeology and Nature Conservation: The Responsibility of the National Trust in, Lambrick, G. (ed) *Archaeology and Nature Conservation*. Oxford University Department of External Studies. 51-58.

The National Trust Acts. 1907-1971.

Tourism and the Environment Task Force. (1991) *Report of the Heritage Sites Working Group*. Department of Employment and English Tourist Board.

● Appendix One

● Land and landscape properties protected by the National Trust

Land owned: 234,853ha
Land under covenant: 31,627ha
Coastline: 861km
Coastal land protected through the Trust's Enterprise Neptune Appeal initiative: 47,346ha
Percentage of total coastline protected in England, Wales and Northern Ireland: 17.4%
Gardens open in 1992: 161
Landscape parks/Deer parks open in 1992: 189
Farms managed "in hand" by the Trust: Wimpole Hall, Home Farm, Cambridgeshire.
Farms leased to tenants, with and without buildings: 1,217

● Nature reserves and habitats protected by the National Trust

National Nature Reserves (NNRs) owned by the Trust: 26
Sites of Special Scientific Interest (SSSIs) wholly or partially owned by the Trust in England: 327
SSSIs partly or wholly owned by the Trust in Wales: 67
Areas of Special Scientific Interest (ASSIs) owned by the Trust in Northern Ireland: 5
Upland heath: 20,000ha
Lowland heath: 3,600ha
Chalk and limestone grasslands: 3,100ha
Unimproved pastures and meadows: 1,600ha
Peatlands: 14,700ha
Common Land: 64,500ha
Freshwater lakes and ponds: 1,600ha
Fen: 400ha
Limestone pavement: 100ha
Sand dunes: 800ha
Saltmarsh: 900ha

● Woodlands protected by the National Trust

Area of woodland owned by the Trust: 25,000ha

Broadleaved woodland: 15,500ha including:
Ancient semi-natural woodland: 8,500ha
Western sessile oak woodland: 2,400ha

● Archaeological sites protected by the National Trust

Number of sites within the Trust's care (approximate): 40,000
Scheduled Ancient Monuments (approximate): 1,000
- on 250 Trust properties.

World Heritage Sites owned wholly or in part by the Trust: 5
(Stonehenge, Avebury, Fountains Abbey, Giant's Causeway, Hadrian's Wall)
- out of a national total of 14.

The Countryside Stewardship Scheme: Testing the Way Forward for Integrated Countryside Management

Maddy Jago

Countryside Stewardship Adviser for Dorset, Somerset and Wiltshire

The views expressed in this paper are those of the author and do not necessarily represent the opinions of the Countryside Commission.

● Introduction

Conservation of ancient monuments needs to be integrated into wider countryside management. Until very recently archaeology has been rather isolated from broader principles of countryside appreciation and conservation. The development of the Countryside Stewardship pilot scheme by the Countryside Commission has provided opportunities to explore the practicality of fully integrating conservation of archaeological and historic elements of the landscape within an overall management package.

● Why is Integrated Management Necessary for Effective Conservation of the Archaeological Resource?

In the UK the majority of the countryside is cared for by farmers. Agricultural advances over the past fifty years, coupled with more recent economic changes, have led to a radical change in the scale of operations on

Plate 1. Fencing has effectively isolated this burial mound from active management.

farms. Today, agriculture only supports a very small workforce so that manual labour is a thing of the past. This rapid practical and social change in agriculture has also been partly responsible for a very substantial erosion of the archaeological resource and has largely "marginalised" areas important for wildlife and archaeology. This may have reinforced our culture of site based non-intervention management of ancient monuments, which can take various forms, such as the total exclusion of a site from the surrounding land management by fencing, or less radically by removing the threat of the plough.

The results of this approach will vary depending upon the archaeology under consideration:

● Small, well-defined monuments

Plate 1 illustrates a burial mound which has been fenced to exclude it from the management regime within a field, sometimes subject to grazing, sometimes cropped with maize. Its condition is now deteriorating with the growth of scrub and tree cover. The monument has been isolated from active management and therefore has no obvious link with the present. It is also visually isolated from its surroundings so that it has no context

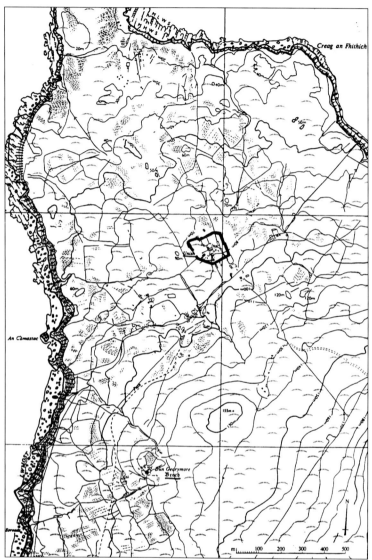

Figure 1. Plan of Unish Township, Isle of Skye. Only the outlined area at Unish and the Broch and Dun Gearymore are scheduled. From the RCAHMS Waternish Afforestable Land Survey and relevant scheduling documents. © RCAHMS Crown copyright.

within the landscape in which it sits. The potential to manage it effectively or to understand more about the historic development of the landscape is consequently reduced. One might pose the question *"For whom or for what purpose is this monument being preserved?"* In this case it might be argued that the benefits are purely archaeological, but with the growth of bracken, scrub and tree cover, root damage and the danger of windthrow affect its archaeological value. It is useful to consider the probable perceptions of the farmer/land manager in this example:

- 1) Perception of responsibility - The land manager sees the monument as something that a specialist is interested in. The authority or responsibility for the care of this feature has been diluted. The physical division of the feature from its surroundings removes it from day-to-day decision making;

- 2) Perceived value - The monument has been fenced from the surrounding land and no longer forms part of the actively managed farmland. It has no part to play within the farm economy or the practical running of the farm. It is probably regarded as of no value or even as a liability for the farm;

- 3) The practical management problem - The economics of farming today allow very little scope for manual work. A small monument that is permanently fenced from the surrounding land is dependent on occasional intervention management, such as scrub clearance. This is both difficult to plan/predict and to sustain. It requires regular specialist input both in terms of advice and financing. In the absence of specialist advice, a requirement for a monument to be fenced from a grazing system would probably imply to a farmer that scrub growth was desirable.

- More complex and extensive archaeological features without clear boundaries

In Figure 1 the boundaries of the Scheduled Ancient Monument are shown by a thickend line. The figure illustrates two things:

- 1) The relationship between the settlement site and its fields;

- 2) The development of the field and settlement pattern through time.

The scheduling of part of this landscape creates an artificial boundary between the settlement site and its fields and appears to focus on one period within the development of this landscape. In this area there are opportunities to integrate management with conservation of wildlife and landscape. There are also very good opportunities for creating more awareness and understanding about the historical development of the landscape both amongst visitors and people local to the area. The boundary of the scheduled monument may disguise these opportunities and reduce the potential for sympathetic and sustainable management over the wider area. In this situation the response of the land manager may be rather different:

• The scale of the site means that management may still include some grazing. The land manager has therefore not relinquished control of the management and day-to-day decisions about the use of the area. The area retains some perceived value within the farming framework;

• The land manager may be conscious of the fieldsystems and other features in the vicinity of the scheduled monument, but the legal protection conferred on the settlement site probably suggests that the surrounding area has no archaeological importance. Damage may result outside the scheduled boundary.

In both of these examples, opportunities to actively conserve the archaeological interest of the area are being lost. The examples also serve to illustrate that many other opportunities are also being lost which may have a direct or indirect effect on the long-term well-being and appreciation of the archaeological resource. An integrated management system could solve problems in both cases.

• Countryside Stewardship - An Experimental Tool for the Integrated Management of the Countryside

In 1991 the Countryside Stewardship scheme was launched by the Countryside Commission in partnership with English Heritage and English Nature. The aim is to develop a flexible, nationwide system of incentives to encourage land managers to integrate conservation and public enjoyment of the countryside with commercial farming and land management. The Countryside Commission is running the scheme as a five year pilot study with funding from Government, under its experimental powers described within Section 4 of the *Countryside Act 1968* as amended by Section 40 of the *Wildlife and Countryside Act 1981*.

The scheme has a number of features which make it different from other countryside conservation packages:

• The approach to countryside conservation is integrated. Archaeology is given equal weighting with three other key considerations. In the scheme literature potential applicants are advised that any proposal must aim to achieve one or more of the following:

• 1) Improve the beauty, diversity and local character of the landscape;

• 2) Conserve or extend wildlife habitats that are in decline;

• 3) Conserve or improve the condition of any archaeological sites and historic features;

• 4) Create new or improved opportunities for public access, informal recreation or educational visits.

In the south west of England interest in the scheme has been high, so that it is often possible to select applications which achieve all four of these objectives.

• The scheme is voluntary and discretionary. Applications are invited from anyone who manages land with a secure tenure of ten or more years. The Countryside Commission then has the discretion to select those applications which best demonstrate the scope of the scheme. In practice, many initial proposals are altered through site meetings and discussion with a Countryside Stewardship adviser before an agreement is offered.

• Eligibility to the scheme is not dependent on designated areas. For the purposes of testing the scheme the experiment has been targeted at particular "landscape types" which have been augmented as the scheme has been developed. At the time of writing there are seven targeted landscapes - chalk and limestone grassland; coastal landscape; lowland heath; uplands; waterside landscape; neutral grassland (only available in Worcestershire and Devon) and historic landscapes. The latter two categories were added to the scheme package in 1992. Regional offices of the Countryside Commission refine these targets in discussion with local partners to provide potential applicants with more detailed guidance on the type of application sought.

These different landscape targets have allowed attention to be concentrated on a particular range of management situations, in turn allowing the development of appropriate management prescriptions to be used in agreements. The intention is to create the basis for a nationwide menu of incentives, that can be tailored to individual circumstances and to achieve specific benefits.

• Agreements are for ten years, which is a sufficiently long period to be able to expect some positive benefits for wildlife, public enjoyment, archaeology and the landscape as a whole.

• Agreements are individually negotiated to create a tailor-made package for each site. All agreements include annual acreage payments in exchange for an agreed management regime. Annual or "revenue" payments can also be made for creating permissive public access which can include areas of open space, paths for the disabled, educational visits, etc. In addition, many agreements include a selection of one-off capital grants towards the costs of various improvement works e.g. hedgelaying; fencing; dry stone walling; scrub management; bracken cutting and spraying; furniture for permissive access and many more. A complete list of the incentives

offered can be found in the scheme handbook (Countryside Commission, 1994). In instances where an applicant submits a proposal not covered within the handbook menu, it is possible to offer grant-aid using the scheme's "Special Project" facility. This has proved particularly useful in designed parkland, for example.

• Countryside Stewardship is looking for measurable benefits from agreements, and the scheme is presented in this way. The whole emphasis is on the land manager being offered incentives to provide certain products which might include on-going scrub clearance of scheduled monuments, or perhaps producing interpretation about an historically important area of landscape to improve public enjoyment and understanding. This approach moves away from the idea of a compensation-led approach. In a Countryside Stewardship agreement the responsibility for the positive care of the land lies firmly with the land manager/farmer.

• The scheme looks at conservation in a practical way. The system of management for each area is discussed and agreed with the land manager. In each case, practical and sustainable solutions are explored within the context of the limitations of an individual situation.

• Issues Raised

The Countryside Stewardship scheme has been in operation since 1991. Its use to try and achieve positive benefits for archaeology as part of an integrated management package, has raised a number of issues:

• Identifying the resource

At present it is not easy to identify the historic/archaeological resource. Countrywide sources of information are limited to English Heritage's Schedule of Monuments, the Sites and Monuments Records usually held by the County Councils and the National Monuments

Record managed by the Royal Commission on Historical Monuments for England.

English Heritage's Schedule relates to monuments identified through national scheduling criteria and so offers guidance on the most important archaeological resources in the country. Unfortunately, the scheduling process itself may create uncertainties about the area of the site that should be cared for, as already illustrated. Many of the entries are very old and sometimes the boundaries seem almost arbitrary. This concern is being addressed by English Heritage's "Monuments Protection Programme" which is reviewing scheduled monuments across England.

The County Sites and Monuments Records, although more comprehensive, (i.e. containing both scheduled and unscheduled monuments and sometimes other historic features in the landscape such as water meadow systems), have not reached a common standard of data collection and presentation. Different counties will offer different strengths and weaknesses both in the quality of information available and in the breadth of historic information presented. For example, some counties may include areas of ridge and furrow within the record whilst others do not. It is also unlikely that many records are able to offer any evaluation of the relative importance of different sites, nor to articulate the criteria on which any such assessment should be based. For the most part, information seems to be haphazard to the extent that a dense cluster of archaeological information may merely point to a higher density of archaeologists rather than a richer resource area. Interpretation by an archaeologist of the record entry is usually required.

The most comprehensive information on ancient monuments is found in those counties covered by the RCHME inventories of historical monuments. Where this information is available, the countryside adviser or manager is able to incorporate the archaeological dimension within the management planning process with some degree of confidence.

Even before the addition of the "Historic Landscape" category to the Countryside Stewardship package, there was a sense of frustration in usually being unable to track down sources of information on historic landscape features e.g. historic field patterns, important boundary features, etc. Comprehensive historic landscape surveys are rare and are usually confined to relatively small areas e.g. a single parish or estate. Examples include the Weld Estate Survey (Keen and Carreck, 1987) and the whole parish surveys undertaken within the Bedfordshire Parish Survey Programme (Bedfordshire County Council, late 1970s to early 1980s).

● Sources of advice

There is a need for an increase in the number of people able to give advice from a broadly-based archaeological/historic landscape training. There are some wonderfully enthusiastic archaeologists, who are wholeheartedly taking a wider and more pragmatic view of countryside conservation. But equally, there are still a proportion of specialists who wish to preserve the professional mystique of archaeology at all costs, in turn stifling the possibilities for a wider recognition of the historic dimension in countryside conservation. This protectionism, that has kept the dialogue about active conservation of monuments to a minimum, does archaeology no favours. In a densely populated country the wider ownership of the archaeological resource needs to be acknowledged, and our management decisions need to address a range of benefits that go beyond the preservation of the stratigraphy of ancient monuments.

● Identifying historic landscapes and recognising the opportunities

The introduction of the Historic Landscape category in 1992 led to a more intense analysis of how the resource might be identified. There was also a need to establish the conservation objectives and opportunities for historic features in the landscape. Graham Fairclough was seconded to the Countryside Commission from English Heritage partly to assist this process. Discussions and training sessions were arranged between Countryside Commission staff and locally-based archaeologists.

In the south west region two practical workshops were arranged in 1993 by the Countryside Stewardship team and local archaeologists to examine what was meant by the term "historic landscape," and to discuss recognition, evaluation and conservation measures for historic features including ancient monuments. The issues of public access and interpretation were also raised and discussed.

Two National Trust sites were visited to inform the discussion: Turnworth in Dorset (N.G.R. ST 810 085), a site rich in archaeology, wildlife and landscape interest; which includes the scheduled earthwork remains of a late Iron Age Romano-British settlement and associated fields and an area of likely ancient wood pasture. This contrasted well with the second area to be visited: Stonehenge (N.G.R. SU 123 422), an area of critical archaeological interest but particularly difficult to interpret to the public and a difficult landscape to appreciate and conserve.

The seminars resulted in the production of two checklists: one to assist with the production of management plans for archaeological earthworks (discussed below); the other to assist in the preliminary identification and evaluation of areas of particular historic interest (Appendix One). This latter checklist was further refined for use at a second training event chaired by Graham Fairclough, when two regional Stewardship teams met with local archaeologists. This evaluation approach has been devised in conjunction with John Wood. It is presented here as an example of a method that could be used in the following ways:

• To assist in recognition of areas rich in historical/archaeological interest;

• To help evaluate the quality and potential of the area particularly within the parameters of the Countryside Stewardship scheme;

• To help define objectives for the conservation of the area;

• To assist in the process of drawing up management plans for large and small areas.

The rationale for using the checklist is to look at ways in which "value may be added" to an historic feature or group of features, the premise being that the conservation value of an area of historic landscape will increase as more of the listed criteria are satisfied. For Countryside Stewardship purposes, the checklist offers the added advantage of assisting in guiding the area of search, where the boundary of land for entry into the scheme may be negotiable. The order in which the criteria appear has not at this stage been based on any ranking or prioritisation. This type of approach combines both "academic" and "aesthetic" criteria as described by Lambrick (1992), but has a wider application than simply evaluating an historic area of landscape. By virtue of its evolution to support a particular field application, it perhaps follows most closely the approach described in Lambrick's paper as organically expanding from one original point or focus, rather than relying on some other method for choosing "sites" and their boundaries.

• Agreeing positive management programmes for ancient monuments and historic landscapes

The non-intervention tradition towards the preservation of ancient monuments cannot incorporate a multiple-objective philosophy, and seems to have stifled active research into sustainable management practices. The Council for British Archaeology (CBA) in its revised policy publication undertakes to *"propose research into the suitability and effectiveness of specific management techniques"* (CBA, 1993), but fails to comment on the value of pooling expertise between archaeologists and those with an expertise in land management. There is a real need for closer liaison between archaeologists and land managers from different disciplines to explore different management techniques that can achieve integration of a range of conservation objectives.

For example, it is common practice in nature conservation for a land manager to make subtle adjustments to grazing patterns in order to secure particular benefits for flora/fauna: different types of livestock will select different types of vegetation, and successful grazing of specific problem plants may be achieved through manipulation of livestock numbers and timing of grazing. Sheep introduced into ragwort (*Senecio* spp.) infested pastures in spring will nibble the plants at the rosette stage, thus inhibiting further spread through seeding. Consequently, downland areas badly infested with ragwort tend to indicate that they have received little or no spring sheep grazing over a long period. Cattle can be particularly effective at controlling the invasion of grassland by coarse grasses and scrub. A number of wildlife conservation bodies are studying the results of using different breeds of sheep to control scrub invasion on heathland. On the Dorset coast, the National Trust have introduced Exmoor ponies to assist in the control of the invasive coarse grass *Brachypodium pinnatum* which threatens to overwhelm the other limestone grassland species. Control of unpalatable species is an important component of any land management strategy since these species may ultimately render the area unsuitable for management by livestock.

This type of sensitivity can also be tailored to accommodate the historic/archaeological resource and has been attempted on some Countryside Stewardship areas.

Meetings set up between local Countryside Stewardship staff and archaeologists in the south west of England resulted in attempts to produce an *aide memoire* for the

management of earthworks. The intention was to explore positive approaches to management that might be incorporated into an integrated management agreement to cover a ten year period. Simultaneously, a checklist was produced by Countryside Commission headquarters for use by all Countryside Stewardship advisers. I have attempted to amalgamate the two and the resulting list is included in Appendix Two. This is at an early stage, based largely on current knowledge and practical experience in land management for nature conservation purposes, but could be further developed through co-operation between skilled land managers and archaeologists, backed by relevant research.

Each Countryside Stewardship agreement is site specific, so although a number of standard clauses exist, there is scope to include variations, as well as more detailed management plans within the agreement text. In practice, an agreement document tends to be a mixture of "don'ts" and "do's". The non-intervention clauses are clearly beneficial to any archaeological interest. Examples include; *"no ploughing or other cultivation"; "no new drainage"; "no pigs and poultry"*. These types of restrictions are a familiar feature of different types of management agreement. It has proved much more difficult to agree "positive" management works for the archaeology and historic interest of an area. The criteria checklist previously described may have a role to play in helping define the objectives to be followed through.

Our discussions suggested that the earthworks are the easiest area to agree on. Discussions become much less lucid when, for example, hedge banks, stone walls and fish ponds are mentioned. The tendency is for a blanket decision of "no management", unless a detailed archaeological survey has been carried out. A standard response of this nature is very protectionist and allows no acknowledgement of wider values.

● Survey requirements

The frequent need for more detailed information on historic features in the landscape has already been mentioned. Current mechanisms to secure this extra detail are limited. Up to 100% grant is available from English Heritage for survey for public interpretation purposes, but this is a very large scale and time-consuming exercise which requires a known high quality archaeological resource to justify expenditure.

The need was identified for a more rapid mechanism to undertake small-scale survey work which could inform multiple-objective management plans. The Countryside Stewardship scheme incorporates a small payment of £300 grant towards the production of management plans and the scope to use this payment is currently being investigated in Somerset with advice from Somerset County Council. For this purpose a survey brief has been compiled in conjunction with Peter McCrone of Somerset County Council (see Appendix Three).

● Conclusion

The Countryside Stewardship scheme is making good progress in setting up integrated countryside management agreements and the archaeological and historic landscape element is being taken very seriously by the Countryside Stewardship team. Efforts to consult on, and set up agreements have highlighted various difficulties of operating within the existing framework of archaeological legislation, information and advice, but great efforts have been made on both sides to create better systems for this process. The use of the Countryside Stewardship tool has allowed active debate on the identification and evaluation of historic landscapes, although the evaluation methodology described has not been adopted as a national approach. Some progress has been made in identifying sustainable active management systems for archaeological

features resulting in an earthworks checklist. There is still a very long way to go and much scope for a new generation of historic landscape experts to work hand in hand with archaeologists and specialist land managers.

● Acknowledgements

I am very grateful to André Berry, David Whelon and Tim Allen who encouraged me to write this paper. I must also particularly mention my husband John Wood with whom I have developed my interest and ideas about historic landscapes over the last nine years.

● References

Council for British Archaeology. (1993) *The Past in Tomorrow's Landscape*.

Countryside Commission. (1994) *Countryside Stewardship Handbook*. CCP 453.

Keen, L. and Carreck, A. (1987) *Historic Landscape of Weld, The Weld Estate, Dorset*. Lulworth Heritage Ltd.

Lambrick, G. (1992.) The Importance of the Cultural Heritage in a Green World: Towards the Development of Landscape Integrity Assessment in, Macinnes, L. and Wickham-Jones, C.R. (eds) *All Natural Things: Archaeology and the Green Debate*. Oxbow Monograph, 21. 105-126.

Lipe, W.D. (1984). Value and Meaning in Cultural Resources in, Cleere, H. (ed) *Approaches to the Archaeological Heritage*. Cambridge: Unwin Hyman.

• Appendix One

• Historic landscape evaluation - a checklist

• Archaeological value

Based on English Heritage's scheduling criteria including elements such as rarity, fragility, survival, condition, etc. These criteria may be used to assess any historically important feature including those perhaps not traditionally regarded as "archaeology", for example ancient boundaries, pollards, etc.

• Visibility

Features to be distinguished as visible i.e. upstanding; or invisible i.e. beneath the ground surface, perhaps only visible through crop marks or pottery traces. A very visible historic landscape may offer more scope for public interpretation or for educational purposes. Earthworks are also more likely to have an associated wildlife interest. Visibility may therefore influence the range of management objectives for a site or area.

• Historic management system (active or relic)

May include water meadow, strip cultivation systems, ancient hay meadows, etc. A complete management system or even a substantial part, may have low archaeological value but a particularly high aesthetic, wildlife and educational value. A functioning or recently derelict system may be worth reinstating for some of these non-archaeological objectives. Maintenance of a traditional hay making system sustains complex wildlife ecosystems and provides a tangible link with the past.

• Number/density of historic features

A straightforward tally of features including both archaeological and notable historic landscape features. If they are visible only as crop marks this will be picked up under 2, and will obviously affect the scope of any integrated management proposals.

• Diversity of features

Includes both synchronic features, i.e. those illustrative of a particular period or event and diachronic features, i.e. those that belong to different periods or illustrate change through time.

• Distribution of features across/beyond area

Drawing up a management proposal for an area of land requires the definition of a boundary. Modern field boundaries may cut important historic features.

• Documentation

May include a wide range of sources including old maps, title deeds, legal and taxation records, drawings and paintings, literary references, etc.

• Inclusion/proximity of any designated area/site

May include landscape designations such as Heritage Coast and Area of Outstanding Natural Beauty; wildlife designations such as Sites of Special Scientific Interest, Ramsar site, Biogenetic Reserve, National Nature Reserve, Local Nature Reserve, County Wildlife sites, archaeological designations such as Scheduled Ancient Monuments and World Heritage Sites; other designations such as Nitrate Sensitive Areas and Environmentally Sensitive Areas.

• Proposal conserves a well-defined historic land unit

For example, an Anglo-Saxon estate or an industrial landscape. This places a particular value on important historical boundaries.

• General heritage values

Loosely based on ideas presented by Lipe (1984), including information/evidence value, aesthetic (e.g. evocative/emotive), ecological, economic, recreational, associative, symbolic, etc.

- The potential for beneficial and possibly sustainable management

May be an important added value to justify use of public money. In this instance it could be seen as an investment for the future.

- The potential for immediate public benefit

For example, improved or new public access and interpretation.

• Appendix Two

- An *Aide Memoire* to assist in drawing up management plans for earthworks

- Manage, if possible, in context with the surroundings. For example, establish permanent pasture around monuments; allow light grazing; only fence monuments out on a temporary basis, where necessary;

- Assess condition - stable or deteriorating, using the following clues:

- 1) Loss of vegetative cover? Will it recover naturally, or does it need help? Avoid further erosion. Natural regeneration is the preferred method in areas of high nature conservation interest but, on heathland sites for example, importing a protective cover of heather, bearing ripe seed in autumn-winter may be an option. A range of other techniques will be possible. For example, spreading herb-rich hay; sowing seed mix; sowing an annual "nurse crop", such as Westerwolds ryegrass, to establish a rapid cover which can be superseded by more indigenous species if managed correctly;

- 2) Scrub encroachment. Consider best removal technique and what, if anything, will grow in its place. Look around to see what may colonise once the existing cover is removed, noting any aggressive colonisers such as sycamore, *Acer pseudoplatanus* (on most soil types); rhododendron, *Rhododendron ponticum* (on light, acid soils); bramble, *Rubus fruticosus* agg., (on most soil types); bracken, *Pteridium aquilinum*, (mainly on acid soils), etc.

- 3) Holes, burrows, vehicle ruts;

- 4) Rubbish in hollows?

- 5) Type of vegetation cover. Stable perennial vegetation or invasive species such as nettle (*Urtica dioica*); creeping thistle (*Cirsium arvense*); annual meadow grass (*Poa annua*), etc. indicating ground disturbance;

- Grazing. Consider types of stock, stocking numbers and timing. Heavier grazing animals may help control specific scrub encroachment problems and will not damage earthworks if the numbers and timing of grazing are strictly controlled. Note the different grazing patterns, vegetation preference and grazing techniques of different livestock, even down to different breeds of sheep which may be selected to graze specific vegetation types. Also consider the enclosure pattern of the grazing, for example, allowing grazing animals to move freely between several fields at once may lead to the development of well-worn tracks to water supplies, etc. There is much more known about the use of cattle and sheep for specific management purposes than other possible grazing animals, such as deer.

- Think about possible causes of damage. For example, fences; water supply; stiles; interpretation panels; siting of trees; stock feeding areas, etc; direct physical damage from tree roots; rubbing by stock; erosion/poaching; paths developing through passage of human/animal feet;

- Vehicular access may be necessary. Agree optimum timing and route;

- Trees can become collection areas for livestock and may cause substantial damage if susceptible to windthrow. Careful tree surgery may avoid this. It may be possible to find suitable sites for tree planting, seek advice;

- Avoid ground disturbance, but if already damaged seek advice on how to fill holes; etc.;

- Incremental management is often favoured for nature conservation purposes, for example, phased cutting/burning programmes. This can fit in with care of earthworks, perhaps prioritising sensitive areas for clearance of damaging scrub. Also be aware of:

- 1) Past management practices and how successful they have been;

- 2) If burning is too intense it may lead to bare areas developing, followed by erosion;

- 3) Phasing tree clearance may lead to problems of windthrow.

• Appendix Three

• Countryside Stewardship archaeological/historic landscape survey: brief for consultants

• Background

Countryside Stewardship offers 10 year management agreements to farmers and land managers to enhance and conserve some important English landscapes and their wildlife habitats. It aims to integrate conservation and informal recreation with commercial farming and land management. The scheme is run by the Countryside Commission in partnership with English Nature and English Heritage.

Countryside Stewardship is a pilot project to develop a flexible, nationwide system offering incentives wherever they are an appropriate way to help land managers improve the countryside and opportunities for people to enjoy it. The scheme is targeted at seven landscape types throughout England. The Commission selects those schemes which offer most benefit for public enjoyment of the countryside and restoration/conservation of wildlife, landscape and historic/ archaeological interest. The Countryside Stewardship Handbook (CCP 345) gives more details about the scheme.

Traces of human activity over the past 10,000 years are found almost everywhere in the countryside. In many cases these remains are invisible or visible only using specialised techniques. It is often the case even with visible remains that they have not been recognised or recorded at all.

The area for consideration may contain remains relating to the historic use of the landscape. It has, therefore, been recommended that an archaeological field assessment be carried out to obtain further information to assist the future management and presentation of the site.

• Survey objectives

The objectives of the survey are to gather sufficient information to establish the presence/absence, character, extent, state of preservation and date of any archaeological or other historic features within the area of application/agreement, and to identify any areas where management changes would benefit their survival. A checklist of factors to be considered is included at the end of this appendix. Any opportunities for public presentation and interpretation should be identified and outlined.

• Stages of work and techniques

For all sites the following is required:

- Assessment of recorded information including, as appropriate, consultation of the Sites and Monuments Record, published material, archive/unpublished reports, aerial photographs and early maps. Sources for this material may include the County Sites and Monuments Record, Local History Library and County Record Office;

- Visual inspection of the entire site and location and recording of any historic features;

- An assessment of management issues and potential for presentation;

The following additional requirements may also apply:

- Measured survey;

- Geophysical survey (presented as raw data and interpretative scale plan);

- Photographic survey;

59

- Fieldwalking.

- Reporting requirements

The survey should result in a report including:

- Site location and description, including current land-use;

- Review of published, archive and SMR information;

- A description of the methodology employed;

- Plans at an appropriate scale showing surveyed features, including profiles as appropriate;

- A description and interpretation of features identified, including photographs as appropriate;

- A description of conservation issues identified, including locations marked on plan;

- Recommendations for management;

- Recommendations for presentation/interpretation.

Three copies of the report are to be produced; one to be supplied to the client; one to the Countryside Commission; one to the County Archaeological Officer. If a photographic survey has been carried out, the photographic archive should be lodged with the County Records Office. Where a fieldwalking survey is to be undertaken appropriate arrangements should be made, before commencement, for the deposition of finds in the appropriate Museum.

- Checklist of factors for assessment and monitoring

- Poaching. Resulting from overgrazing/over stocking;

- Scrapes. Animals rubbing against areas leading to loss of vegetative cover, resulting in an expanding area of bare and eroding substrate;

- Burrowing animals. Rabbits, badgers, etc. leading to the destruction of archaeological stratigraphy;

- Animal tracks. Persistent use of the same track by livestock leading to erosion and gullying;

- Footpaths. Erosion caused by heavy pedestrian use or focal erosion around gates, stiles or interpretation locations;

- Woody growth or encroachment. Trees, shrubs or scrub growth or encroachment on or adjacent to a monument, causing root damage or disturbance;

- Focal point erosion. Alongside or behind walls, fence lines or fence posts; erosion in gateways, around water troughs, supplementary feed locations or other areas where livestock may gather;

- Inappropriate erosion repairs. Alien materials (e.g. stone chaffer into an earthen mound); methods (e.g. heavy machinery) or without appropriate advice;

- Vehicular damage. Machinery erosion caused by driving across or too close; by nicking with agricultural implements whilst working nearby; or, by working on or adjacent to a site when ground conditions are unsuitable.

- Natural erosion. Damage caused by water or wind erosion, perhaps originating as a result of human activity on the site;

- Fire Damage. Camp fires, rubbish burning, etc. leading to damage to vegetation cover and erosion. This can include burning management, e.g. on grouse moors, leading to fire damage to monuments;

- Quarrying/dumping/fly tipping. Removal of parts of the monument or burial under tipped material;

- Defacement/disturbance. Illicit excavations, e.g. metal detecting holes; interference by others, e.g. walkers' cairns added to high points, defacement by paint daubing, etc. or any other activity which changes the nature or form of the monument.

Plate 1. A wide range of plants grow on ruined buildings. This group at Buildwas Abbey, Shropshire (N.G.R. SJ 642 044), includes maidenhair spleenwort and wild strawberry (*Fragaria vesca*)

The Nature Conservation Importance of Standing Remains

John Thompson

Nature Conservation Adviser to English Heritage

● Introduction

Ruined historic structures exist in many forms and all support some kind of plant and animal life. A stone circle or a megalith may only have a covering of lichens and some bryophytes, but if these have been present for hundreds of years the species or communities are likely to be of great interest or rarity. It is unlikely that they will damage the stone; indeed they may help to protect it from weathering. At the other extreme are large complex structures, such as some castles or abbeys, which may additionally support large and diverse populations of annual and perennial flowering plants as well as numerous forms of animal life. Even relatively recent industrial remains can be of considerable natural interest. Taken as a whole, "standing remains" are a large and significant resource for nature conservation.

● The Fauna and Flora of Ruins

The extent to which buildings support plants and animals will vary depending on their design and materials, age and condition. Most standing remains are ancient and incomplete; many are ruinous. As such they will tend to support far more than well-maintained modern buildings (Plate 1). For example, at Jervaulx Abbey (N.G.R. SE 175 860) no less than 176 species of ferns and flowering plants have been recorded (Rob and Holloway, 1983).

A wide range of habitats will often be present, coupled with marked differences in aspect, producing both sun-baked and densely-shaded areas in close proximity. Surfaces may be horizontal, vertical or sloping. The type and condition of any mortar is critical; lime mortar, particularly if it is weathered, will often support

Plate 2. At Sherbourne Old Castle, Dorset (N.G.R. ST 647 167), a population of clove pink has been carefully protected for many years.

(N.G.R. NY 293 236) and Rollright (N.G.R. SP 329 318) stone circles has been elucidated by studying growth-rates in relation to aspect (Winchester, 1988).

Numerous mosses occur on ruins and typically these include *Bryum argenteum*, *Bryum capillare*, *Barbula convoluta*, *Barbula recurvirostra*, *Homalothecium sericeum* and *Schistidium apocarpum*. Common liverworts on damp walls include *Conocephalum conicum*, *Lunularia cruciata* and *Plagiochilla porreloides*.

The flowering plants are numerous and include many common and widespread species, particularly those whose propagules are dispersed by wind or birds. Some of these plants can be harmful to structures and need to be controlled. Obvious examples are various trees and shrubs, but perennials such as red valerian (*Centranthus ruber*) also develop a woody rootstock which can be damaging. Most plants, however, are more benign and some may actually protect the masonry.

One of the earliest vascular plants to colonise ruins is often the procumbent pearlwort (*Sagina procumbens*). Others are the ferns wall rue (*Asplenium ruta-muraria*) and maidenhair spleenwort (*A. trichomanes* ssp. *quadrivalens*). As pockets of decaying leaves, crumbling mortar, roots and detritus accumulate on ledges and in crevices, so other plants will be able to establish. Many of these are ubiquitous, but some are particularly associated with walls and other masonry. These include, for example:

Pellitory-of-the-wall (*Parietaria judaica*)

Ivy-leaved toadflax

Wall lettuce (*Mycelis muralis*)

Wallflower (*Cheiranthus cheiri*)

Annual wall rocket (*Diplotaxis muralis*)

Perennial wall rocket (*D. tenuifolia*)

Wall pepper (*Sedum acre*)

Navelwort (*Umbilicus rupestris*)

Hairy rock-cress (*Arabis hirsuta*)

calcicolous ("lime-loving") species in areas where they do not otherwise exist.

Whether or not a particular plant occurs will obviously depend on the presence of spores or seeds and their ability to become established. Propagules of algae, mosses, liverworts and ferns are all wind-borne and so arrive easily. So also do the seeds of ash (*Fraxinus excelsior*), sycamore (*Acer pseudoplatanus*), sallow (*Salix cinerea*), buddleia (*Buddleia* spp.), willow-herbs (*Epilobium* spp.) and many other plants. Some frequent colonisers, such as hawthorn (*Crataegus monogyna*), yew (*Taxus baccata*) and elder (*Sambucus nigra*) are brought in by birds. Voles, mice and other mammals bring in hooked seeds. Some seeds are known to be carried by ants; one example being the ivy-leaved toadflax (*Cymbalaria muralis*) (Gilbert, 1992).

The first plants to colonise masonry are algae, such as *Pleurococcus* spp., lichens and a variety of bryophytes. Most lichens are very susceptible to pollution and so their presence or absence can often be a useful indicator. Many species are long-lived and knowledge of their growth rates can assist in establishing and dating past events. For example, the re-siting of stones at Castlerigg

Wall speedwell (*Veronica arvensis*)

Fern grass (*Catapodium rigidum*)

Walls and other forms of masonry are, in many areas, the principal habitat for a number of plant species. Gilbert (1992) lists eighteen species that are largely dependent on walls, although ten of these are not native to Britain. Nevertheless, walls are the optimum habitat for a significant number of native species and play an important role in their conservation. Examples are the clove pink (*Dianthus caryophyllus*) (Plate 2), wall bedstraw (*Galium parisiense*), wall germander (*Teucrium chamaedrys*) and wall brome (*Anisantha madritensis*).

Ferns are an especially important feature of many standing remains. Apart from those already mentioned, several others are particularly associated with old walls:

Black spleenwort (*Asplenium adiantum nigrum*)

Lanceolate spleenwort (*A. obovatum*)

Sea spleenwort (*A. marinum*)

Brittle bladder-fern (*Cystopteris fragilis*)

Rustyback (*Ceterach officinarum*)

Hart's tongue (*Phyllitis scolopendrium*)

Polypody (*Polypodium vulgare*)

Intermediate polypody (*P. interjectum*)

In addition, a number of rare or local fern species, sub-species and hybrids occur in these habitats. Southern polypody (*Polypodium cambricum*) occurs at Berry Pomeroy (N.G.R. SX 839 623) (Plate 3), Carew (N.G.R. SN 045 030) and Wigmore Castles (N.G.R. SO 408 693); the confluent maidenhair spleenwort (*Asplenium trichomanes x Phyllitis scolopendrium = A. x confluens*); and Lady Clermont's spleenwort (*A. trichomanes x A. ruta-muraria = A. x clermontiae*), which has only ever been recorded with certainty from a wall (Page, 1988).

A surprisingly large variety of animals are also associated with ruins. Some indication of the diversity of such assemblages is given by Simmons (1976) and Darlington (1981), but no detailed studies appear to have been reported. Near to the base of the food-chain are creatures such as members of the *Collembola* (springtails), *Thysanura* (bristletails), snails, slugs, woodlice, bees and various insect larvae. These are followed by predators such as spiders, ants, wasps, reptiles, amphibians, mammals and birds such as owls and the kestrel (*Falco tinnunculus*). Many of the lower forms are cryptozoic and hence well-suited to using cracks and voids in old masonry. In doing so they assist the establishment of plants by bringing in seeds and soil particles, decomposing debris and raising fertility through their excreta.

Amongst the very numerous insects associated with old buildings are *Diptera* (flies) of various sorts, breeding in debris, feeding on flowers, or basking; midges, forming plant galls; *Coleoptera* (beetles), particularly predatory species such as the Devil's coach-horse (*Staphylinus olens*) and the glow-worm (*Lampyrus noctiluca*). Butterflies which use buildings include the large white (*Pieris brassicae*), which frequently pupates on walls; the wall butterfly (*Lasiomata megera*) and Grayling (*Hipparchia semele*), which bask on sunny

Plate 3. The very local southern polypody growing on the boundary wall at Berry Pomeroy Castle, Devon.

masonry; and the small tortoiseshell (*Aglais urticae*) and peacock (*Inachis io*), which hibernate in roof spaces and other dry sheltered areas. Amongst the moths, the herald (*Scoliopteryx libatrix*) is frequently found hibernating in buildings, whilst a number of moths rest on masonry in the daytime, using their cryptic coloration to avoid being predated by birds. Such species include the red underwing (*Catocala nupta*), garden carpet (*Xanthorhoe fluctuata*), various pugs and the willow beauty (*Peribatodes rhomboidaria*). Amongst the micro-*Lepidoptera* are *Crambus falsellus* (Schiff) and several species of *Scoparia*, all of which breed in mosses such as *Tortula* and *Grimmia* (Darlington, 1981) or on lichens (Emmet and Heath, 1992).

Many of the *Hymenoptera* (ants, bees and wasps) are associated with masonry. Amongst the social wasps, the hornet (*Vespa crabro*) the common wasp (*Vespula vulgaris*), the German wasp (*V. germanica*) and the red wasp (*V. rufa*) will all breed in voids. The queens will also overwinter there. The semi-social and solitary bees and wasps include a number of species that are particularly associated with buildings. Examples are the bumblebees (such as *Bombus pratorum*); the mason bees (*Osmia* spp.), which will tunnel into sand and soft mortar; and various mason and digger wasps, of which *Crossocerus tarsatus*, *Ancistrocerus antilope* and *A. parietum* are examples. In addition to these, other wasps such as the spider-hunting wasps (*Pompilidae*) and the ruby-tailed wasps (e.g. *Crysis* spp.) prey on, or parasitise, other fauna occurring there.

Ants are also frequent inhabitants of walls. Species using such habitats include the common black ant (*Lasius niger*), *Myrmica rubra* and *Lasius fuliginosus*.

Darlington (*loc. cit.*), estimates that as many as sixty-six species of spider out of a total British list of nearly six hundred (i.e. more than 10%) are closely associated with walls. Amongst these, the zebra spider and other species of *Salticus* are well-adapted to surviving on walls, making use of the heat of the sun to assist in catching their prey.

Other Arthropods associated with masonry include several species of woodlouse, centipede, millipede and earwig.

Some of the most easily seen wall-dwellers are the snails. In most areas the garden snail (*Helix aspersa*) and the banded snails (*Cepea hortensis* and *C. nemoralis*) are commonly found, but a number of smaller species also occur, such as the scarce *Clausilia dubia* which occurs on ivy-clad walls at Dover Castle (N.G.R. TR 326 416).

Amongst the reptiles, the common lizard (*Lacerta vivipara*) will often bask on wall-bases and the slow worm (*Anguis fragilis*) has been recorded sheltering under ivy on the tops of walls. Amphibia also make use of ruins; newts, frogs, toads and snakes all use cavities in which to shelter or overwinter. All of these are legally protected to varying degrees.

Many birds will use ruined buildings either for roosting, breeding or feeding. Nesting species include rock- (*Columba livia*) and stock doves (*C. oenas*), swift (*Apus apus*), swallow (*Hirundo rustica*), house martin (*Delichon urbica*), blue - (*Parus caeruleus*) and great tits (*P. major*), wren (*Troglodytes troglodytes*), blackbird (*Turdus merula*), house sparrow (*Passer domesticus*), pied wagtail (*Motacilla alba*), spotted flycatcher (*Muscicapa striata*), robin (*Erithacus rubecula*), jackdaw (*Corvus monedula*), kestrel and barn owl (*Tyto alba*). Also, but less commonly, wheatear (*Oenanthe oenanthe*), dipper (*Cinclus cinclus*) and nuthatch (*Sitta europaea*). In coastal areas even the fulmar (*Fulmarus glacialis*) and herring gull (*Larus argentatus*) have been recorded nesting on ruins. The rare black redstart (*Phoenicurus ochruros*) almost always uses buildings for its nest and is known to nest regularly at certain historic sites.

Amongst the mammals, common- (*Sorex araneus*) and pigmy shrews (*S. minutus*), bank voles (*Clethrionomys glareolus*) and field- (*Apodemus* spp.) and yellow-necked mice (*Apodemus flavicollis*) will search crevices for food. Stoats (*Mustela erminea*) and weasels (*M. nivalis*) hunt there, as will polecats (*M. putorius*) and even pine martens (*Martes martes*) where they occur. However, it is the bats which are most dependent on buildings (see Hutson - this volume), and their ability to fly makes it possible for them to utilise areas which are out of the reach of other animals. Although some species mainly use trees, all fourteen British species do occur in buildings and some use wells, tunnels, ice-houses or caves for hibernation. All bats are now protected by law, so any work on standing remains must have regard for the possibility that bats may be disturbed or harmed, and proper advice sought.

Plate 4a. Fountains Abbey, North Yorkshire (N.G.R. SE 278 684), has a particularly diverse flora as well as notable bat populations.

● Impact of Fauna and Flora on Conservation of Standing Remains

All remains tend to decay over time and so the object of conservation work will usually be to manage that process. Whether the presence of fauna or flora affects it will depend on the particular circumstances. Deep-rooted woody plants are obviously harmful, but the effects of most organisms are less clear.

Lichens, for example, may help to protect a surface, or they may cause slight damage. If water is trapped behind the lichen thallus, it can result in damage through freeze-thaw action. Such water contains dissolved carbon dioxide which, as carbonic acid, affects calcareous materials. Some lichens produce weak organic acids which may have the same effect, although whether this is by chelation or chemical reaction is not clear. Additionally, lichens adhere to the surface and may pull some of it away if they die and desiccate; or may loosen particles of stone as they contract and expand in response to wetting and drying (Hale, 1974). Krumbein (1987) describes in some detail how complex epilithic (on the surface), chasmolithic (in crevices and

Plate 4b. This wall face, at Sherbourne Old Castle, is being thoroughly consolidated, but a protective capping of vegetation remains on its top.

fissures) and endolithic (within the material or interstitial spaces of material) microbial communities interact with both a stone and its environment. But whilst such systems can be "biodeteriorating", he notes that they may also be protective.

All plants will tend to accumulate debris and dust, so forming a primitive soil as time goes by. This will accumulate in crevices and on ledges and so enable plants to colonise. Ants contribute to this process by transporting mineral particles. At the same time a multitude of decomposer organisms are recycling vegetable matter, thereby reducing such deposits. Excreta of all kinds contribute to these processes, adding fertility and increasing growth rates. For example, guano has been shown experimentally to increase the growth rate of lichens.

Snails utilise the lime from limestone or mortar to form their shells and they make a watertight seal when at rest. But, although some snails return to the same spot after feeding they do not create a shaped recess, as happens with the common limpet (*Patella vulgata*).

Some mining bees and wasps will tunnel into mortar and occasionally very soft sandstone. Whilst this obviously hastens the weathering process it is only significant where decay is already advanced.

The damaging effects of tree roots and ivy stems can be very serious, levering apart masonry and dislodging corework and mortar. Their weight also affects stability and wind action can exacerbate the damage. Where trees are subject to windblow, they can dislodge large areas of masonry.

So, despite their aesthetic value, trees and shrubs must usually be removed from standing remains before they cause significant damage.

As already mentioned, some long-lived herbaceous plants also develop a woody rootstock which can cause damage.

However, annuals and many perennials cause little or no damage and may help to protect the fabric. There is some evidence that a "soft capping" of vegetation on a wall-top may be beneficial in this respect (Plates 4a and b). The plants provide insulation against extremes of temperature, thereby reducing shattering due to frost or heat. They also intercept precipitation, returning some of it to the atmosphere by evapo-transpiration, and can help to shed run-off away from the face of the wall.

There is considerable scope for research into the possible benefits of plants on walls and for experiment with methods of establishing and maintaining beneficial plant cover. One way of achieving this is to lift existing vegetation, inserting a membrane before replacing the vegetation mat. At Jervaulx Abbey, vegetation has been set aside during repair work and then re-established in concrete "trays" formed *in situ* on the wall tops (A Davidson, pers. comm.). At Bolingbroke Castle, Lincolnshire (N.G.R. TF 349 649), soil has been added to hollowed-out wall tops and the surface turfed (Wimble and Thompson, 1993). Similar work has been undertaken at Kirkham Priory, North Yorkshire (N.G.R. SE 735 657), where subsoil has been used in order to discourage rank growth. Other examples are to be found at Tintagel (N.G.R. SX 048 891), Bury Court (N.G.R. SX 224 974) and Battle Abbey (N.G.R. TQ 749 157).

Whether or not such cappings are effective in reducing deterioration of the fabric, they do not necessarily offer any nature conservation benefits. If fertile soil is used, there may be rank growth of coarse, competitive vegetation including weed species such as thistles and docks. Or a dense species-poor turf may be created.

In order to investigate possible ways of achieving a covering of vegetation which will meet the architect's requirements whilst retaining existing floral diversity, English Heritage is carrying out trials in the Isles of Scilly. The extensive walls of the 18th century garrison on St. Mary's (N.G.R. SV 898 104) support a diverse and colourful flora (Plate 5) including a number of species that are rare or of special local interest. They run for roughly 1.6km around the St. Mary's peninsula and are an important feature of a popular scenic walk. Built of granite blocks, with a core of rubble and stone, their top surface is exposed to salt-laden winds and, in places, eroded by walkers. Some sections have been soiled and re-seeded and are now of little botanical interest, but the majority has only a very thin soil or none at all.

Surveys commissioned by English Heritage in 1991 confirmed the importance of the flora and emphasised the harm that had been done where re-soiling had been carried out. Typically, the flora includes maritime species such as thrift (*Armeria maritima*), scurvy-grasses (both *Cochlearia officinalis* and *C. danica*), sea fern-grass (*Catapodium marinum*), buckshorn plantain (*Plantago coronopus*), rock sea-spurrey (*Spergularia rupicola*), sea stork's-bill (*Erodium maritimum*) rock samphire (*Crithmum maritimum*) and the fern sea spleenwort (*Asplenium marinum*). The more unusual species include the rare four-leaved allseed (*Polycarpon tetraphyllum*), autumn lady's-tresses orchid (*Spiranthes spiralis*), early meadow-grass (*Poa infirma*) and parsley (*Petroselinum crispum*). A variety of annual and perennial clovers include subterranean clover (*Trifolium subterraneum*), rough clover (*T. scabrum*), western clover (*T. occidentale*), hare's-foot clover (*T. arvense*), suffocated clover (*T. suffocatum*) and bird's-foot clover (*T. ornithopodioides*), in addition to the commoner species. Most of these plants require dry, infertile, conditions and could not compete with a vigorous turf.

Because of the paucity of soil and the generally concave profile of the wall-top it was necessary to supplement the rooting medium and form a convex surface to assist the shedding of water. The use of soil was undesirable due to fertility problems and the risk of introducing weeds. Peat was

Plate 5. Bird's-foot trefoil (*Lotus corniculatus*) enhances the setting of the Garrison Walls, St. Mary's, Isles of Scilly. Photograph: André Berry.

Plate 6. Thrift and other plants being lifted for replanting along the edges of trial plots at the Garrison Walls on St. Mary's, Isles of Scilly.

ruled out on environmental grounds. After careful consideration it was decided to use "DANU", a by-product of the brewing industry consisting of spent roasted barley and pulverised oil-seed rape straw. This had already been used on a small scale by the Cornish Archaeological Unit in the repair of another scheduled ancient monument on the nearby island of Tresco (King Charles' Castle, N.G.R. SV 882 161). In the St. Mary's trial, the DANU was mixed in the ratio of two parts to one with a locally-obtained grit, formed from the weathering of the granite. This was expected to increase its stability and permanence. The result was a dark, fibrous, gritty material similar in appearance to the existing soil. Although higher in nutrient content, it was expected that this would quickly fall in the exposed conditions and that plant roots would soon make contact with the base-rich core of the wall.

Three treatments were applied at each of three sites, having different degrees of exposure and different aspects:

• 1) Turfed using commercially-grown turf composed of three salt-tolerant strains of red fescue (*Festuca rubra*);

• 2) Seeded with the same three cultivars as 1) and protected with a polypropylene fleece to assist germination and reduce wind erosion;

• 3) Seeded as 1), without the fleece, but watered with a starch-based adhesive ("Scanbinder") at 5g/sq.m.

At each plot some of the existing plants were first dug up and then replanted at the landward edge of the completed plot to act as a source of colonisation (Plate 6).

The initial work was undertaken in November 1992. The damp, frost-free, conditions favoured growth and germination and early indications were that a close knit sward would be established. However, by September the following year most of the turf was severely browned and the seeded areas were reduced to between 20% and 60% cover. Despite this, the "compost" was still intact. Some

colonisation, mainly buckshorn plantain, was occurring and many of the plants that had been placed along the edges had survived. Earlier tests had shown that the litter on the wall-tops contained a variety of viable seeds. Some of this litter was swept up during September 1993 and used to inoculate the treated areas after scarifying their surfaces.

It had been expected that the turf might prove too dense for many of the indigenous herbs to become established. However by May 1994 the most diverse vegetation cover was on the turfed areas. On present indications it seems likely that the best solution will be to use a combination of purpose-grown turf, over-sowing with local seeds and retention of mature plants at the margins of the turfed areas. Depending on how much growth occurs, the sward will need cutting occasionally to prevent the smothering of seedlings and small herbs.

• Summary and Recommendations

A wide variety of plants and animals occur on standing remains. Some of these are dependent on such habitats for their continued survival and distribution. It follows, therefore, that the integrated management of standing remains is essential to ensure the conservation of these species. The plants and animals also enhance the beauty and interest of such places and are an important aspect of "romantic ruins". In order to ensure that these benefits are taken into account and that valuable features are not unwittingly destroyed, the following recommendations are made:

• All standing remains should be surveyed for bats, newts and plants prior to undertaking repairs or consolidation;

• Plants and animals should be conserved unless causing specific damage or obscuring particular features of importance;

• If protected organisms are present, the relevant statutory authority must be consulted. This should be undertaken at an early stage of planning;

- If vegetation does have to be removed, every effort should be made to retain unusual species and the conditions which they require. As a last resort, this may involve transplantation;

- Entrances and voids used by animal life should be retained, wherever possible;

- The use of herbicides should be avoided, except for the spot treatment of cut stumps of woody plants which cannot be removed;

- Only approved insecticides or fungicides of low mammalian toxicity should be used for the control or prevention of insect or fungal attack.

● References

Darlington, A. (1981) *Ecology of Walls.* London: Heinemann Educational Books.

Emmet, A.M. and Heath, J. (1992) *The Moths and Butterflies of Great Britain and Ireland* Vol.7, Pt.2. Harley Books.

Gilbert, O. (1992) *Rooted in Stone.* Peterborough: English Nature.

Hale, E.M. (1974) *The Biology of Lichens.* London: Edward Arnold.

Krumbein, W.E. (1987) Microbial Reactions with Mineral Materials. *Biodeterioration,* 7. 78-100.

Page, C.N. (1988) *Ferns.* London: Collins.

Rob, C.M. and Holloway, J.M. (1983) *Guide Book of Wildflowers and Other Plants in Jervaulx Abbey.* The C.M. Rob and the Harrogate and District Natural History Societies.

Simmons, G.E. (1976) *Plant and Animal Habitats in Town and Country.* Approaches to Environmental Studies, 23. Blandford.

Simmons, G.E. (1976) *Looking at Walls.* Natural Science in Schools, Vol.14, No.2. 35-41.

Wimble, A. and Thompson, J. (1993) *Natural Wall Cappings.* English Heritage Scientific and Technical Review, 2.

Winchester, V. (1988) An Assessment of Lichenometry as a Method for Dating Recent Stone Movements in Two Stone Circles in Cumbria and Oxfordshire. *Botanical Journal of the Linnean Society, 96.* 57-68.

● Bibliography

Suggested additional texts:

Anon. (1975) *The Wall- A Starting Point for Environmental Studies.* Council for Environmental Education.

Anon. (1990) *Wildlife on Walls.* Avon Wildlife Trust.

Green, W. (1974) How do your Lichens Grow? *Surveyor.* December 1974.

Hosking, R. (1990) The Wildlife of Old Barns. *Birds.* Sandy: The Royal Society for the Protection of Birds.

Kent, D.H. (1961) The Flora of Middlesex Walls. *The London Naturalist,* 40. 29-43.

Lewis, F.J., May, E. and Browery, A.F. (1987) Metabolic Activities of Bacteria Isolated from Stone and their Relationship to Stone Decay. *Biodeterioration,* 7. 107-112.

Miles, P.M. and Miles, H.B. (1967) *Town Ecology.* Hulton Educational Publications.

Nicholson, A. (1990) Tidiness and the Trust. *The National Trust Magazine,* No.58.

Raistrick, A. and Gilbert, O. (1962) Malham Tarn House, Its Building Materials, their Weathering and Colonisation by Plants. *Field Studies* 1, No.5. 89-115.

Richardson, B.A. (1987) Control of Microbial Growths on Stone and Concrete. *Biodeterioration,* 7. 101-106.

Segal, S. (1969) *Ecological Notes on Wall Vegetation.* Junk, The Hague.

Woodell, S. and Rossiter, J. (1959) The Flora of Durham Walls. *Proceedings of the Botanical Society of the British Isles,* 3. 257-273.

Conservation of Bats in the Management of Ancient Monuments

A.M. Hutson

Conservation Officer, The Bat Conservation Trust

● Introduction

Fourteen species of bat *(Mammalia: Chiroptera)* are resident in the UK. They are considered to be particularly threatened and are given special consideration in national legislation and international treaties. All are insectivorous and need an abundance and diversity of insects to sustain them. Changes in landscape and land use and the use of pesticides have affected their food supply. Bats need a range of roost sites for use at different times of year and under different weather conditions. The preferred roost sites vary between species, but all species are particularly vulnerable during summer, when females collect into maternity colonies, and in winter, when all bats hibernate and some species often concentrate in underground habitats. Many of these roosts are in buildings or other artificial structures where they may be affected by deterioration, renovation work and other management practices.

All bats and their roosts are given very full protection under the *Wildlife and Countryside Act 1981* (in Northern Ireland *The Wildlife [Northern Ireland] Order 1985* and in the Isle of Man the *Wildlife Act 1990*). The Act places special emphasis on the conservation of bat roosts in buildings and other artificial structures because of the increasing reliance on such structures by bats. Their colonial breeding behaviour and hibernation requirements render them especially vulnerable to building work. The legislation demands that if work is intended and might affect bats or their roosts, the relevant statutory nature conservation

organisation (SNCO) must be consulted and be allowed reasonable time to give advice on procedures that will accommodate, where appropriate, the conservation requirements of the bats. If such advice is sought early, the SNCO is better able to acquire relevant information and offer well-considered advice that takes account of the nature of the proposed work. Thus, it is advantageous for surveyors and architects to involve the nature conservation authorities at the planning stage of intended work.

A review of the current state of bat conservation in the UK and proposed requirements to improve the status of bats is given in Hutson (1993). General information and an outline of the legislation is given in leaflets or booklets published by the SNCOs and by The Bat Conservation Trust (BCT), whose addresses are given in an appendix to this volume. Details of contacts and resources are given in *The Bat Worker's Guide* (BCT, 1993). A policy for the management of bats in its properties is available from The National Trust (Anon, 1993) and can be applied more widely to artificial structures of conservation concern where bats may be present. Further information on the conservation of bats in buildings can be found in Hutson (1987), for underground habitats in Hutson, Mickleburgh and Mitchell-Jones (1990) and for woodland in Mayle (1990). The BCT intends to provide wider guidelines on habitat management for bats.

As a general principle, older structures have a greater variety of bat species using them than newer ones. Thus, ancient monuments can play a key role in providing roost sites for many of our rarer species. The requirements of the *Ancient Monuments and Archaeological Areas Act 1979* now include the need to consider obligations under the *Wildlife and Countryside Act 1981*. General features of ancient monuments that make them attractive to bats include the greater use of natural stone and large hardwood timbers, a wide range of constructional features, limited human disturbance and a certain amount of "weathering". It is also a notable feature that bats show a greater degree of site fidelity in ancient monuments than they do in modern buildings.

Frequently, the management of the areas around ancient monuments is based on a traditional form of land management that would retain features suitable for bats and their insect food (such as trees, permanent pasture and water bodies). Intense management to provide a particularly "orderly" site may involve use of pesticides that may affect the bats as well as their food supply, or may remove landscape features important to bats.

● The Law in Action

Conservation problems arise through the use of chemicals highly toxic to mammals and applied for the preservation of timbers or stonework; through renovation or protection that excludes or entombs bats or renders the roost site unsuitable or inaccessible; or through deterioration of the structure to the point where it no longer provides the required protection from the external environment. The opening of the site to the public may also bring levels of

human activity that are unacceptable to the bats.

To help the SNCOs to discharge their advisory role, they may call upon the services of local volunteer bat groups. About 90 such groups exist throughout the UK and these are co-ordinated through The Bat Conservation Trust. Trained members can visit sites to give a first-hand assessment of the situation as it pertains to bats, the bat species involved and possibly the purpose for which bats use the site. The SNCO can then provide appropriate advice, which would take account of the planning process for the site. The advice may include recommendations about the timing of work; the risks of exclusion, entombment or deterrent in the proposed work; how to maintain the bat interest once the work is completed (if that is appropriate); and about the range of chemicals that is now available for the treatment of insect and fungal infestations in buildings and considered suitable for use in sites used by bats.

Some local bat groups can undertake surveys that would provide a valuable foundation of information to be included in management plans. They may also be available to help with the monitoring of progress once the work has started.

● Case Studies

● Carew Castle, Pembrokeshire (N.G.R. SN 045 037) (Plate 1).

This important archaeological site is open to visitors between Easter and October, and is used by theatre and school groups. Bat interest centres on its use as an important temporary "gathering" (pre-breeding) roost in spring and post-breeding roost in autumn for the endangered greater horseshoe bat (*Rhinolophus ferrumequinum*) and as a maternity roost for Natterer's bat (*Myotis nattereri*) (Plate 2). Altogether, nine of the UK's 14 bat species have been recorded in or around the castle. Integrated management proposals have been agreed

Plate 1. An integrated programme of restoration work has taken account of the bats using Carew Castle and its grounds, with particular reference to its importance as a roost for the endangered greater horseshoe bat. Photograph: H. Schofield

Plate 2. Natterer's bat - a species for which the UK may have internationally important populations. Many known summer roosts are in ancient buildings and important winter sites include mines in chalk and other rock, kilns and other underground structures. Photograph: F.R. Greenaway

between Pembrokeshire Coast National Park (which manages the site), Countryside Council for Wales and Cadw: Welsh Historic Monuments. In recognition of the importance of the site for bats, local bat groups and park staff are involved in survey work and management recommendations.

Management includes the introduction of an appropriate grazing regime and avoidance of the use of pesticides, both helping to enhance the local insect food supply for bats. Much of the site has been threatened by deterioration. Consolidation of walls has involved removal of shrubs and ivy, but many herbs and other wall flora have been replanted, maintaining the high botanical and associated invertebrate interest.

In a tower where Natterer's bats were known to roost, bat group and park personnel surveyed and marked used crevices; consolidation work was carried out when the bats were least likely to be present and procedures avoided the blocking of those identified roost sites and hence the risk of excluding or entombing bats. The status of these bats has shown some improvement following renovation. Further survey work identified crevice roosts of a total of four bat species.

Another tower is currently undergoing the same renovation procedure.

A nearby mill store has been converted for staff use and the conversion has allowed the incorporation of a wide range of features appropriate for bats (with special emphasis on encouraging horseshoe bats). In re-roofing the three attic areas, special crevices were left at the eaves and larger holes in the walls to allow specified access points for different bat species. The roofs were lined to retain heat and loft hatches designed to allow inspection without disturbance.

● Fountain's Abbey, North Yorkshire (N.G.R. SE 275 683).

The Fountain's Abbey and Studley Royal Estate contains a mixture of structures used by bats. The Harrogate Bat Group surveyed the estate and identified about 20 roost sites, including a tree, rock shelters, grottoes and tunnels, and ancient and more modern buildings. The Group's report has enabled the National Trust and English Heritage to work with English Nature to ensure that essential renovation work on buildings was carried out with due regard for their use by bats. By the Water Gardens, the Temple of

Plate 3. Careful restoration of this cellarium at Fountain's Abbey has left gaps used by Daubenton's bats. Photograph: R. Deaton

Piety was a summer roost site for a colony of brown long-eared bats (*Plecotus auritus*) and re-roofing was carried out in winter when the bats were absent.

In the cellarium of Fountain's Abbey itself (Plate 3), a colony of more than 100 Daubenton's bats (*M. daubentonii*) (Plate 4) and a small colony of Natterer's bats used gaps in the stonework. As with Carew Castle, the bat group identified the individual holes used by bats and restoration work left those holes and crevices open. The bat group co-operated closely with the stone-masons throughout these renovations. Nevertheless, there was an initial decline in the number of bats using the site following renovation.

Such considerations do catch the public imagination and so these projects have generated extra publicity (and, one hopes, understanding) for the work on the sites, for the bats and for the organisations involved.

● Bodiam Castle, Sussex
(N.G.R. TQ 785 255).

Bodiam Castle highlights inconsistencies in the wisdoms of bat conservationists! It is

home to very significant maternity colonies of Natterer's and Daubenton's bats (perhaps 400 bats altogether), with some use by pipistrelles (*Pipistrellus pipistrellus*) and brown long-eared bats. Despite the frequent (and, for the most part, justified) claims that bats are extremely prone to disturbance, here they occupy gaps in the ceilings of rooms visited by some 160,000 visitors per year, many of whom ignore notices, playing radios, smoking and carrying out a range of other activities in these rooms that might normally be expected to deter bats. The droppings and noise of the bats are obvious in these rooms and in June, the appearance of baby bats that have fallen from the maternity colony to the floors has caused concern to visitors and passing members of the local bat group. For the most part these young bats are recovered by their parents, but one room is usually kept gated during this period and there has been pressure to rope off sensitive parts of other rooms.

The Castle authorities (for The National Trust) have always been ready to explain the situation to visitors and now carry appropriate leaflets on bat conservation. They are currently reviewing their policy on interpretative notices, including the consideration of incorporating an educational notice about the bats and an explanation of the authority's policy on the conservation of bats in the Castle. There is, of course, an obvious conflict here in providing an explanation for those who are aware of the presence of small animals (even if they are not aware of their identity) and drawing attention to something that may then suffer from increased direct public attention.

A recent concern here arose from the Fire Brigade wishing to hold a rescue exercise with smoke in the Castle, but the exercise was timed and organised to avoid unnecessary disturbance to the bats.

● Clayton Church, Sussex (N.G.R. TQ 299 139).

Realising the special place of medieval churches in the English scene, as well as their importance to bats and the occasional special problems that bats cause in churches, The Bat Conservation Trust established a *Bats in Churches* project in 1991 with the aims of assessing the use of churches by bats, the attitudes to bats of those responsible for churches and to investigate ways of managing bats where they are a problem. Happily, most incumbents with bats are at least tolerant of them, but there remains a core of situations where bats are responsible for unacceptable damage to fabrics within the church.

One such example concerns medieval wall paintings. Now it seems that bats, which have probably lived with the paintings since their creation and have "seen" them subjected to so many perturbations over the centuries, are regarded by some as the last problem in the restoration and conservation of these important historical artefacts. Bat conservationists have worked hard in some churches to try to resolve such problems, but it has to be admitted that at Clayton Church, despite a considerable but varied amount of effort over several years by the author and other members of the Sussex Bat Group, it has

not been possible to establish the pattern of usage of the church by bats or even their means of access. Currently, the cleaners are keeping a log of bat activity (as recorded from the droppings) and with their help it is hoped to develop a management plan that will ensure that the bats are not a problem to the wall paintings. In 1994, a data logger will record the bat activity within the church through the summer and human observation will be intensified to establish the pattern of use.

The co-operation of those in day-to-day contact with churches and any associated bat problems is, of course, crucial to the development of any solutions, so it is unfortunate that the *Bats in Churches* project has seen the creation of a

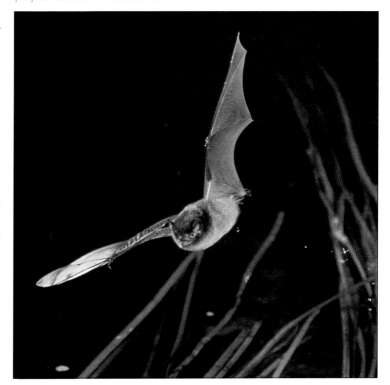

Movement Against Bats In Churches whose aims include the statement that, in its opinion, *"there is no place for bats in English churches"*. Likewise, misrepresentation of the law as it pertains to bats, the objectives of the BCT's project and, indeed, of the bats

Plate 4. Daubenton's bat - trees are probably the most important summer roost sites for this species, but many known roost sites are in older stone-built structures. Photograph: F.R. Greenaway

themselves (as in Paine, 1993), does not help to resolve these problems.

● Grimes Graves Flint Mines, near Thetford, Norfolk (N.G.R. TL 817 897).

These Neolithic flint mines are used by bats for winter hibernation (Green, 1993). Five species have been identified in recent surveys. A sixth species, Bechstein's bat

Plate 5. Lesser horseshoe bat - one of the UK's most endangered bat species, often associated with buildings of historic importance in summer, whilst hibernating in caves and artificial underground structures. Photograph: F.R. Greenaway

(*M. bechsteinii*), is no longer recorded in the area, but archaeological material (bones) found in the mines (and in some other sites) suggests that this bat was once a common resident species. The periodic blocking and opening of shafts has presented the bats with mixed fortunes. In recent years, more or less solid caps have restricted bat access and effected changes to the microclimate within the mines. A novel way of capping shafts to enhance the bat usage, while maintaining air flow and protecting the site, has been introduced at one pit but has not proved as successful as hoped. Such shafts have been fitted with a horizontally-set grille which some authorities feel bats might have difficulty in negotiating. Here, a small concrete surface structure allows a vertically-set grille with a short

horizontal passage opening into the top of the mine.

Grimes Graves has one curious significance to bat conservation. It is often difficult to assess the relationship between the numbers of bats counted at sites and the number of bats actually using such a site. This is particularly so in rather rough-dug mines of chalk and sandstone and in natural caves. One shaft at Grimes Graves had regular winter counts of up to 10 bats, but during one winter a shed was built over the shaft and in spring it is estimated that a minimum of 120 bats was found trying to emerge (Stebbings, 1993). Thus, in this instance, the number of bats counted at the site was only at best about 10% of the numbers actually present.

● Dene Holes, Grays, Essex (N.G.R. TQ 631 794).

A similarly constructed complex of mines dug for chalk was suffering degradation from dumping of refuse and from frequent visits of tour groups, many arranged by the local council. Following better protection of the site, agreements on visiting practices and rubbish clearance, the numbers of hibernating bats counted here has increased from just over 20 to more than 70.

● Hoffmann's Kiln, Settle, North Yorkshire (N.G.R. SD 823 663).

It is hoped that the proposals for the management of this site (see White - this volume) can take account of its use by hibernating bats. Kilns, ice-houses, fortifications and a range of other underground structures can provide important hibernation sites where bats roost in gaps in brick- or stone-work, behind walls and in a range of other cavities. Restoration work can exclude or entomb bats and opening the site to the public may render it unsuitable for use by bats. The extra "exuberant" level of restoration work required for safety reasons if the site is to be opened to the public may itself restrict its suitability for bats. Nevertheless, there are many examples of where time-sharing allows access to the bats in the winter and humans in the summer, or space-sharing retains parts of the structure available for humans and parts left for bats.

● Cefn Caves, Clwyd (N.G.R. SJ 021 701).

Sometimes, there are almost insurmountable difficulties in accommodating the conservation of bats with the management of ancient monuments. Bat conservationists would like to see the installation of grilles to protect bats from disturbance at sites such as these caves in Clwyd where the endangered lesser horseshoe bat (*R. hipposideros*) (Plate 5) roosts in winter. Archaeologists want a dig completed at the site first, but it is not a priority for them. They also consider that the engineering work in installation might inflict unacceptable damage on the structure of the caves and probably all interested parties would agree that the grilles would remove some of the aura of the site. But grilles and doors are installed on such sites for their own protection and there are usually ways of blending such structures in where they are necessary, or of positioning them so that they are not so visually intrusive. In some cases sites have been gated, grilled or blocked in such a way as to exclude bats. If gates or grilles are to be applied to sites known to be used by bats, the SNCO should be consulted. If the site appears suitable for bats it may also be worth seeking advice and remembering that the increased security afforded to a site through such measures may make unused or little-used sites much more suitable for bats.

● Wider Habitats

The conservation of bats and their roosts is of little value if the available habitat is unsuitable for them to find their insect food. This may mean a suitable range and number of insects, which will vary from bat species to bat species. For most species it also

means suitable safe routes for passage between roosts and feeding sites. Relatively little work has been carried out in the UK on this due to the difficulties of studying small night-flying animals. However, a three-year *National Bat Habitat Survey* to identify the relative importance of the range of habitats in different parts of the country and to try to identify landscape features of importance to bats has recently been completed (Walsh, Hutson and Harris, 1993). Elsewhere in Europe (particularly in the Netherlands) methodology is advancing rapidly to identify the landscape and habitat characteristics required by different bat species (Kapteyn, 1993). The UK project highlights areas for further research and the BCT is now providing a series of *Bat Detector Training Courses* to encourage a greater and wider ability to use these machines (which convert the ultrasonic sounds of bats to an audible signal) for species distribution, identification of habitat requirements, survey work and roost finding.

The *Wildlife and Countryside Act* does not provide for such wider habitat conservation, but it is required for certain species by the *EC Directive on the Conservation of Natural Habitats and Wild Species of Fauna and Flora 1992* ("The Habitats and Species Directive"). It is also required for all species by the *Agreement on the Conservation of Bats in Europe* (an Agreement under the *Bonn Convention on the Conservation of Migratory Species of Wild Animals*). This Agreement came into effect in January 1994. As explained above, the identification of precise habitat requirements is a major practical problem and one subject to strenuous efforts to develop better understanding. At present we have limited knowledge with which to lobby or advise governments and landowners on habitat management, and limited information on how Government expects to exercise its obligations in this respect under these international treaties. That is not to say that we are wholly ignorant in this area. We do have understanding of general principles of preferred habitat and landscape features that are important for bats, as well as some of the special requirements for some species, and we are anxious to see bats' requirements becoming a more integral part of landscape management practices.

● Acknowledgements

Information for the case studies discussed here has come from R. Deaton (North Yorkshire), J. Dobson (Essex), J. Goldsmith (Norfolk), G. Hinchcliffe (Durham), J. Hodges (Dyfed), H. Schofield (Clwyd) and the respective local bat groups, and from The National Trust. I am also grateful to Dr A. J. Mitchell-Jones and Professor P. A. Racey for comments on the manuscript. Thanks must also go to all those people working at or responsible for the many sites where bats have been accommodated in their management procedure; that goes far beyond the examples discussed here.

● References

Anon. (1993) *Bat Pack - The Conservation of Bats and their Legal Status.* Cirencester: National Trust.

Green, B. (1993) *Grimes Graves.* London: HMSO/English Heritage.

Hutson, A.M. (1987) *Bats in Houses.* London: Fauna and Flora Preservation Society (Reprinted by The Bat Conservation Trust).

Hutson, A.M. (1993) *Action Plan for the Conservation of Bats in the United Kingdom.* London: The Bat Conservation Trust.

Hutson, A.M., Mickleburgh, S. and Mitchell-Jones, A.J. (1990). *Bats Underground - A Conservation Code.* London: Fauna and Flora Preservation Society.

Kapteyn, K. (ed) (1993) *Proceedings of the First European Bat Detector Workshop.* Wageningen: Netherlands Bat Research Foundation.

Mayle, B.A. (1990) *Habitat Management for Woodland Bats.* Forestry Commission. Research Information Note 165.

Paine, S. (1993) The Effects of Bat Excreta on Wall Paintings. *The Conservator,* 17. 3-10.

Stebbings, R.E. (1993) *The Greywell Tunnel.* Peterborough: English Nature.

The Bat Conservation Trust (1993) *The Bat Worker's Guide.* London: The Bat Conservation Trust.

Walsh, A.L., Hutson, A.M. and Harris, S. (1993). UK Volunteer Bat Groups and the British Bats and Habitats Survey in, Kapteyn, K. (ed) *Proceedings of the First European Bat Detector Workshop.* Wageningen: Netherlands Bat Research Foundation. 113-123.

Caer Drewyn: Hillfort and "Boulder Field" Habitat

André Q. Berry and Brian W. Fox

Clwyd Archaeology Service, Clwyd County Council and British Lichen Society

● Introduction

Caer Drewyn, located above Corwen (N.G.R. SJ 088 444), is Clwyd's finest example of a stone-ramparted hillfort and is a Scheduled Ancient Monument (Cadw ref. Me12).

Bowen and Gresham (1967) have suggested four phases. An early, small earthen enclosure occupies the crest of the hill and is overlain by the much more extensive stone ramparts of the Iron Age fort with remains of the inturned gateway to the north east. Adjoining this gateway is a smaller enclosure, attributed to the Romano-British period, which uses sections of the stone rampart and earlier earthen enclosure to provide its defences. This "annex" displays the apparent foundation courses of a number of roundhouses. The final phase comprises the remains of a platform of a medieval "longhouse" located in a break in the rampart to the south, and apparently associated with a period when the rampart of the hillfort still stood to a height that enabled the fort to serve as an enclosure for livestock.

The monument, together with the immediately surrounding hill land totalling 17.7ha, was acquired by Clwyd County Council in 1990 following episodes of damage involving the construction of an agricultural access road and harrowing of some two-thirds of the interior (Plate 1).

The objectives of acquisition may be defined as:

● To enable conservation of the archaeological and natural heritage of the hillfort and surrounding hill land;

● To contribute to the maintenance and enhancement of the visual amenity of the Dee and Edeirnion valleys;

● To support County Council policy relating to the development of the potential of the A5(T) tourist corridor, particularly the provision of local community recreational access.

Plate 1. Caer Drewyn hillfort, showing the agricultural access track and extent of harrowing in the interior. © Copyright Clwyd-Powys Archaeological Trust Ref. 85-4-32.

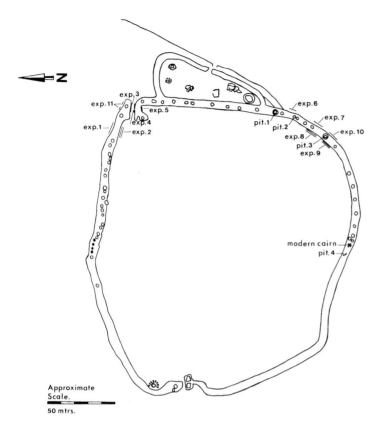

Figure 1. Plan of the hillfort based on Prichard (1887), showing the location of extant facework exposures and key episodes of modern disturbance. Plan drawn by Richard Parry.

investigations undertaken between AD1885 and AD1921 (Prichard, 1887; RCAHM, 1921; Gardner, 1922). Others are of more recent origin, associated with random removal of loose stone by visitors and local youths.

Whilst the latter exposures have not resulted in damage to facework they have exposed such faces to potential damage through weathering, the actions of livestock and vandalism.

Of greater concern is the increasing incidence of cairn and shelter construction in recent years, which has resulted in minor disturbance of inner terraced facework and significant removal of rubble corework. The majority of such disturbance is located along the eastern rampart, the area in which public access is focused due to the line of the agricultural access track.

The presence of such structures is seen to encourage further damage as features are added to or replicated elsewhere. Consequently, a programme of dismantling cairns and shelters was identified as desirable, coupled with the burial of selected facework exposures.

Given the historic significance of a number of the facework exposures, and the impact of the more significant recent episodes of cairn and shelter construction, a programme of works was undertaken as follows:

• Desk-top study to establish the extent of published records relating to archaeological investigations at Caer Drewyn;

• Field-based assessment to enable the plan location of all features and the correlation of such features with information derived from the desk-top study. This phase included a full photographic record of all features supported by scale drawings of all significant areas of exposed facework. The study was implemented in June/July 1993 and has established a baseline survey of exposures to facilitate future monitoring of site condition, thereby enabling evaluation

The site is now managed as a public open access area and is subject to an agricultural tenancy providing grazing for sheep only. The County Council reserves the right to define maximum stocking densities in accordance with the stated objective of ensuring conservation of the archaeological integrity of the monument.

• The Stone Rampart

The collapse of the ramparts at Caer Drewyn has afforded protection to substantial sections of intact facework behind extensive spreads of loose stone, particularly on the outer face. Whilst the upper courses of such extant facework are generally exposed, in some areas the exposure has been deliberately increased through the removal of the protective collapsed material. It is apparent that many of the significant exposures owe their origins to successive episodes of antiquarian of the impact of proposed increased recreational access.

11 exposed sections of facework were identified, together with 5 key episodes of modern disturbance in the form of 4 shelters/pits and 1 walkers' cairn (Figure 1). These were plotted on Prichard's (1887) plan of the fort to facilitate correlation of extant features with known antiquarian investigations.

History of Antiquarian Investigation at Caer Drewyn

Thomas Pennant's description of Caer Drewyn dated circa 1780 (RCAHM., 1921) notes the remains of "apartments" evident within the thickness of the wall, undoubtedly a reference to the pits which remain a significant feature of the rampart to this day. Whilst hinting at the antiquity of some of these pits, the description does not permit accurate correlation with extant features.

Comparison suggests that Prichard's (1887) stylised plan of the fort, dated to the summer of 1885, establishes the location of pits with some reasonable degree of accuracy.

Prichard also provides the first documented reference to antiquarian investigations at Caer Drewyn which he describes as *"a few tentative clearances along its wall"*. Five key areas of clearance are identified (correlation of these exposures with extant facework exposures is identified in parentheses):

• 1) North-eastern gateway. In a central part of the gateway *"the upper loose stones"* were removed from each side so as to *"bring to view its masonry, and of ascertaining its width"* (correlation: exp.3, exp.4);

• 2) Northern outer face of gateway (eastern exposure). Facing masonry collapse cleared to reveal *"good uncemented work with well placed stones, the interior of the wall*

being filled with dry rubble" (correlation: exp.11);

• 3) Northern outer face (western exposure). 18ft [5.49m] of wall was cleared to a depth of 4ft [1.20m] (correlation: exp.1);

• 4) Northern inner face. 60ft [18.29m] of the ramparts length were cleared revealing *"two or more lines of masonry contiguously built. The present height of the terrace next to the enclosure is 3ft [0.90m]. Measured across its top, its thickness varies from 4 to 5ft (1.20 - 1.50m), the lines being very irregular. The second wall, as seen at the back of the first, ascends 2ft (0.60m) higher; and its upper face has much the appearance of having supported another step or terrace, 4 or 4.5ft (1.20 - 1.35m) wide"* (correlation: exp.2);

• 5) South-eastern rampart inner and outer faces. *"A length of several yards of the lowest step on the inner face was uncovered, and its.....height was ascertained to be 3ft (0.90m), with a width at top of 5ft (1.50m). Beyond and above this first terrace, the main wall attains the height of 3 additional feet (0.90m)....."* (correlation: exp.9 and exp.10).

Gardner (1922) notes that the clearances made by Prichard in 1885 had been maintained in a *"partially visible"* state by Mr J. Salisbury Roberts of Corwen, apparently up until the time of Gardner's investigations in 1921. The Commission's description (1921), however, suggests that Salisbury Roberts actions may have been somewhat more intrusive in nature, with *" a good deal of tidying.....done"* exposing what Salisbury Roberts referred to as *"the fighting platform"*, *"finding the total width of wall and platform to be 18ft (5.49m)"*. This work is dated to 1912 and is unpublished except for four photographs reproduced in the Commission's inventory (correlation: exp.2).

Gardner's investigations were principally restricted to those clearances made previously by Prichard, described above at 1), 3), 4) and 5) (correlation: exp.3 and exp.4; exp.1 and exp.2; exp.9 and exp.10). *"By uncovering Mr. Prichard's clearances of*

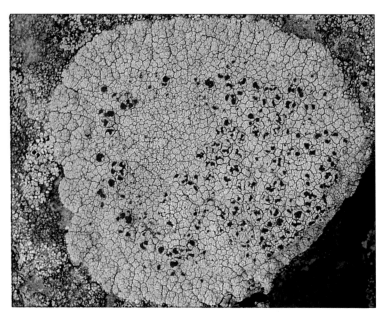

Plate 2. A fine example of fruiting Ophioparma ventosa var. ventosa. The presence of usnic acid gives an overall yellow-green colour to the thallus. 05.1993.

years ago, the upper courses of wall faces were revealed to view". Gardner also revealed facework located on the southern face of the southern inturned section of the north eastern gateway (correlation: exp.5) and within the guard chamber of the same section.

• The Lichen Interest

During the course of studying facework exposures it became apparent that the rampart of the hillfort comprised a significant expanse of "boulder field" habitat and as such supported a diverse saxicolous lichen flora. Proposals for the deconstruction of walkers' cairns and shelters were perceived as having a potential adverse affect on the lichen interest if undertaken with an inadequate knowledge of the significance and distribution of lichens on the site.

Preliminary survey was therefore undertaken on the 27th October 1993 and 24th June 1994 to identify the range of species represented and their frequency and distribution across the site. Sixty species of lichen were identified (listed as an appendix to this paper).

A clear distinction between the lichen flora associated with the collapsed rampart and that of the natural rock outcrops of the fort interior and adjoining hillside was noted and there is increasing richness in the flora as one ascends the hill.

Ophioparma ventosa is a dominant species (Plate 2). Both usnic acid positive (subsp. *ventosa*) and negative (subsp. *subfestiva*) forms were present in quantity, and one example of an usnic acid positive plant was seen at the time of survey to have hemispherical usnic acid free thalli, approximately 0.5-1.0cm in diameter, growing on its surface. *Pertusaria corallina* was present in sometimes very large thalli approaching 30cm in diameter, and in some cases was conspicuously isidiate-coralloid. *Tephromela atra* was abundant everywhere.

Stereocaulon vesuvianum appeared to be the dominant *Stereocaulon* species present, together with a variety *Stereocaulon vesuvianum* subsp. *nodulosum*. There were some fine groups of *Sphaerophorus fragilis* on some of the stones of the southern rampart and the southern edge of the northern rampart.

On the soil and amongst the moss (mainly *Rhacomitrum* spp.) between the stones, there were several species of *Cladonia*, including *Cladonia portentosa, C. squamosa, C. fimbriata, C. coccifera, C. subrangiformis* (rare) and, most interestingly, *C. luteoalba* of which only one isolated colony was recorded (Plate 3).

Other species noted on the ramparts were *Lecidia fuscoatra, L. lapicida* (or *lactea*, a thin lens section is required to confirm identification), *Schaereria fuscocinerea, Rhizocarpon oederi, R. geographicum* (various morphs), *R. obscuratum, Parmelia saxatilis, P. fuliginosa, Lecanora intricata* and *Hypogymnia physodes* (infrequent).

On isolated boulders within the fort area were noted *Parmelia conspersa* (common) with *Trapelia involuta, Lecanora intricata* and *L. polytropa*.

On outcrops of sandstone in an old quarry occurred *Lecidea orosthea.*

An outcrop of shale between Tan-y-Gaer farm and the summit, surrounded by bracken (*Pteridium aquilinum*) and western gorse (*Ulex gallii*), provided the only record of *Lasallia pustulata.*

Of particular note from the above outline description is the colony of *Cladonia luteoalba* situated in a shallow hollow on the north eastern rampart adjacent to the "annex" and occupying an area of approximately 45cm x 30cm. This species, *Lasallia pustulata* and *Stereocaulon vesuvianum* var. *nodulosum* have not previously been recorded from the grid square and represent the most westerly record of their Welsh distribution (c.f. Wilkinson, 1900; Armstrong, 1974).

A number of the older pits/depressions in the eastern rampart serve to augment and enhance the range of habitats by providing cooler and more humid conditions which favour species intolerant of desiccation, particularly the bryophytes. One pit, again located on the north eastern rampart adjacent to the "annex", provided the location for the only record for the site of the dog lichen *Peltigera didactyla.*

● Conclusion

Works have provided a baseline survey of the extent of exposed facework which will facilitate future monitoring. Evidence as to the degree of structural stability of these exposures, derived from a comparison of extant exposures with documentary evidence from earlier episodes of archaeological investigation, is somewhat conflicting.

Exposure 1 shows a high degree of structural stability which may be clearly established from published sources to 1921, a period of at least 72 years. Given the correlation of this exposure with Prichard's works in 1885, it is not unreasonable to suggest that substantial parts of the

facework may well have survived for a period of 108 years since re-exposure.

Elsewhere, facework exposures have been subject to partial collapse and/or reburial by corework from above over the same time period.

The degree of preservation of facework exposures, the incidence of modern disturbance/construction and the relationship between these and the proximity of the access track seems more than coincidental. Modern disturbance and the location of constructed shelters/cairns is clearly focused along the length of the eastern rampart where the course of the access track brings visitors into first close contact with the rampart. The location of exp.1 appears to afford it a degree of protection from such disturbance, whilst key exposures within the north eastern gateway (exp.3 and exp.4) and along the eastern rampart (principally exp.9 and exp.10) fall within the perceived zone of disturbance and have thus been subject to damage. Whilst the access track is a recent phenomenon (i.e. within the last 15 years), historically the definitive right of way has brought visitors close to the rampart along the eastern side.

Plate 3. The identified colony of *Cladonia luteoalba* **amongst corework on the rampart section adjoining the "annex". 24.06.1994**

Modern shelter/cairn construction has not resulted in other than minor disturbance of extant facework. It is apparent, however, that where such features are allowed to remain they encourage further episodes of enhancement or construction which have the potential for significant damage to surviving facework. A programme of works to deconstruct all modern features has therefore been implemented, the masonry derived therefrom being used to refill any associated hollow, with the remainder spread across the area of surrounding masonry collapse. Where individual masonry elements support a good surviving lichen flora they are to be positioned so that this lies on the upper face. Spread masonry will also be placed in areas of obvious recent disturbance rather than on areas supporting established lichen cover.

The apparent restricted distribution of *Cladonia luteoalba*, *Lasallia pustulata* and *Peltigera didactyla* at Caer Drewyn provides a salutary lesson in the need to ensure adequate survey of nature conservation interest prior to the management of ancient monuments. Both the *Cladonia* and *Peltigera* could so easily be buried and ultimately rendered extinct at the site through the dispersal of stone during deconstruction of cairns or shelters. Similarly, the apparent limited occurrence of *Lasallia pustulata* on a single boulder outcrop amongst bracken and gorse has implications for vegetation management. Farmers in the region traditionally manage gorse by burning, an action which may damage or even eradicate *Lasallia* if undertaken at Caer Drewyn.

● Acknowledgements

The baseline survey of facework exposures was funded jointly by Clwyd County Council and Cadw: Welsh Historic Monuments. Thanks are due to Dr. Sian Rees of Cadw for her support and assistance with the project. The survey was undertaken by Richard Parry. Thanks are also due to Dr. John Osley of the Countryside Council for Wales for his valuable assistance in arranging and contributing to the survey of lichens.

● References

Armstrong, R.A. (1974) The Descriptive Ecology of Saxicolous Lichens in an Area of South Merionethshire, Wales. *Journal of Ecology*, 62. 33-45.

Bowen, E.G. and Gresham, C.A. (1967) *History of Merioneth* Vol.1 Dolgellau. The Merioneth Historical and Record Society. 144-148.

Gardner, W. (1922) The ancient hillfort known as Caer Drewyn, Merionethshire. *Archaeologia Cambrensis*, 77. 108-125.

Prichard, H. (1887) Compound walls in North Wales: Caer Drewyn, Pen y Gaer, Craig y Ddinas, and Tre'r Ceiri. *Archaeologia Cambrensis*, Vol.4 5th Series. 241-259.

RCAHM. (1921) *Inventory of the County of Merioneth*, Vol.6. The Royal Commission on the Ancient and Historical Monuments and Constructions in Wales and Monmouthshire. London: HMSO. 13-16.

Wilkinson, W.H. (1900) Merionethshire Lichens. *Journal of Botany, London*, 38. 182-184.

● Appendix One

● Preliminary list of lichen species recorded at Caer Drewyn.

Key to notation:

Frequency on site: (f) frequent; (i) infrequent; (r) rare - only one or two records.

Location on site: w - rampart; b - boulders within fort; o - outcrops outside fort.

Acarospora fuscata (f) w,b,o.
Buellia aethelia (f) w,b,o.
Candelariella vitellina (i) w,b.
Cladonia chlorophaea (f) w.
Cladonia coccifera (f) w.
Cladonia fimbriata (f) w.
Cladonia floerkeana (f) w.
Cladonia furcata (i) soil at base of rampart.
Cladonia luteoalba (r) w.
Cladonia portentosa (f) soil at base of rampart.
Cladonia squamosa (f) w.
Cladonia subcervicornis (r) w.
Cladonia subrangiformis (r) w.
Cladonia uncialis (r) w.
Coelocaulon aculeatum (f) w.
Fuscidea cyathoides (f) w.
Hypogymnea physodes (i) w.
Lasallia pustulata (r) o.
Lecanora intricata (f) w,b,o.
Lecanora muralis (i) b,o.
Lecanora orosthea (i) o.
Lecanora polytropa (f) b,o.
Lecanora soralifera (f) w.
Lecidea fuscoatra (f) w.
Lecidea lapicida/lactea(? thin lens section required to determine species) (i) w.
Lepraria incana (i) w,o.
Micaria lignaria (i) w (on mosses).
Ochrolechia androgyna (i) b.
Ophioparma ventosa var. *ventosa* (f) w.
Ophioparma ventosa var. *subfestiva* (f) w.
Parmelia conspersa (i) b.
Parmelia fuliginosa (f) w,b,o.
Parmelia omphalodes (f) w,b,o.
Parmelia saxatilis (f) w,b,o.
Peltigera didactyla (r) w.
Pertusaria corallina (f) w,b,o.
Pertusaria dealbescens (f) w.
Pertusaria lactea (r) b.
Pertusaria pseudocorallina (r) w.
Platismatia glauca (i) w,o.
Porpidia cinereoatra (f) w.
Porpidia macrocarpa (i) w.
Porpidia tuberculosa (f) w.
Psilolechia lucida (r) w (north facing).
Rhizocarpon geographicum (f) w,b,o.
Rhizocarpon obscuratum (f) w,b,o.
Rhizocarpon oederi (f) w.
Schaereria fuscocinerea (f) w (north facing).
Sphaerophorus fragilis (f) w.
Sphaerophorus globosus (r) (base of rampart).
Stereocaulon dactylophyllum (i) w.
Stereocaulon evolutum (i) w.
Stereocaulon nanodes (r) w.
Stereocaulon vesuvianum (f) w.
Stereocaulon vesuvianum subsp. *nodulosum* (f) w.
Tephromela atra (f) w,b,o.
Trapelia involuta (f) w,b,o.
Tremolechia atrata (i) w (north facing).
Umbilicaria cylindrica (i) w.
Umbilicaria polyphylla (i) w.

Preliminary Species Count: 60

Langcliffe Quarry: A Balancing Act

Robert White

Archaeological Conservation Officer, Yorkshire Dales National Park

The views expressed in this paper are the personal views of the writer and not necessarily those of the National Park Authority.

● Introduction

Limestone is the dominant rock over much of the Yorkshire Dales. It has been exploited for centuries and used as building and walling stone; as a source of lime for agricultural, building and industrial processes; and, most recently, as an aggregate for the road building and construction industries.

Early limestone quarries were relatively small, particularly those which provided walling stone or the raw material for field lime kilns. 1187 lime kilns were mapped by the Ordnance Survey in the Yorkshire Dales in the 1850s. The transport opportunities created by the development of the railway system led to the demise of the small, often farm-based, lime production industry and its replacement by a modern capital and labour intensive quarrying industry. The area of the Yorkshire Dales was served by four standard gauge railways: along the Lune Valley and Airedale gap (the Ingleton Branch of the London and North Western Railway); along Ribblesdale (the Settle-Carlisle line of the Midland Railway); along Wensleydale (the Hawes branch of the North Eastern Railway); and the Grassington branch (Midland Railway). Of these, only the Settle-Carlisle line and the Grassington branch to Swinden quarry (N.G.R. SD 984 614) were still operating in 1994, the Ingleton and Wensleydale branches having closed in the early 1960s. Large limestone quarries and commercial lime kilns developed near each railway,

sometimes as at Moor Quarry, Leyburn (N.G.R. SE 098 909) and Threshfield (N.G.R. SD 977 645), linked to the standard gauge lines by light mineral railways. A handful of quarries have continued in use, but now distribute all of their product by road or, in the case of Swinden quarry, 75% by road.

● Langcliffe Quarry: Its Historical Development

Langcliffe Quarry (N.G.R. SD 925 663; Plate 1), beside the Settle-Carlisle route, is believed to have ceased lime production in the 1930s. Today it is best known for its Hoffmann lime kiln, the largest and best preserved such kiln in England.

The Langcliffe complex lies in Langcliffe and Stainforth townships and developed in the 1870s as two separate quarries: the Craven Lime Works and Murgatroyd's Limeworks. The complex has been described in detail by Trueman (Trueman *et al* 1989; Trueman 1990, 1992) following a survey by the Lancaster University Archaeological Unit (LUAU).

The principal components of Murgatroyd's Limeworks include a traditionally designed,

Plate 1. An aerial view of Langcliffe Quarry, showing the Hoffmann and triple kilns and the encroaching rubbish tip. SD 824663 ANY 333/21. 04.03.1988.

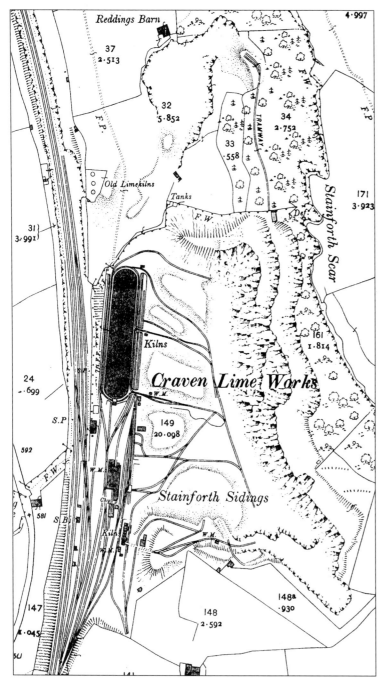

Figure 1. The quarry complex as shown on OS 1:2500 map, Yorkshire West Riding sheet 132.2. Surveyed in 1907, published 1909.

though massively scaled, set of three draw kilns, constructed in the side of a cutting beside the main railway line; a now heavily revegetated quarry at the base of Winskill Scar; and an inclined plane. Extraction probably began in 1872-3 and the limeworks was certainly in operation in 1876 but had closed by 1907.

The Craven Lime Works began at about the same time but quarrying continued until after the Second World War. The principal components of this part of the site are the Hoffmann lime kiln; the base of a later vertical steel lime kiln; a complex tramway system including an inclined plane and a tunnel; railway sidings and office buildings. The 1909 OS 25" map gives a good indication of the scale of this part of the complex (Figure 1).

The Hoffmann lime kiln was built in 1873. It consists of a series of 22 firing chambers, in total 242m long but arranged in an elongated oval, inside a 128m long structure. It was a continuous process kiln but, unlike the Murgatroyd's lime kilns, operated horizontally.

Limestone, quarried on site, was brought to the kiln via a horse drawn narrow gauge tramway and carefully packed into the chambers which, when empty, formed a continuous tunnel. Coal, brought by the main railway line, was raised to the top of the kiln by a water balance hoist and fed into the firing chambers through a series of feeder holes. Draught was controlled by a network of flues and a central 69m high chimney. By opening and closing the network of flues and controlling the fuel supply, the fire or fires could be advanced around the kiln. Fresh limestone would continually be packed in front of the burning zone and burnt lime extracted behind it. Hoffmann type kilns were very fuel efficient and produced a high quality lime but were labour intensive.

The Langcliffe Hoffmann kiln (Figures 2 and 3) remained operational until 1931 and was relit for a brief period in 1937. It is believed to have been used as an explosives and

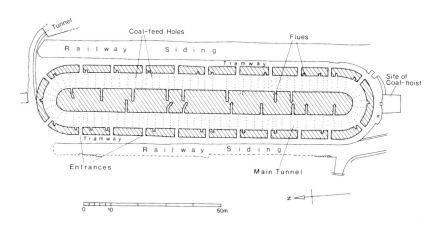

Figure 2. Ground level plan of the Hoffmann lime kiln. Courtesy of Lancaster University Archaeological Unit.

chemical store during the Second World War. After the War, the Craven Lime Works complex passed through various ownerships until it was acquired by the then Settle Rural District Council, passing in 1974 to Craven District Council. The red brick chimney of the Hoffmann kiln, with the date 1873 picked out in white brick, was demolished in 1952, supposedly finally falling after the insertion of explosives while the demolition workmen were having tea. Under Council ownership the quarry gained a new use as a landfill site for domestic and local trade refuse and the sidings and office buildings developed as a works area for Council workmen.

● Recognition of the Asset - Tip or Totem?

The importance of the Hoffmann kiln began to be recognised in the 1970s, largely through the efforts of Griff Hollingshead and Arthur Raistrick. The first moves to protect the kiln came in 1981 when a restoration and interpretation project utilising Manpower Services Commission (MSC) labour was mooted. This was discussed by both Craven District Council, the owners, and the Yorkshire Dales National Park Authority (YDNPA), a department of North Yorkshire County Council, as the quarry complex lay within the National Park. It did not proceed, although some vegetation clearance was

undertaken on and around the Hoffmann kiln and the kiln was proposed for scheduling.

At the same time the County Council Highways Department was also granted planning permission for an extension to the refuse tip which would have brought tipping right up to the kiln. A planning condition imposed by the National Park as the local planning authority specifically sought to protect the "channel" immediately east of the kiln (actually a loading bay positioned to allow easy loading of standard gauge railway wagons) but the likelihood of other features within the quarry complex being important, either in their own right or by association with the kiln, was apparently not recognised. When the kiln was finally scheduled in 1985, the boundary was drawn very tightly around the main structure and excluded the loading bays.

Figure 3. A section through the Hoffmann lime kiln. Courtesy of Lancaster University Archaeological Unit.

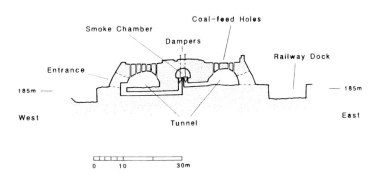

Plate 2. The Hoffmann lime kiln from the spoil heap to the north west, prior to scrub clearance. LQ20. 03.12.1986.

In 1986 a privately funded feasibility study into socio-economic prospects in Ribblesdale identified the quarry as a possible site for a visitor centre devoted to extractive industry (Wakeford and Whitelegg, 1986). The Ribblesdale Trust was formed to help revitalise the area by pursuing this and other projects identified by the report. These initiatives developed awareness of both the kiln and the Settle and Carlisle Railway (at that time under threat of closure by British Rail). In 1988 a commercial Community Programme operator, Jarvis plc, financed a more detailed feasibility study of the training, employment and enterprise potential within the Settle to Carlisle corridor which would use the Langcliffe Quarry complex as a pivotal all-weather tourist attraction. This study envisaged the development of a visitor centre, incorporating a rebuilt Hoffmann Kiln with a superstructure and a rebuilt chimney as the main visitor centre space and providing conference and exhibition facilities, etc. The report (Brooks-Rooney, 1988) envisaged a major programme, using MSC labour on both Langcliffe Quarry and Hellifield Station (a formerly important railway junction 11km to the south), with a gross budget of over £4.2m of which £3.0m was to represent the MSC input. The report was initially enthusiastically received

by the MSC and a project manager was appointed by Jarvis. In late 1988, however, the Community Programme rules were changed and the company immediately abandoned the scheme.

The Ribblesdale Trust again took up the initiative. An oral history project based on interviews with former workers at the complex had been carried out (Elliott, 1989) and, with the assistance of the YDNPA and English Heritage, the Trust sponsored an archaeological survey of the quarry complex (Trueman et al, 1989). This survey confirmed the archaeological importance of the site as a whole, not simply as an example of one stage of the economic and industrial development of the Pennines but in an international context with the contemporary Murgatroyd's quarry draw kilns as an essentially outdated example of British technology and European techniques indicated by the Hoffmann kiln and the later steel kiln.

Practical work inspired by the Ribblesdale Trust and the YDNPA included further clearance of scrub vegetation growing on the kiln, carried out by the Yorkshire Dales Conservation Volunteers in 1990. (Plates 2 and 3) This work was initially programmed for the winter but was delayed until mid-March and thus some of the sycamore (*Acer pseudoplatanus*) and hazel (*Corylus avellana*) scrub was coming into bud. The clearance resulted in a dramatic change in the appearance of the kiln, not totally appreciated by some users of the footpath which runs alongside the kiln, and there were also complaints that some bee orchids (*Ophrys apifera*) growing on the kiln, not then in flower, had been trampled.

A modified planning permission for the refuse tip had been granted in 1988 and subsequently implemented. This had the effect of limiting the area for landfill, keeping the edge of the tip away from the kiln. The tip has since closed and has been replaced, in the short-term, by a refuse transfer site, a series of skips in which local residents can dump domestic waste.

The EarthWorks UK project, initiated by Public Arts and sponsored by various bodies including the YDNPA and the Henry Moore Sculpture Trust to devise more imaginative, sculptural landforms for land reclamation sites used Langcliffe Quarry as a competition site but it did not prove possible to implement any of the entries or the concept to enhance the final profile of the landfill area (Israel, 1989).

• The Development Potential

The Ribblesdale Trust still wanted to pursue the idea of an interpretation centre or more extensive development and commissioned another commercial viability study. Central Government money through the Rural Development Commission was available to pay consultants for this but not to help finance the salary of a project officer to develop the ideas generated by previous reports and seek funding for their implementation. The summary of this third study recognised that *"a delicate balance needs to be struck between preserving the natural and man-made heritage of the National Park and providing tourism developments which stimulate wider interest and awareness in these special qualities*

without detracting from them" (LUC 1990, 5), although this was not necessarily obvious from the proposals.

Four development options for the kiln were identified:

• A: "basic preservation" of the Hoffmann Kiln, manned by volunteers, attracting 5,000 visitors *per annum*;

• B: "a low key attraction" of the Hoffmann and Murgatroyd's kilns, fitting out part of the Hoffmann kiln as an exhibition and display centre, manned by paid and unpaid staff attracting up to 25,000 visitors *per annum*;

• C: "modest development of a visitor attraction", building on B but adding development of the depot buildings into bunk barn accommodation; a visitor centre; cafe/bar; restaurant; craft shops and the development of a new railway halt attracting up to 50,000 visitors *per annum*;

• D: "a major visitor attraction" attracting in excess of 50,000 visitors incorporating a newly built Victorian railway station, Victorian "heritage" village shops and a mineral railway ride round the quarry complex. It was suggested that this would create up to 50 full time job equivalents.

Plate 4. Part of one of the better preserved entrances to the firing chamber showing brittle bladder fern and problems with the brick arch.

central chimney and the coal feeder holes are possible bat roosting sites, three species having been observed inside the kiln (Daubenton's bat [*Myotis daubentoni*]; Natterer's bat [*M. nattereri*] and brown long-eared bat [*Plecotus auritus*]), albeit in small numbers. It is also home to a colony of bee orchids which grow on the now exposed top of the kiln (on an area which would be built over if plans to re-create the superstructure were implemented); brittle bladder fern (*Cystopteris fragilis*; Plate 4) and other species grow on the brick entrances to the firing chambers; it is a hibernating spot for Herald moths (*Scoliopteryx libatrix*); and a rare cave dwelling species of spider, *Meta menadii*, recorded at only nine locations in Great Britain, has been provisionally identified here.

At this time neither the quarry nor the kiln had been subject to a detailed ecological survey, although over eighty two species of flowering plant had been recorded in a preliminary survey in May 1986 (Wakeford and Whitelegg, 1986). The cliffs above the quarry are also of avian interest, with breeding peregrines (*Falco peregrinus*) possibly attracted by the food supply generated by small mammals living on the recently closed refuse tip.

● A Way Forward? Balancing the Interests

The "Victorian village" proposal was not favourably received by the National Park Authority. Ecological and archaeological factors were major considerations balanced against the possible employment benefits. The proposals were subsequently scaled down but then fell victim to the recession. Another commercial developer expressed interest at the beginning of 1993 with a proposal to create a holiday complex, supposedly based on the attraction of the kiln, with hotel and time share accommodation and a chair lift to the top of the cliffs.

This study was followed up by a commercial developer who proposed the creation of a "Victorian" tourist village, exploiting the quarry's position in the National Park adjacent to the Settle-Carlisle railway. The initial proposal, which incorporated a "scale" model of the Settle-Carlisle railway inside the kiln, completely failed to take into account the archaeological and ecological importance of the site.

● Development Constraints

The Hoffmann kiln is scheduled; its flues which connected the firing chambers to the

After indications that this and similar scale developments would be unlikely to receive planning permission, the owners, Craven District Council, discussed the future of the complex with the National Park Authority and resolved:

"That, subject to (a) adequate safeguards for the Council's continued use of the Langcliffe Depot and house; (b) the National Park Committee's undertaking to preserve and restore the Hoffmann Kiln and subsequently to open it to the public as a heritage/visitor centre; (c) full consultation with the District Council on all proposals for development of the Quarry and Kiln; (d) the continued use by the North Yorkshire County Council of part of the Quarry as a civic amenity site; and (e) the consent of the Secretary of State, the Council agrees in principle to transfer ownership of the Craven Quarry site, including the Hoffmann Kiln, to the Yorkshire Dales National Park Committee at nominal cost."

Discussions are now taking place to clarify these conditions, the area to be transferred and arrangements for the future of the refuse transfer site and works depot. In the meantime a pre-intervention survey of those parts of the Hoffmann kiln, principally the surviving length of parapet wall and the decaying entrances to the firing chambers, which need consolidation work in the short-term whatever the future plans for the site, has been commissioned by the National Park from the Lancaster University Archaeological Unit. The need for more detailed ecological survey was also recognised but, prior to a brief being prepared, the Authority was approached by a newly qualified professional ecologist seeking suitable case studies for career development. The opportunity was therefore taken to acquire further ecological information on the site, at a minimal cost to the Authority, with the additional data being plotted on the archaeological survey drawings prepared by LUAU. This work, however, is concentrating on botanical aspects and there is still a need for further entomological investigation.

The findings of this botanical survey will undoubtedly influence both the consolidation of the kiln and the development of the site as a whole. In the short-term there is unlikely to be a conflict - the sycamores and brambles (*Rubus fruticosus* agg.) provide some wildlife cover but in the long-term will smother the more important limestone flora of the site and therefore need to be controlled.

There will be a more serious conflict over the long-term protection of the kiln. As constructed, the sides of the kiln appear to have been flush pointed and subsequently at least partially coated with bitumen. The pointing has now partially failed, providing niches for a variety of plants of which probably the most damaging are sycamore and bramble. These two can relatively easily be controlled by periodic weeding although this will be labour intensive. It may be necessary to point some of the most hungry joints but more comprehensive flush pointing would dramatically affect the appearance of the monument, part of whose charm is its colonised state. The twenty two entrances to the firing chamber will be one of the first parts of the kiln to be reconsolidated. The brick linings of these arches, attractively colonised by ferns (refer Plate 4) were subject to frequent temperature changes and repairs and are now often fractured or badly bonded.

The top of the kiln however, when built, and perhaps until the 1930s, was at least partially roofed above the firing chambers. Rainwater falling on the kiln would thus have been shed and any which reached the surface would have rapidly evaporated because of the heat loss from the burning process. Water is now able to soak into the body of the kiln, although some evaporates or transpires through the vegetative cover. Lime is now being deposited on the firebricks covering the firing chamber. Freeze-thaw action is also weakening the brick lining of the loading arches and the entrances to the smoke chamber. Long-term protection of the kiln body may thus be best achieved by re-roofing the kiln or by making the top of the kiln watertight - both actions which would destroy its present bee orchid habitat.

One measure, necessary in the short-term on safety grounds, may improve the attractiveness of the kiln for bats by reducing draughts. This is the replacement of steel covers to those smoke chamber entrances which are at present open to the elements and create hazardous 3m deep holes in the top of the kiln, although even this work will impinge on fern and spider habitat. At present the limited evidence suggests that the kiln is not of major importance as a bat roost, as not more than 5 bats have been observed inside the kiln on recent inspections (although the kiln's scale and number of possible openings means that it is a difficult site to survey). There is, however, some concern that the number of bats may be declining - local residents describe the kiln as having been *"black with bats"*. If so, this may in part be due to increased activity at the kiln during the winter (G. Hinchcliffe, pers. comm.). But, as yet, there has not been any attempt to attract or encourage visitors into the kiln. Any confirmation of this decline or increase in bat numbers will increase their importance as a constraint on development. An alternative explanation is that many of the entrances to the firing chamber were bricked up after the kiln fell into disuse and this reduced the airflow inside the kiln. These blocking walls have now mainly collapsed, partly no doubt assisted by visitors wishing to get more light into the firing chamber, thus increasing the airflow and making the internal temperature less stable.

A number of mature sycamores growing in the walls of the triple kiln have been felled and their stumps chemically treated in advance of more detailed consolidation proposals for this privately owned structure. Regrettably, however, the owners have carried out some limited demolition, stone robbing and dumping within the Murgatroyd's Quarry area but they are now discussing a woodland management scheme

for the cliffs above this part of the site. The opportunity is therefore being taken to ensure that no further damage to the archaeological features takes place.

Development of the Langcliffe Quarry complex, i.e. anything other than basic presentation of the site (LUC option A), is likely to be prejudicial to the conservation interests of the site as a whole unless very carefully handled. Options C or D would certainly have a major impact. It should, however, be possible to implement some limited development and still retain most of the ecological and archaeological interest of the complex.

Some of the depot buildings could be converted into a workshop for the National Park's Area Field Team. This would ensure that there would be a National Park presence on site, desirable for security and day-to-day management, and would also provide a base for guided tours of the complex, the most effective form of interpretation. These would take place outside the nesting and roosting seasons. One building could also be developed as an interpretation/exhibition centre, possibly unmanned but with the Field Team presence providing some security. This would remove the need to develop the interior of the kiln and limit the impact on the ecological and archaeological interest. Part of the yard area could be developed as a Lime or Building Resource Centre, explaining the importance of lime as a building material, and providing a base for running occasional courses in practical building conservation and the use of lime for mortars, renders and washes.

There is, however, local political support, even momentum, for greater development of the site to create a significant all-weather tourist attraction, perhaps including partial reconstruction or loading of one or more of the burning chambers to illustrate how the kiln worked, as well as the cafe/restaurant, craft workshops, etc envisaged by the LUC option C. In part this is due to the potential for increasing traffic along the Settle and

Carlisle railway and thus helping to ensure its survival. This in itself is an important conservation aim. The railway provides non-car borne access to the countryside and, equally important for rural communities, from the countryside, and is a monument in its own right - a formally designated linear conservation area which includes three viaducts scheduled as ancient monuments. A major development would be required to justify any investment in new railway facilities but the proximity to the main road along Ribblesdale suggests that most visitors would continue to come by road unless car-borne access was restricted. Development of the Langcliffe Quarry complex offers the opportunity to increase the local employment base and of utilising European Union Structural Funds as the Yorkshire Dales area now has Objective 5(b) status. There is therefore a growing need for a balancing act, balancing the pure interests of conservation of the archaeological and ecological resource with the potential that the site has for explaining and illustrating technological and ecological processes and with the economic benefits that external investment would bring to the area.

● References

Brooks-Rooney, M. (1988) *A Feasibility Study on the Training, Employment and Enterprise Potential within the Settle to Carlisle Corridor.* Jarvis plc: Unpublished report.

Elliott, S. (1989) *Working in a Limekiln.* Oral history project. Lancaster University: Unpublished report.

LUC. (1990) *Langcliffe Quarry Visitor Centre. A Commercial Viability Study.* Unpublished report by Land Use Consultants for The Ribblesdale Trust.

Trueman, M. (1990) A Lime Burning Revolution. *Association for Industrial Archaeology Bulletin,* 17.2. 1-2.

Trueman, M. (1992) The Langcliffe Quarry and Limeworks. *Industrial Archaeology Review,* XIV, 2. 126-144.

Trueman, M; Isaac, S and Quartermaine, J. (1989) *The Langcliffe Quarry Limeworks, Settle. An Archaeological Survey of the Site and Hoffmann Limekiln.* Unpublished report by the Lancaster University Archaeological Unit for The Ribblesdale Trust.

Wakeford, J. and Whitelegg, J. (1986) *The Ribblesdale Project Feasibility Study.* University of Lancaster.

Israel, T. (1989) The Art of Restoration? *Mineral Planning,* 41. 16-19

Correspondence and papers relating to Langcliffe Quarry are on YDNP file B614801. After Craven District Council agreed to transfer the quarry complex to the YDNP, The Ribblesdale Trust decided that it had achieved its main objective and wound itself up. Its archive was transferred to the care of the YDNP.

Forestry Management and Archaeology

Graham Lee

**Archaeological Conservation Officer,
North York Moors National Park**

● Introduction

The creation of commercial coniferous plantations in England has occurred predominantly in the uplands on poor soils and steep slopes, areas of marginal land and moor where land values are lowest. These same areas can often, however, be extremely important for the archaeological remains that their relative lack of value has helped preserve.

Within the North York Moors the extensive remains of early agriculture and settlements exist widely across what is now moorland, at altitudes of up to c. 320m OD.

Dated mainly to the Bronze and Iron Ages, occupation of the uplands was assisted by climatic improvements and large tracts of the natural forest which once covered the area were cleared away. Soils, however, would have been relatively poor and thin, prone to erosion and leaching. As they were worked out and became exhausted (at the highest altitudes this may have been quite rapid) entire landscapes came to be abandoned. This probably also coincided with the climatic deterioration at the beginning of the Iron Age. But for later mineral extraction and activities such as rabbit warrening which have all left their own distinctive remains, most of these landscapes were left virtually undisturbed for centuries until modern society found another use for the land. The impetus for the creation of twentieth century forests came at the end of the First World War which had caused a serious depletion of native stocks of timber and highlighted Britain's dependence on imports.

Figure 1. Land managed by Forest Enterprise within the North York Moors National Park.

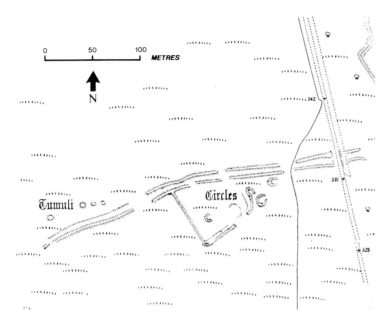

0   50   100
METRES

N

Tumuli

Circles

Figure 2. Ordnance Survey County Series Second Edition 25" map (1928) showing enclosure and putative hut circles attached to a cross-ridge dyke at N.G.R. SE 956 874.

The scale of the survival and significance of the forests' archaeological resource was brought to wider attention during part of a survey of the Wykeham Estate, near Scarborough. This includes some 6.5ha of coniferous plantations which are leased to the Forestry Commission and managed by Forest Enterprise, the arm of the Commission which cares for their own forests.

Over 15% of the North York Moors National Park is actually managed by Forest Enterprise (part lease-hold, part directly owned). The majority of the holding, 12.9% of the National Park, is predominantly coniferous plantations and represents an area of some 71 square miles (Figure 1).

The Wykeham survey highlighted the inadequacy of the existing records which were found to be out of date (many by 20-35 years), confused and inaccurate. It was quickly realised that many sites recorded on the Ordnance Survey second edition County Series 25" maps, dating from 1912-1928, which had been written-off by modern Ordnance Survey fieldworkers as destroyed by afforestation (and hence omitted from the modern maps) survived as originally shown, albeit planted over with

trees. These monuments could be "rediscovered" from an examination of the County Series maps and accurately located by underlaying them to the existing 1:2500 sheets, where available. This provides both positions for sites within the current forest layout and national grid co-ordinates. Sites formerly written-off above and rediscovered by the survey include an enclosure (Figure 2 and Plate 1) which shows a clear relationship to the adjacent cross-ridge dyke (the ditch of the enclosure cuts through the southern bank of the dyke) and is associated with what appears to represent at least one house site visible as a slight extant ring ditch.

Although often noted as a destructive agency, the early forest plantings, undertaken before the use of deep ploughing as a method of ground preparation, have actually preserved many archaeological landscapes which would otherwise almost certainly have been lost to agricultural improvements and intensification.

This is not to say that damage did not occur in the past. For example, round barrows were bulldozed to accommodate the required line of forest tracks and entire cairnfields, even when scheduled, have been ploughed virtually to obliteration. However, significant changes have occurred in recent years and environmental conservation, which includes archaeology, is now firmly established in Forest Enterprise objectives.

The Wykeham survey did reveal, however, that monuments were continuing to suffer damage and erosion during a wide range of even relatively minor forestry operations due to the lack of detailed information available to contractors. This is especially significant since the bulk of such work is now carried out by independent operators rather than Forest Enterprise staff. The most damaging operations involve the movement of vehicles and equipment and the extraction of timber, especially when the latter is performed by skidding (chain-dragging trunks behind a tractor). Care is also required with the stacking of timber or dumping of brash (the branches cleared from the trunk to encourage a healthy main stem, or stripped off during felling), since these can mask remains and make them more vulnerable to future damage.

● The North York Moors Forest Survey Project

These factors prompted the establishment in 1992 of the *North York Moors Forest Survey Project*, jointly funded by the National Park, Forest Enterprise and English Heritage. The objectives were:

● to carry out a (condition) survey of all known monuments within all Forest Enterprise properties;

● to record any unknown sites recognised during the course of the project;

● to draw up recommendations on the future management of the archaeological resource.

Detailed topographical surveys were not required, although some sketch-plans were compiled in order to clarify site characteristics.

Work has been split into two phases. Fieldwork has been restricted to the period of late winter through to early summer, when existing vegetation has died back and before features are masked by dense new growth, particularly of bracken which can grow to at least 2m high making site evaluation impossible without clearance. Recorded monuments are graded into one of five categories, utilising the same non-statutory criteria as applied by English Heritage in the scheduling of ancient monuments, to assist in the process of drawing up management recommendations and priorities, based on a method successfully adopted in a survey of the Weld Estate in Dorset (Keen and Carreck, 1987):

● Level. I Archaeological and historical features of special importance which warrant the greatest possible protection;

● Level IB. Level I monuments which appear to have been badly damaged or destroyed;

● Level II. Archaeological and historical features but of lesser significance;

● Level IIB. Level II monuments which appear to have been badly damaged;

● Level III. Former archaeological and historical features for which there is confidence that no coherent archaeological remains (including buried features) are recoverable.

By definition most Scheduled Ancient Monuments should fall within Level I unless they have been badly damaged or where, after careful survey, no obvious signs of the monument can be located; in which case they would be categorised as Level IB.

Work has been carried out by independent archaeological consultants to a detailed specification, citing precisely what information should be recorded since many

Plate 1. Perimeter of south east sector of enclosure in Figure 2, showing central ditch and slight internal and external banks. Photographed from east north east 10.07.90.

of these monuments may not be re-examined for at least a further decade. A cut-off date for the definition of archaeological features was given as 1945, thus including all industrial and warrening remains, together with historic watercourses, sheepfolds, boundary stones, kilns and clamps. Information on the condition of sites includes a description of vegetation and tree cover, together with details of the effects of any forestry ploughing.

Reports produced include:

• A brief outline of survey techniques utilised and limitations/problems encountered;

• A brief summary of archaeological monuments encountered, by period, to assess the diversity and survival of the resource;

• A catalogue to include the following fields of information on each site: site reference (including SMR and SAM numbers), national grid reference (minimum of eight figures plus grid letters), condition, land-use and

grading plus a concise summary and description of key features (incorporating classification, factors affecting condition, vegetation/tree cover and dimensions);

• Management recommendations (to include some form of marking for sites which are difficult to identify or locate) and review of grading system;

• Series of base maps to show distribution and relative gradings of the resource (at 1:10000 scale), referenced to the catalogue.

The distribution maps and associated catalogue are obviously the most important product of the survey as far as Forest Enterprise and the practical management of sites is concerned. Management recommendations vary from maintenance of the *status quo*, to careful clearance of tree cover planted or self-seeded on Level I sites, movement of tracks away from monuments, to the establishment of permanent markers (see Appendix One) where important monuments are slight and likely to be masked by vegetation.

The survey has, in fact, recorded over 2000 archaeological sites and features, a number of which are new discoveries, including several possible round barrows. Examples of other monuments encountered range from square barrows to embanked enclosures, field systems (both historic and prehistoric), hollow-ways and also a large number of industrial monuments. These comprise quarries, lime kilns, mines (particularly for jet) and warrening remains. The latter include boundary banks, turf and stone-walled enclosures and a variety of rabbit traps known as a "type", some of which were still in use this century. Although the results have yet to undergo detailed analysis, they will be used to produce implications reports on each of the forest areas surveyed. That produced for Harwood Dale Forest (N.G.R. SE 99 NE) has been appended as an example (see Appendix Two). Such summary reports and the survey results will be used by Forest Enterprise in their forest design plans and to help guide future management operations in

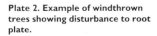

Plate 2. Example of windthrown trees showing disturbance to root plate.

order to reconcile and integrate the needs both of timber production and archaeological conservation.

The mechanics of this integration can be quite complex. Archaeological monuments, in particular less discrete sites such as enclosures or elements of field systems, when properly respected, will act as significant constraints to conventional forestry operations. From the archaeological perspective, however, trees even where sensitively planted and without ground preparation by ploughing, will eventually disturb archaeological layers through root development, a problem seriously compounded by windthrow where the entire root plate and attached section of a monument can be ripped from the ground (Plate 2). Also to be considered is future access, for thinning and extraction of timber, and other requirements such as drainage.

In the long-term even the creation of conservation areas to carefully exclude important monuments from areas of planting is not without its difficulties unless subject to regular labour intensive clearance. This is due to the very invasive nature of regeneration by shrubs and trees. Where carefully managed though, such areas also offer a range of habitat and feeding opportunities for wildlife. Experience has shown that the most stable environment for monuments in forestry appears to be within an area of thinned semi-mature/mature plantation, provided that the trees are not growing on or too close to sensitive areas. Where this is possible the existing canopy can help to shade out and reduce the invasive growth of other vegetation. Such an arrangement, however, would require considerable planning to perpetuate and would increase the frequency of forestry operations in the vicinity. This, in turn, could increase the chances of accidental damage occurring.

It is clear from the survey that any failure to respect monuments during forestry operations can prove very serious, particularly with regard to vulnerable

earthwork features. There is, therefore, a need for careful supervision of all operators in the forest, and it would obviously be beneficial if this could be linked with some form of increased promotion of awareness. Since such supervision may prove difficult to achieve, especially if there is no regular workforce, the author favours the imposition of a penalty clause on all forestry contracts which would financially penalise contractors for any damage caused to monuments during forest operations (or to other environmentally sensitive locations which would all obviously need to be clearly indicated). Although a bonus system to reward careful operators would represent a more positive approach, this seems less likely to be feasible, whilst a potential reduction in profits is in itself a positive way to make most contractors take archaeology more seriously.

One of the first results of the early survey work was the production of a set of recommended guidelines to protect archaeological sites during forestry operations:

• All archaeological features within a work area should be located and clearly/securely marked in an appropriate manner prior to the commencement of operations;

• There should be no vehicular movement or the dragging of timber over/across monuments;

• Timber growing on monuments should be cut off at the base and lifted clear, avoiding any disturbance to the monument and leaving the stump in situ;

• Monuments affected by windblow should have the root pad replaced in as close to its original position as possible;

• Monuments should be kept clear of brash dumps and timber piles;

• During replanting operations, monuments and a protection zone which should extend to at least 5m beyond known limits around the site, should be left unploughed and unplanted;

Although mostly practical, it is acknowledged that a number of these recommendations will have direct or indirect cost implications, particularly number four which, although a preferred option, may not be at all straightforward.

● Conclusion

Future work will now focus on the completion of the implications reports for the remainder of the twenty two defined survey areas (which range in size from one to thirty five square kilometres) and the practical management of vegetation on a selection of nationally important monuments which lie in areas which have recently been clear-felled. This will concentrate on clearing brash left on site during felling operations and on controlling the growth of obscuring vegetation, particularly bracken and brambles, and the regeneration of trees. This work will involve the services of the British Trust for Conservation Volunteers as well as other local assistance.

The up to date archaeological information provided by the survey will also enable a more detailed archaeological evaluation of human activity in these parts of the Moors to take place. The survey has brought to light a number of previously unrecognised monuments and facilitated the re-interpretation of others, affecting particularly the known distribution of upstanding square barrows.

There is thus considerable potential for the presentation of monuments on a series of guided trails and this topic has been under discussion between Forest Enterprise and the National Park for a number of years now. It is recognised that this requires care so as not to increase the risk of erosion or other forms of damage, particularly to rare or vulnerable monuments. However, the diversity of the resource within the forests could support a number of themed trails

and these will hopefully be progressed over the next few years.

● Acknowledgements

It is important to note that none of this work would have been possible without the co-operation, assistance and interest of John Mackenzie, the regional Forest District Manager and his staff, and this is gratefully acknowledged

● References

Crew, P. (1994) Personal Communication. Archaeology Officer, Snowdonia National Park.

Iles, R. (1989) Danby Moors Archaeological Survey 1988-89, North York Moors National Park Report.

Keen, H. and Carreck, A. (1987) *Historic Landscape of the Weld Estate, Dorset*

North York Moors National Park. (1977) *North York Moors National Park Plan.* Helmsley: North York Moors National Park.

● Appendix One

● The Marking of Monuments

Although it has been a policy of the North York Moors National Park (since the first National Park Plan appeared in April 1977) that monuments should be marked, to aid location and to help prevent accidental damage, few attempts at permanent markers have been made. This has been largely due to the problem of finding an acceptable design.

Temporary markers, using wooden posts and fluorescent tape, around the periphery of monuments have frequently been used in the past to help protect sites during operations. Such markers continue in use today and can be surprisingly long-lasting, as site visits have demonstrated.

It is clear that, in addition to temporary marking of monuments during operations, important sites which are slight or tend to be masked by vegetation would benefit from permanent markers (Iles, 1989). These should not cause damage to the sites in question and although they should be instantly recognisable by all people working within the forests, they should not attract unwanted attention. The author favours the use of a series of low marker posts, located around the periphery of the known or suspected archaeological interest of the monument, but substantial enough to dissuade vehicular access. However, an interesting new idea which is currently being put into practice in the Snowdonia National Park utilises hardwood trees as markers planted at a safe distance around the perimeter of appropriate monuments (Crew, pers. comm.). In time these should offer the double advantage of both standing out clearly within coniferous plantations and of helping to shade out future regeneration.

● Appendix Two

● Phase I results: Implications for archaeological resource and site management. Sample exercise, Harwood Dale Forest

The survey produced 197 records for Harwood Dale forest. Of these 33 records (or 17%) can be discounted as having very minor or no practical implications for future Forest Enterprise activities. These comprise four records outside the survey area; four sand pits; four quarries; three ponds; a well; a bridge; and 13 boundary stones of which 11 could not be located and two which were incorporated within a drystone wall. A further two records represent cairnfields where the sites are also dealt with individually, and there is one duplicate record. Nearly two thirds of the remaining 164 records are located within the two cairnfields. The forest has therefore been dealt with below in three sections: the forest excluding the two cairnfields, and then each of the cairnfields in turn.

● Harwood Dale forest.

Harwood Dale forest has been shown by the survey to contain a core of 58 sites (excluding Hardhurst Howes and Standingstones Rigg cairnfields). These break down into the following groups:

- Level I - 21
- Level Ib - 9
- Level II - 27
- Level IIb - 0
- Level III - 1 (This record refers to a Round Cairn/Barrow that appears to have been completely ploughed out).

Recommendations relating to the future management of these features fall into the following categories:

- Sites to be marked - 4
- Sites obscured by windthrow, not yet recorded - 6
- Sites to be cleared of planted trees - 4
- Sites to be cleared of regenerating trees - 4

- Decision on site prior to ploughing/replanting - 1

- Hardhurst Howes Cairnfield.

Records were compiled for a total of 49 cairns which can be subdivided into the following groups:

- Level I - 0
- Level Ib - 0
- Level II - 16
- Level IIb - 9
- Level III - 24

These figures reveal that up to 49% of the cairnfield appears either to have been destroyed by deep ploughing or to have had all surface traces removed, with a further 18% recorded as badly damaged (although two of these feature in the recommendation below):

- Sites to be marked - 2
- Sites to be cleared of debris/vegetation to better evaluate - 3

- Cairnfield on Standingstones Rigg.

Records were compiled for a total of 57 features (56 cairns and one cup-marked stone) which can be subdivided into the following groups:

- Level I - 2
- Level Ib - 55
- Level II - 0
- Level IIb - 0
- Level III - 0

This grouping occurs because the cairnfield is a scheduled ancient monument. The survey, however, reveals that only one cairn (2%) appears to have survived undamaged. The majority of the remaining 98% have all been affected by deep ploughing - up to 65% appear to have had all surface traces totally removed, 29% show slight traces (a single stone or stone scatter amidst the furrows) while 4% (two sites) show slight remains. The management recommendations of the report have therefore been amended slightly to include the latter two sites (as rare survivals) amongst those for marking:

- Sites to be marked - 3
- Sites to be re-erected and marked - 1 (Cup-marked stone)
- Sites to be cleared of debris/vegetation to better evaluate - 1

- Conclusion

The known archaeological resource for Harwood Dale forest can therefore be broken down into the following totals:

- Level I - 23
- Level Ib - 64
- Level II - 44
- Level IIb - 9
- Level III - 25

These totals show that up to 1992, some 50% of the previously known or recorded features, have been severely damaged (Ib and IIb) or lost (III), although this figure is particularly influenced by the current condition of the two cairnfields. This situation is considered to be exceptional and not likely to be repeated in other forest areas. Standingstones Rigg obviously requires its status as a scheduled ancient monument to be re-assessed, but with particular attention taken to mark the three extant sites: the Level I site should be preserved and a decision taken on the future of the two Level Ib sites in association with English Heritage, in advance of further forestry operations.

There is also a small group of scheduled barrows which were obscured by windthrown trees and not recorded. This area obviously requires careful clearance prior to ascertaining the condition of these monuments.

Practical recommendations for management, therefore, include a total of ten sites for marking, eight sites to be cleared of planted or regenerating trees (these are all "discrete" sites of limited size), ten sites to be cleared of windthrow/debris or vegetation, one stone to be re-erected and three scheduled sites to be assessed in association with English Heritage prior to future operations.

"Hen Caerwys": A Deserted Medieval Settlement Under Woodland

André Q. Berry

Clwyd Archaeology Service, Clwyd County Council.

• Context

The case study described within this paper forms part of Clwyd Archaeology Service's on-going sites and landscapes management programme, the aims of which are to undertake the integrated management of ancient monuments and historic landscapes and to promote the inter-relationship of archaeology and countryside. Other case studies demonstrating this approach, together with more detailed discussion of the programme, are given elsewhere (this volume; Berry 1992; 1993a; 1994a; 1994b).

• Introduction

The remains of banks and walls within the woodlands of Coed y Marian and Coed Gerddi-gleision, near Caerwys, Clwyd (N.G.R. SJ 138 743) (Plate 1) were first reported by W.J. Hemp in 1960. In consultation with Canon Ellis Davies, a well-known local historian, the site was named "Hen Caerwys" (Rogers, 1979).

Limited excavation at the site, of one platform house (Plate 2) undertaken by G.B. Leach and T.T. Pennant Williams between 1962 and 1966 (Archaeology in Wales, 1962-6), recovered in excess of 1,000 pottery sherds which, in general form, were equated with wares from late fifteenth century contexts known from Flint Castle, Clwyd. A bronze religious token of possible French origin, together with the general standard of construction of an annex, led

Plate 1. "Hen Caerwys", situated within the main block of woodland, forms part of a more extensive historic landscape. The two narrow linear woodlands beyond and to the left of "Hen Caerwys" and the triangular area of rough pasture in the right foreground contain similar earthworks. © Royal Commission on the Ancient and Historical Monuments (Wales). Ref. 945167-51. 13.08.1994.

Plate 2. House platform excavated by Leach and Pennant-Williams in the 1960s. 10.11.1993.

105

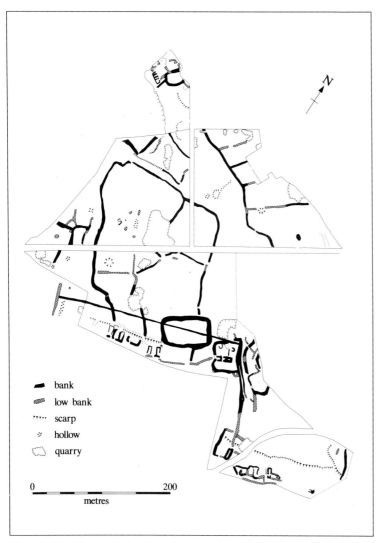

bank
low bank
scarp
hollow
quarry

0   200
metres

Figure 1. "Hen Caerwys": plan of the earthworks. Plan prepared by Pete Muckle, Gwynedd Archaeological Trust.

included iron knives, arrowheads and numerous pieces of wrought iron, together with much slag and coal suggesting that a coal-burning forge was in use.

Other than some limited survey work undertaken in the early 1980s (Hill, pers. comm.), no attempt had been made to establish the nature and extent of the archaeological remains at "Hen Caerwys". An EDM survey of the extent of the scheduled area was therefore commissioned by Clwyd Archaeology Service in 1993 to provide a plan of the earthworks so as to enable the formulation of detailed management proposals on behalf of the landowner. The survey, undertaken by Gwynedd Archaeological Trust, has revealed (Figure 1) two discrete groups of house sites with associated enclosures and network of fields and access ways. This apparently contemporary system is overlain by a complex of small mounds and hollows believed to be associated with piecemeal mineral exploration in the late 18th/19th centuries (Hughes, pers. comm.). A number of quarries of similar date are potentially related to episodes of housebuilding.

Analogy with an adjacent area of fieldsystem preserved beneath pasture (Marian Drew, part scheduled ancient monument F163, N.G.R. SJ 143 745) and believed to be contemporary with "Hen Caerwys" suggests that the fieldbanks comprise the remains of collapsed stone-faced earthen banks the profiles of which are now much softened by many years of accumulated leaf litter.

"Hen Caerwys" remained as common land until 1852 when it was the subject of an enclosure award under Act 49, Geo.3. (Clwyd Record Office, Hawarden ref. QS/DE/25). This episode in the history of the site is witnessed by the straight drystone wall bounded public highway and access to the property of Marian Bach (which form an inverted 'T'-shape in Figure 1; Plate 3), together with a collapsed length of field boundary running roughly east west which

the excavators to attribute a mid-fifteenth date to the site (Rogers, *ibid*).

The house site, one of a cluster of four, comprised a more or less level platform cut into the steeply sloping south facing bank. Excavation revealed the surviving lower courses of the limestone walls of the house leading the excavators to the opinion that there was a change in construction, from stone walls within the cutting to a timber-framed structure, resting upon a dwarf wall, outside. A central line of postholes indicated a ridged roof, probably thatched. An adjoining annex, of later construction, comprised two rooms and evidence

Plate 3. The enclosure road - this characteristic straight, drystone wall bounded highway contrasts markedly with the sinuous hedgerow flanked sections which approach the former common on either side. 22.06.1994

overlays and bisects the principal enclosure. The largest of the quarries lying immediately north west of the public highway may have provided the source for the limestone used in the construction of the drystone walls which bound the enclosure roads.

● The Monument as Woodland

79% (8.77ha) of the extent of the Scheduled Ancient Monument (Cadw ref. F162) is located under mature broadleaved woodland which, in general character, is dominated by ash (*Fraxinus excelsior*) and sycamore (*Acer pseudoplatanus*) with oak (*Quercus* spp.). Scattered larch (*Larix* spp.) indicate a failed attempt, in the early years of this century, to increase the productive value of the woodland for timber. The density of the canopy is variable, with more open areas dominated by a dense understorey of hawthorn (*Crataegus monogyna*), hazel (*Corylus avellana*) and blackthorn (*Prunus spinosa*). Elsewhere, the understorey is sparse. Overall, structural diversity is good, though age class amongst canopy trees is restricted.

The woodland, though obviously secondary for the most part, is long established and supports a diverse flora including the early purple orchid (*Orchis mascula*), common twayblade (*Listera ovata*), common spotted orchid (*Dactylorhiza fuchsii*) and greater butterfly orchid (*Plantathera chlorantha*) (Plate 4). A number of the more common species often associated with ancient woodland sites but more appropriately recognised regionally as indicators of long established or rich woodland sites also occur, including bluebell (*Endymion non-scriptus*), perennial dog's mercury (*Mercurialis perennis*), wood sorrel (*Oxalis acetosella*), sanicle (*Sanicula europaeus*), moschatel (*Adoxa moschatellina*), wood avens (*Geum urbanum*) and an isolated example of wood anemone (*Anemone nemorosa*).

Beyond the limits of the earthworks within Coed y Carreg, a colony of herb paris (*Paris quadrifolia*) has been identified. This species, which is much more reliably indicative of ancient woodland sites in north east Wales, may indicate an area of undisturbed ground or woodland cover that co-existed with the medieval settlement of "Hen Caerwys".

Plate 4. Greater butterfly orchid in Coed y Marian. 22.06.1994

area as a habitat for wildlife and the relative scarcity of this resource in both a regional and national context (only 3% of the land area of Clwyd is occupied by broadleaved woodland [Forestry Commission, 1985]).

The opportunity existed therefore to develop an integrated programme of management to address four principal objectives:

• the conservation of the archaeological integrity of the monument;

• the conservation and enhancement of the woodland as a habitat for wildlife;

• the enhancement of the quality of the woodland as a timber resource;

• and, the conservation of the woodland as a landscape feature.

• Conservation of the archaeological integrity of the monument

It is apparent that the stratigraphy of occupation areas such as those excavated by Leach and Pennant Williams is being greatly degraded by the actions of uncontrolled scrub colonisation and associated rootgrowth. Damage to fieldsystem earthworks, although less critical, is still apparent where there is direct colonisation of the features by canopy trees. In addition to damage through physical displacement of stonework by expanding roots and buttresses there is an attendant risk of windthrow.

EDM survey has identified five key areas of archaeological sensitivity (Figure 2) - the two discrete groups of house sites; an enclosure with possible foundations of buildings; the principal enclosure with substantial enclosing earthworks, function unknown; and a primary enclosing field boundary. The latter, although undoubtedly containing limited information of archaeological interest, is a well-defined earthwork for the most part and is diagnostic of the structure and form of the

The remainder of the scheduled extent supports permanent pasture which is subject to grazing by sheep and cattle.

• The Objectives of Management

The regional importance of "Hen Caerwys" as the only identified deserted medieval settlement site in Clwyd must be balanced against the significance of the woodland complex of field boundaries that occur at "Hen Caerwys".

In general terms, the management plan proposed that the five key archaeological areas be subject to immediate clearance of all understorey species, together with regenerating trees. Those "mature" canopy trees showing evidence of decay or instability are to be felled and removed from site. Stumps are to be left *in situ*, with regrowth chemically controlled by spot application of glyphosate.

The condition of retained trees is to be closely monitored for evidence of decay or instability with the long-term objective of a phased removal of all canopy trees. Long-term, it is proposed that the key archaeological areas be managed as glades within the woodland, thereby eliminating root disturbance to stratified archaeological deposits whilst providing areas of managed limestone grassland and transitional zones into woodland cover suitable for ecotone species such as migrant warblers and butterflies. "Long-term" in this context is defined as in excess of ten years and within the natural, stable lifespan of the retained trees.

Glades are to be strimmed/brushcut once per year in late autumn (October) to control recolonisation by trees, shrubs and brambles whilst permitting flowering and seeding of the native herbaceous species. Where such regrowth is vigorous, it may prove necessary to increase cuts to twice per year (October and early March). In such cases, all cut regrowth is to be removed from the extent of the compartment so as to avoid nutrient enrichment of the substrate and a concomitant decrease in species diversity of the sward and increase in dominance of a coarse, more competitive flora.

● Conservation and enhancement of the woodland as a habitat for wildlife

Works in the remainder of the woodland are designed to enhance the value of the

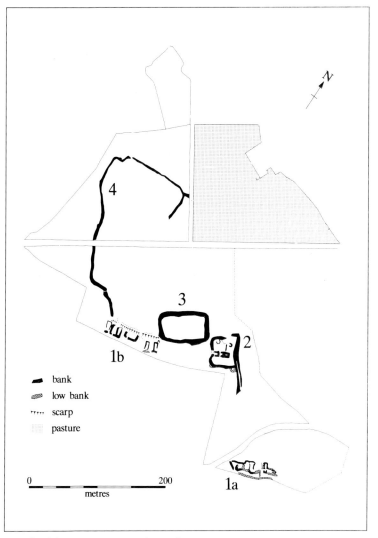

woodland for nature conservation and timber production.

As noted above, whilst the works within the five areas identified as being of archaeological sensitivity are primarily designed to achieve enhanced conservation of the monument they are seen as being an integral component of works intended to diversify the habitat of "Hen Caerwys" by providing areas of open grassland habitat.

Elsewhere, the woodland is to be subject to selective group felling of canopy trees to provide coupes for restocking by natural regeneration. In general terms, it is

Figure 2. The five identified key areas of archaeological sensitivity. 1a and b - house sites; 2 - enclosure with remains of possible internal buildings; 3 - principal enclosure; 4 - primary fieldbank. Plan prepared by Pete Muckle, Gwynedd Archaeological Trust.

proposed that selective felling be focused on sycamore; a non-native species of invasive habit the presence of which can lead to a reduction in diversity of the ground flora and which, as a timber resource, is prone to severe damage by grey squirrels. However, the value of sycamore as a summer source of insects for young birds is recognised and the species will be retained as an element of the canopy, felling being undertaken so as to result in an overall reduction in the proportion of sycamore as a component of the stand in the long-term.

It is anticipated that natural regeneration will be principally of ash, with oak and wild cherry.

Where sycamore regeneration occurs it will be controlled. Once regeneration has been achieved, the opportunity will be taken to augment species composition through the selective planting of 60-90cm fieldgrown transplants of oak and wild cherry, where the proportion of these species is not adequately represented through natural regeneration. As a guide, it is intended that oak should comprise 20% of species composition with wild cherry not exceeding 10%.

All understorey species will be coppiced, with selected stumps of hawthorn to be chemically controlled by spot treatment with glyphosate, the overall objective being to increase the proportion of hazel in the long-term. This proposal is intended to meet the landowner's request for an increase in productive hazel stools so as to enable sustainable harvesting for craft use.

The overall aim is to further diversify the structure of the woodland and to increase the age range of timber trees to enable the development of sustained low intensity harvesting of timber. It is proposed that the proportion of hazel be increased to enable the adoption of regular coppicing of the understorey and, in part, to develop a coppice with standards system. Such diversification of structure will result in increased feeding, roosting and nesting opportunities for woodland wildlife, whilst the development of a low intensity harvesting system will reduce the impact of forest operations on wildlife by ensuring continuity of woodland cover.

A proportion of larch is to be retained in the short/mid-term to further diversify opportunities for wildlife. It is recognised, for example, that the expanding distribution of siskin (*Carduelis spinus*) noted in recent years has been assisted by the planting of commercial conifer trees (Holden and Sharrock, 1988). Short/mid-term is defined in this context as at least for the duration of the initial five year plan and not exceeding such time as trees become unstable, show evidence of degradation or are required for farm use thereafter.

● Enhancement of the quality of the woodland as a timber resource

Works to achieve the enhancement of the quality of the woodland as a timber resource are integral with proposals set out above for the enhancement of nature conservation interests.

Such works are intended to increase the age range of timber trees and, through active long-term management, to secure an increase in the proportion of broadleaved trees of good form. It is intended that ash will comprise the dominant species, with oak, wild cherry and sycamore.

● Conservation of the woodland as a landscape feature

Coupes are to be restricted in size to ensure continuity of woodland cover.

Natural regeneration is intended to ensure a semi-natural woodland canopy in keeping with the landscape character of the Caerwys area.

● Conclusion

The mechanics of funding the initial programme of management have been relatively straightforward, thanks to the progressive attitude of officers in Cadw: Welsh Historic Monuments and the Forestry Authority. The entire wooded extent was submitted to the Forestry Authority under the Woodland Grant Scheme, those areas of archaeological sensitivity being defined under the category of "Other Land". This effectively has meant that the need to meet obligations regarding the licensing of felling under the *Forestry Act 1968* have been addressed. However, grant-aid from the Forestry Authority is only payable on those areas not defined as "Other Land". This has enabled the more intensive and costly works associated with the areas of archaeological sensitivity to be funded by Cadw without creating the problem of double-funding. To enable works to be implemented sooner rather than later, Cadw is providing a 100% grant to cover the costs of the initial programme of management through Section 24 of the *Ancient Monuments and Archaeological Areas Act 1979* ("Grants to Owners"). The on-going programme of maintenance designed to prevent recolonisation by scrub and to meet wider nature conservation objectives is being addressed through a Section 17 management agreement.

The initial five year programme of management described in this paper commenced in late autumn 1994 and a number of issues of more long-term significance remain to be addressed. Fundamental amongst these is the provision of defined lines of vehicular access to enable the implementation of the proposed programme of low-intensity sustainable harvesting of timber (including an evaluation of the need for the creation of a sacrificial surface to protect the underlying archaeological deposits?). Extraction of timber to be harvested as part of the initial programme of felling, particularly in respect of the identified areas of archaeological sensitivity, is to be converted "at stump" for manual extraction to road or fieldside. Such an approach is proving possible at this early stage because of the overall low quality of timber suitable mostly only for firewood.

However, as active management increases the proportion of good quality timber so the need to extract in butt lengths rather than as cut rings or logs will render manual extraction impossible.

"Hen Caerwys" also raises important questions and possibilities concerning the techniques for the identification of "ancient" woodland at a regional level. Technically, convention (Walker and Richardson, 1989) would define the three component woodlands of "Hen Caerwys" (Coed y Marian, Coed Gerddi-gleision and Coed y Carreg) as "ancient semi-natural woodland" (ASNW) - such woodland being defined as having a continuous history since at least 1600. Given the mid-fifteenth century date derived from the only excavation undertaken at "Hen Caerwys" and the apparent abandonment of the site shortly thereafter, on this basis it is entirely reasonable to define the woodland as ASNW. It clearly is not "ancient" in the true sense however, as the earthworks of the fieldsystem attest. The site does, nevertheless, support a number of wildflower species that would be generally taken as indicative of long-established or "ancient" woodland at a regional level, as described earlier. The presence of herb paris is of particular interest given its obvious, apparently exclusive, association with "ancient" woodland in Clwyd. "Hen Caerwys" therefore offers opportunities to test and refine our suite of indicator species to provide a tool for the identification of "ancient" woodlands elsewhere, where other means (earthworks or documentary sources) are unavailable.

The development of management proposals for "Hen Caerwys" has, from the outset, been one of the integration of the many varied interests of the site - the desire to achieve enhanced conservation of a nationally important monument, of a scarce habitat for wildlife, and the landowners' interest in creating an economic resource in the long-term. The latter may be seen as fundamental in securing the long-term, sustainable management of the site. A resource that has "value" is "valued". Whilst the present landowners are more than usually sympathetic and active in the conservation of our archaeological and natural heritage, who is to say that those who come afterwards will be equally supportive? In developing the value of the woodland as a timber resource it is intended that the site will, in time, become an integral component of the farm economy and therefore, of day-to-day farm management. Only at the stage when the conservation of the monument becomes an inherent part of agricultural operations will the integrated management of the site truly have been achieved.

● Acknowledgements

The programme of survey and management at "Hen Caerwys" would not have proved possible without the keen interest and support of the landowners Clwyd and Mags Owens and their son Michael. The author's development of the management plan was enormously assisted by Dr. Sian Rees (Cadw: Welsh Historic Monuments) and Les Starling and Arthur Miller (Forestry Authority). EDM survey of the site was undertaken by Gwynedd Archaeological Trust, more especially Pete Muckle, Andy Shallcross and Roland Flook, the expertise of the former contributing significantly to the detail and success of the survey. Figures 1 and 2 were prepared for publication by Pete Muckle with the support of Dave Longley. Access to part of the monument was with the kind permission of Mr. and Mrs. Brooke. Initial survey was funded jointly by Clwyd County Council and Cadw, whilst implementation of the plan is being supported by Cadw and the Forestry Authority. Many thanks to all involved.

● References

Archaeology in Wales 1962, 1963, 1964, 1965, 1966.

Berry, A.Q. (1992) Integrating Archaeology and the Countryside: Clwyd County Council's Approach to Archaeological Sites Management in, Macinnes, L. and Wickham-Jones, C.R. (eds) All Natural Things: Archaeology and the Green Debate. Oxbow Monograph 21. Oxford: Oxbow. 155-160.

Berry, A.Q. (1993a) From Burrowing Bunnies to Wayward Wildwood in, Swain, H. (ed) Rescuing the Historic Environment. Hertford: RESCUE, The British Archaeological Trust. 71-5.

Berry, A.Q. (1994a) Counting the Cost of Erosion on Archaeological Earthworks in, Berry, A.Q. and Brown, I.W. (eds) Erosion on Archaeological Earthworks: Its Prevention, Control and Repair. Mold: Clwyd County Council. 1-4.

Berry, A.Q. (1994b) Counting the Cost - the Sequel in, Berry, A.Q. and Brown, I.W. (eds) Erosion on Archaeological Earthworks: Its Prevention, Control and Repair. Mold: Clwyd County Council. 45-56.

Forestry Commission (1985) Clwyd Census of Woodlands and Trees 1979-82. Edinburgh: Forestry Commission.

Hill, M. (1993) Personal Communication. Caerwys.

Holden, P. and Sharrock, J.T.R. (1988) The RSPB Book of British Birds. London: Macmillan. 174.

Hughes, T. (1994) Oral history evidence provided by Tudor Hughes, Gors, Babell.

Walker, G. and Richardson, C. (1989) Clwyd Inventory of Ancient Woodlands (Provisional). Peterborough: Nature Conservancy Council. 4.

Rogers, T. (1979) Excavations at Hen Caerwys, Clwyd, 1962. Bulletin of the Board of Celtic Studies, 28. 528-533.

Heathland and Grassland Management for Conservation

Robin J. Pakeman

Plant Ecologist, Institute of Terrestrial Ecology

● Introduction

Many archaeological sites have considerable ecological interest. This is less a product of any particular feature of the archaeological site, but rather the result of the preservation of semi-natural communities as a consequence of the presence of such structures in the landscape. These communities can be remnants of vegetation types that were at one time more widespread before the modernisation of agricultural practices, and are hence valuable as a result of their rarity. For example, chalk grassland that was once common throughout south east Britain is preserved in areas of arable farming by the presence of such earthworks as the Black Ditches, Suffolk (N.G.R. TL 773 685); Devil's Dyke (N.G.R. TL 623 612) and Fleam Dyke (N.G.R. TL 543 548), Cambridgeshire; and Honnington Camp, Lincolnshire (N.G.R. SK 954 424).

In particular, of the 27 sites where Pasque flower (*Pulsatilla vulgaris*) was recorded (Wells, 1968), 8 were on earthworks (Table 1), with many other sites being on old quarry workings.

Sites for rare species or localised communities are protected as nature reserves or through scheduling as Sites of Special Scientific Interest (SSSIs). However, no mechanism is in place to recognise the other aspects of the site, such as soils or field systems, although geology is included. Similarly, the mechanisms which protect the archaeological interest of a site do not

specify the protection of the ecological features. Calls for the combination of these approaches have been made in the past (Sheail and Wells, 1969; Wells, 1985). Hopefully, there should be the machinery put in place to formally safeguard both sets of interest in the future.

This review briefly covers the ecological importance of semi-natural grassland, heathland and moorland, and discusses the types of management needed to maintain the conservation interest of these communities. The mechanisms of reversing successional change are outlined and the information sources for habitat restoration given. The need for integrating conservation, archaeology and public pressure is discussed and contacts for advice on management detailed.

● The Conservation Value of Heathland and Moorland

Heathlands are a distinctive feature of the Atlantic and sub-Atlantic areas of western Europe, and although floristically rather poor, they have an extremely rich and characteristic invertebrate fauna. The word "heathland" is generally taken to mean an area of land dominated by dwarf shrubs, particularly heather (*Calluna vulgaris*), at low altitude (< 250m) on poor, acidic, mineral soils (Plate 1). "Moorland" usually refers to areas of similar vegetation at higher altitudes (> 250m). The vegetation is similar, although lowland heathland often has a large cover of gorse (*Ulex* spp.) and moorland has a higher incidence of berry-

Table 1. Earthwork sites of Pasque flower in Great Britain (Wells, 1968).

Iron Age Forts	Aldbury Nowers, Herts. (N.G.R. SP 953 128)
	Deacon Hill, Beds. (N.G.R. TL 124 298)
	Honnington Camp, Lincs.
	Ravensburgh Castle, Beds. (N.G.R. TL 097 297)
Defensive Ditches	Devil's Dyke, Cambs.
	Fleam Dyke, Cambs.
Field Systems	Knocking Hoe, Beds. (N.G.R. TL 134 308)
	Royston Heath, Herts. (N.G.R. TL 333 397)

Plate 1. Mature heathland at Cavenham Heath, Suffolk (N.G.R. TL 757 727), dominated by heather. Birch invasion is taking place over a large frontage and is being controlled by hand pulling.

warbler (*Sylvia undata*), nightjar (*Caprimulgus europaeus*), woodlark (*Lullula arborea*), smooth snake (*Coronella austriaca*), sand lizard (*Lacerta agilis*), natterjack toad (*Bufo calamita*), the silver studded blue butterfly (*Plebejus argus*) and marsh gentian (*Gentiana pneumonanthe*), to name but a few. The main conservation importance of moorland derives from the large number of birds that nest on them including curlew (*Numenius arquata*), golden plover (*Pluvialis apricaria*), greenshank (*Tringa nebularia*), hen harrier (*Circus cyaneus*), merlin (*Falco columbarius*), red grouse (*Lagopus lagopus*) and twite (*Acanthis flavirostris*), all of which are included in the EC Council Directive on Conservation of Wild Birds or are British Red Data Book species.

bearing shrubs such as crowberry (*Empetrum nigrum*) and bilberry (*Vaccinium myrtillus*), but the associated fauna are very different.

Over the past century and for a variety of reasons, there has been a massive decrease in the area of heathlands throughout Europe. Sweden has lost 93% of its heathlands, Jutland in Denmark 98% and the Netherlands 95% (Webb, 1986). Similar decreases have been seen in the area of heathland in Great Britain (Table 2), although not to such a large extent. This, however, means that Britain possesses much of the European resource of this habitat type and hence its conservation is important in a European, as well as a national context. Much of this decline has been a result of agricultural expansion, forestry and losses to urban areas. These threats are now less of a problem, with the greatest threats from invasion of bracken, scrub and woodland as a result of poor management. The decline in moorland areas has been much smaller, e.g. 20% lost from 1947 to 1980 in England (Armstrong, 1991), most to forestry and agriculture.

Heathlands are important for conservation for many reasons. As an illustration of their importance, they provide the main habitat for a number of rare species: Dartford

● The Conservation Value of Lowland Grassland

There are many types of grassland recognised by ecologists, such as chalk and limestone grassland; flood, water and hay meadows, and heath grassland. The National Vegetation Classification recognises 36 grass dominated communities, each with various sub-communities, but this review is too short to detail the differences and this has been done elsewhere (Duffey *et al.*, 1974; Rackham, 1986; Rodwell, 1992). Similarly, the conservation value of these grasslands needs many more pages for a full discussion. The Pasque flower has already been mentioned. Another plant that is only associated with ancient grasslands is the fritillary (*Fritillaria meleagris*) which has diminished greatly in the last half century as a result of the drainage and conversion of flood meadows. In particular chalk, limestone and heath grasslands have survived in association with ancient agricultural patterns and remains, for example the preservation of Celtic fieldbanks at Parsonage Down (N.G.R. SU 040 413) (Wells, 1985).

However, what most semi-natural grassland types have in common is their massive decline in area in the last half century (Table 3). In particular, much chalk grassland has disappeared under the plough, with Dorset losing more proportionately of this grassland type (92%) than even heathland (Rackham, 1986). What remains is still at risk from agricultural improvement, the drift of fertiliser or pesticide, and the encroachment of scrub.

• The Need for Management

The current vegetation of Britain is largely a result of the influence of human activity. Only in areas such as high mountains, cliffs or on the coast can the vegetation be said to be natural. Both lowland grassland and heathland are the result of the progressive forest clearance for grazing land - grasslands developing on the better soils, heathland or grass heath on poorer, acidic soils (Gimingham, 1992). Their persistence in the landscape depends on their continual management to prevent the recolonisation of trees - i.e. succession to woodland. This is occurring on many lowland heaths; the area of heath on Lakenheath Warren in Norfolk (N.G.R. TL 749 808) has been reduced by half in the last sixty years (Marrs, Hicks and Fuller, 1986). However, the changes in vegetation as a result of succession must be distinguished from those that result solely due to the normal fluctuations in vegetation composition as a result of weather and other chance events.

It is important that when a site is being managed, whether to conserve the archaeological or floral and faunal interest, that a detailed management plan is drawn up with specific objectives, such as maintaining heathland or grassland diversity, or controlling undesirable species. However, the plan must be adaptable in the light of changing circumstance and must not be seen as something concrete to be followed at all cost. Bound up with this is the need for continual monitoring of the effects of management. These should be in the form of written records of vegetation or faunal

Region	Survey Date	Heathland Area (ha)	Percentage Change in Area Between Surveys
Breckland	1824 1980	16469 4529	- 73
Suffolk Sandlings	1783 1983	16403 1580	- 90
Surrey	1804 1983	55400 5901	- 89
Hampshire	1819 1982	37000 18000	- 51
Dorset	1750 1983	39960 5670	- 86
TOTAL	1830 1980	143250 39450	- 72

Table 2. Changes in the extent of the main areas of lowland heath in Great Britain (Webb, 1986).

Grassland Type	Survey Date	Area ('000 ha)	Percentage Change Between Surveys
Total Grassland	1932 1984	7800 * 4800	- 39
Lowland Rough Grazing	1932 1984	1400 400	- 71
Unimproved Permanent Pasture	1932 1984	5800 200	- 97

Table 3. Changes in the extent of lowland grassland in England and Wales 1932 to 1984 (Fuller, 1987) * Contains land previously arable, but left to revert to pasture during agricultural depression of 1870s.

changes. Only by monitoring the effects of management can its success or failure be determined, and the management plan updated.

● Heathland and Moorland Management

Except in a few areas, particularly on wet ground where layering can take place, heather plants have a finite lifespan. Each plant passes through a number of life-cycle stages (Watt, 1947):

● Pioneer - Establishment phase, growth either from seed or from stem bases surviving after burning;

● Building - Vigorous growth of bushes, producing dense stands;

● Mature - Canopy is more open and taller;

● Degenerate - Branches start dying, gaps open in canopy, eventually the whole plant dies.

Management is needed as the pioneer and, particularly, the degenerate phase are susceptible to invasion by other species (Plate 2), either heathland or moorland

species such as bilberry or wavy-hair grass (*Deschampsia flexuosa*), itself a problem on the Breckland heaths, or by shrubs such as gorse or trees like birch (*Betula* spp.). Management is directed to either maintain the stand in the building or mature phases or to ensure that the heather passes from the mature, through the pioneer, to the building phase as quickly as possible.

All the methods of heathland management detailed below have a similar objective; the maintenance of vegetation dominated by vigorous heather plants and the maintenance of low soil fertility by the continual removal of nutrients. However, it must be stressed that if applied wrongly then they will result in either wide expanses of uniform vegetation with little associated animal or plant diversity or in the wholesale succession of large areas to other vegetation types. Further information will be found in Gimingham (1992) and Michael (1993).

● Grazing

This type of management represents the main traditional management of most heathland and moorland in Britain, although its practice is less common now on lowland heaths than in former times. However, it must be stressed that there must be a correct management of grazing intensity (Gimingham, 1992). If the correct grazing intensity is maintained, then the heather is held in the building phase. If the area is undergrazed, then the heather plants pass through the life-cycle and gaps will appear favouring the appearance of other species. Supplementary management, such as burning or cutting, must then be carried out. Overgrazing damages the heather plants and reduces their competitive ability, eventually leading to the increasing dominance of grass species. Sheep are generally preferred as the agents of grazing, as the heavier cattle or horses can damage old heather plants by trampling. The stocking rate depends very much on the age and vigour of the heathland vegetation and whether the stock are to be grazed

Plate 2. Degenerating heathland with significant invasion of grasses, sheep's fescue (*Festuca ovina*) in the foreground and wavy hair grass (*Deschampsia flexuosa*) in the background.

throughout the year or just during certain seasons.

Two strategies are available; the licensing of the grazing to a nearby farmer, or the ownership of stock by the conservation body. The latter is more controllable as regards to stocking density, but means that alternative sources of grazing must be available and all the associated costs and problems of owning stock must be borne. Although simpler to operate, licensing the grazing must be subject to a clear written agreement, so that the grazing levels can be maintained so as to satisfy both parties to the agreement. For example, higher stocking rates may be needed for management than those which would maximise livestock productivity. Further details are given in Gimingham (1992).

● Cutting

Provided the heather to be cut is not too old, cutting can be used to maintain heather in a vigorous form, as dormant buds below the level of the cut will sprout. It has advantages over burning - it is not restricted to a particular time of the year, it is less detrimental to many forms of wildlife and it can be used where burning could be risky. Like burning, it should be used to produce and maintain small areas of heather in a mosaic of different ages. Cutting produces large amounts of litter and this must be removed to prevent the build up of soil nutrients and to prevent the smothering of any plants regenerating from seed. The cut material must be disposed of, but if cut during October to December can be used as a seed source for heathland regeneration.

The disadvantages of this technique are that it is only possible on sites where vehicular access is possible and not detrimental to the archaeological interest of the site. Also the machinery is expensive and disposal of the cut material may be problematical.

● Burning

Like cutting, controlled burning of building and mature heather results in good

vegetative regeneration from the stem bases (Plate 3). However, if the heather to be burnt is in the degenerate phase then regeneration must come from seed and, as a consequence, will be slower, particularly in the drier areas of southern Britain.

Plate 3. Heather regeneration from stem bases after burning.

This technique has the advantages that it is relatively cheap, although necessitating a large amount of manpower for a short period. It is also easier to carry out whatever the nature of the terrain, prevents invasion by unwanted species and reduces the accumulation of nutrients.

Good burning practice means that only a small proportion of the area is burnt at any one time to produce a mosaic of small patches. Areas should be burnt no more often than once in every twelve to fifteen years and burning should take place only during the legal period (1 November to 31 March in England, with slightly longer periods in the uplands and Scotland). Certain areas of old heather should be left to maintain a diverse ecosystem. The burn should be rapid and, as a consequence, of low temperature so that regeneration comes from the stem bases and so that minimal heating of the soil occurs. Slow, hot burns frequently penetrate the organic surface horizons of the substrate with resultant damage to, or destruction of, both the ecological value and stratified archaeological deposits.

Burning should not be carried out on patches adjacent to stands of bracken, as the lack of competition allows rapid invasion by the bracken; on areas of wet heathland as it will damage the bryophyte flora and on lichen dominated heaths. Burning of heather and grassland is subject to regulation by MAFF or their equivalents, and licences must be obtained from their local office. Further details of management by burning can be found in Gimingham (1992).

● Recommendations for Heathland and Moorland Management

The management of moorland and heathland should be aimed at maintaining the diversity of habitats and species. As the present species compliment is the product of past management then usually continuance with that type of management will be the best choice. However, other methods may have to be used as a result of public pressure or the needs of particular conservation aims. Also local variations in management should be taken into account; cutting and grazing, for example, are the main options used in the drier south of England, burning being used less frequently than in the rest of the country.

Using cutting or burning as the main management tools has the advantage that a wide age range of heather stands can be produced to increase the structural diversity of the site. However, management must be regular enough to prevent the invasion of other species or a decline in heather vigour. Cutting can only be used where ground conditions are appropriate and burning demands high inputs of manpower (although over a short period of time).

Grazing, supplemented by burning, maintains a varied community structure in moorland areas, although its use in the lowlands has fallen into decline as few farmers now graze heathland areas. However, if carefully managed then grazing offers a feasible and sustainable means of heathland management, although the diversity of heathland structure may not be as great as with more direct methods of management. However attractive grazing animals might be as a source of income, it should be borne in mind that they will need alternative grazing, water, fencing, insurance and staff to look after them (Gimingham, 1992).

● Grassland Management

Traditional grassland management takes two main forms, the grazing of pasture and the mowing of meadows, and to maintain conservation interest these two practices should normally be carried out where they have been traditionally used. However, the use of mowing on small sites traditionally used for pasture is an attractive alternative to save money. A study on the effects of cutting and sheep grazing on chalk grassland showed that cutting is an effective substitute for sheep grazing, although some change in species composition resulted (Wells, 1971).

Burning is used in a few situations for grassland management. In the Cotswolds and the Peak District, rough grassland is regularly burned to produce succulent herbage. Burning takes place during the late winter to remove the build up of litter. On undergrazed rough grassland, burning can be used to remove litter build up which tends to suppress low growing species and leads to a poor community of coarse grasses.

Further details of grassland management can be found in Duffey et al. (1974) and in Hillier et al. (1990).

● Grazing

The effects of grazing depends very much on two things, the type of livestock used and the timing of grazing. Sheep tend to be selective, eating the most palatable and nutrient-rich plants first, although grazing the whole area evenly. High stocking densities are necessary to affect coarse dominant grasses such as upright brome (*Bromus erectus*) in chalk grassland. Cattle are less selective and produce a mosaic of short vegetation and taller tufts, as a result of their use of the tongue to grip vegetation. Horses are highly selective and their use will result in some areas becoming rank.

Most archaeological and conservation sites in lowland Britain are too small to allow free range grazing and so must be periodically grazed. Hence they have the same problems as those of grazing management on heathlands sites. Winter grazing will lower the competitive ability of most grasses, reduces the litter present and opens up bare ground for the germination of annuals. However, the poor herbage means that supplementary feeding may also be needed. The potential for surface poaching on sensitive archaeological sites must also be considered. Spring or summer grazing similarly affects the growth and dominance of grasses. The flowering and seeding of most species is reduced, but as most grassland plants are perennial then the reduction in competition from the grasses is more beneficial.

● Mowing

Mowing differs from grazing in two main ways; it is non-selective, and it is possible to remove nutrients in the form of hay. Traditionally, meadows are cut in mid-summer when many of the diverse range of plants present have completed their growth. If traditional cutting is still in use it must be maintained in order to preserve the composition of the plant community and the animals associated with it.

In productive grasslands the cut material must be removed, for if left it smothers the underlying vegetation and reduces the species diversity. On nutrient-poor sites, removal is less important, as long as the material returned is broken up: it is the

defoliation of the dominant grasses that is important.

● Management Problems as a Result of Successional Changes

● Trees, scrub and gorse

The encroachment of scrub and trees has been particularly evident since the introduction of myxomatosis in the 1950s (refer Plate 1). Three problems arise from this conversion of open land to woodland; root damage to archaeological remains, shading out of the previous natural vegetation, and the increase in soil fertility associated with a cover of trees and shrubs (particularly gorse), which can result in the invasion of a "weedy" flora after control. The conversion of open communities to scrub and woodland is prevented by normal management methods, i.e. burning, cutting or grazing. If scrub invasion is a problem, then to minimise soil disturbance the scrub should be cut down and regeneration from the stump prevented by applying herbicides such as ammonium sulphamate, fosamine ammonium or glyphosate (Marrs, 1985). Coniferous plants can be controlled simply by cutting.

The reinstatement of vegetation from a closed canopy of scrub or woodland is more problematical and would require:

● the control of woody species;

● the depletion of nutrients by soil-stripping (on non-archaeological sites), grazing, cropping or burning;

● the addition of suitable seed;

● the implementation of suitable after-management.

● Bracken

Bracken is a major problem in many heathland and moorland areas. It also has the potential to disturb stratified archaeological deposits preserved in the soil. It is almost impossible to eradicate and control is difficult and long-term. The problems caused by bracken and the advantages and disadvantages of the different methods of control have been discussed elsewhere (Pakeman and Marrs, 1992). However, if the bracken stand has developed a deep litter layer and there is little associated vegetation cover then bracken control will not be sufficient to restore heathland or grassland communities. As part of the control process, the litter layer must be disturbed or removed, suitable seed added, possibly with a nurse crop or fertiliser to aid establishment (Pakeman and Marrs, 1992).

● Grass

If the replacement of heather by grassland has been identified before the process has gone too far, then any action to reduce the vigour of the grass (grazing or mowing) should give the natural heathland vegetation time to expand. If the grass, usually wavy hair grass on drier areas and purple moor grass (*Molinia caerulea*) on wet ones, has completely eliminated the heather, then disrupting the grass turf and creating bare areas should allow regeneration from the seed bank, although this must be undertaken with great care on archaeological sites.

● The Restoration of Vegetation

● Reinstatement of vegetation after excavation

Although excavation of archaeological sites is now often in the form of rescuing remains from the bulldozer, many sites are excavated without such pressure. After excavation these sites should, if possible, be restored. The basic techniques for this have been developed for reinstatement of heathland after pipeline laying (Putwain and Rae, 1988) but are applicable in this context and should be applicable for grasslands. The basic message is that topsoil must be preserved so maintaining its seedbank intact. However, some plants and most animals will not survive this storage and must be reintroduced afterwards.

● Re-creation of grassland and heathland

Grassland and heathland vegetation can be created *de novo* in order to enhance the conservation and amenity value of land. Techniques for heathland are detailed in Gimingham (1992) and Putwain and Rae (1988), and grassland in Wells (1989). Both types of communities require the choice of suitable seed mixes or seed sources, the use of nurse crops, careful site and seed bed preparation, and the imposition of a suitable management regime. Grassland diversity can be improved by slot-seeding or inserting pot-grown plants.

● Conclusion

Many sites that are valuable for their archaeological interest are important, either locally or nationally, in terms of their ecological interest. At present no mechanism ensures that the two differing needs are integrated. Until this happens it is the responsibility of those in charge of a site's maintenance to ensure that management is appropriate for its continuing archaeological and conservation value. At the very least, it is aesthetically pleasing for a monument to be preserved with the animal and plant communities it has been associated with over the centuries.

This approach falls down where public access pressure is considerable. Heathland communities are easily damaged by trampling, and although grassland is more resistant, many individual species are not resistant and communities will become dominated by trampling resistant plants. This means that management must be aimed at maximising public access whilst minimising the effects of access on both the monument and its surrounding vegetation.

Advice on the development of management plans for the conservation of heathland and grassland communities should in the first instance be sought from the local office of the relevant statutory body - English Nature, Scottish Natural Heritage, Countryside Council for Wales, or in Northern Ireland the Department of the Environment. Where the site is located in a National Park, the appropriate National Park Authority may also be consulted. More specialist advice should be available from organisations such as the Royal Society for the Protection of Birds, Institute of Terrestrial Ecology or from university researchers. Local wildlife trusts and the British Trust for Conservation Volunteers may be able to help in carrying out the actual management. Contact numbers and addresses are given as an appendix to this volume.

● References

Armstrong, H. (1991) Britain's declining heather moorlands. *Outlook on Agriculture*, 20. 103-107.

Duffey, E., Morris, M.G., Sheail, J., Ward, L.K., Wells, D.A. and Wells, T.C.E. (1974) *Grassland Ecology and Wildlife Management*. London: Chapman and Hall.

Fuller, R.M. (1987) The Changing Extent and Conservation Interest of Lowland Grasslands in England and Wales: A Review of Grassland Surveys 1930-84. *Biological Conservation*, 40. 281-300.

Gimingham, C.H. (1992) *The Lowland Heathland Management Handbook*. Peterborough: English Nature.

Hillier, S.H., Walton, D.W.H. and Wells, D.A. (eds) (1990) *Calcareous Grassland - Ecology and Management*. Huntingdon: Bluntisham Books.

Marrs, R.H. (1985) The Effects of Potential Bracken and Scrub Control Herbicides on Lowland *Calluna* and Grass Heath Communities in East Anglia, UK. *Biological Conservation*, 32. 13-32.

Marrs, R.H., Hicks, M.J. and Fuller, R.M. (1986) Losses of Lowland Heath Through Succession at Four Sites in Breckland, East Anglia, England. *Biological Conservation*, 36. 19-38.

Michael, N. (1993) *The Lowland Heathland Management Booklet*. Version 1.0. Peterborough: English Nature.

Pakeman, R.J. and Marrs, R.H. (1992) The Conservation Value of Bracken (*Pteridium aquilinum* [L.] Kuhn) Dominated Communities in the UK, and an Assessment of the Ecological Impact of Bracken Expansion or its Removal. *Biological Conservation*, 62. 101-114.

Putwain, P.D. and Rae, P.A.S. (1988) *Heathland Restoration: A Handbook of Techniques*. Southampton: British Gas.

Rackham, O. (1986) *The History of the Countryside*. London: Dent.

Rodwell, J.S. (ed) (1992) *British Plant Communities*. Vol.3. *Grassland and Montane Communities*. Cambridge: Cambridge University Press.

Sheail, J. and Wells, T.C.E. (eds) (1969) *Old Grassland - Its Archaeological and Ecological Importance*. Monks Wood Symposium No.5, Huntingdon.

Watt, A.S. (1947) Pattern and Process in the Plant Community. *Journal of Ecology*, 35. 1-22.

Webb, N.R. (1986) *Heathlands*. London: Collins.

Wells, T.C.E. (1968) Land Use Changes Affecting *Pulsatilla vulgaris* in England. *Biological Conservation*, 1. 37-43.

Wells, T.C.E. (1971) A Comparison of the Effects of Sheep Grazing and Mechanical Cutting on the Structure and Botanical Composition of Chalk Grassland in, Duffey, E. and Watt, A.S. (eds) *The Scientific*

Management of Animal and Plant Communities for Conservation. Oxford: Blackwell Scientific Publications. 497-515.

Wells, T.C.E. (1985) The Botanical and Ecological Interest of Ancient Monuments in, Lambrick, G. (ed) *Archaeology and Nature Conservation.* Oxford: Oxford University Department for External Studies. 1-9.

Wells, T.C.E. (1989) The Re-creation of Grassland Habitats. *The Entomologist,* 108. 97-108.

Lordenshaws: A Management Agreement for an Historic Landscape

Paul Frodsham, Andrew Miller and Albert Weir

Northumberland National Park

● Introduction

Lordenshaws Farm is a 409ha hill farm situated on the eastern side of the Simonside Hills near Rothbury (centred on N.G.R. NZ 055 990) (Plate 1). The farm is of national importance, containing part of the Simonside Site of Special Scientific Interest and supporting an outstanding prehistoric landscape, individual elements of which are Scheduled Ancient Monuments. A management agreement has recently been negotiated by the Northumberland National Park Authority with the owner (Northumberland Estates) and the farm tenant. The principal aims of this agreement are the conservation of the archaeological remains, regeneration of heather moorland, improved public access and better interpretation of the area's ecological and archaeological resources.

The Simonside Hills consist of an extensive escarpment of carboniferous fell sandstone rising to a height of 400m OD. Steep northerly facing slopes are covered with shallow, loamy, acid soils colonised by *Calluna-Vaccinium* heath. Blanket peat covers the less freely draining dip slopes and a number of raised bogs, containing locally important mire communities including *Erica tetralix-Sphagnum papillosum* (M18) mire, have developed. The complex mosaic of dwarf shrub-heath and mire vegetation provides an important breeding area for many ground nesting birds such as red grouse (*Lagopus lagopus*), golden plover (*Pluvialis apricaria*) and merlin (*Falco*

Plate 1. Aerial photograph of the Lordenshaws area. Several of the sites referred to in the text are visible here. © Airfotos Ltd, Newcastle upon Tyne.

columbarius). Small areas of ancient semi-natural woodland along the sides of streams encourage upland passerines like redstart (*Phoenicurus phoenicurus*) and provide a link with the wildwood that once covered much of the area. Extensive grazing by sheep has prevented any substantial natural regeneration of the woodland and has contributed to a change in the vegetation of the lower slopes from dwarf shrub heath to acid grassland communities.

The Royal Commission on the Historical Monuments of England (RCHME) has produced a detailed ground survey (Topping, 1993) covering most of the visible archaeological remains (Figure 1) and this has been essential to the production of detailed management and interpretative plans. Whilst several of the "sites" at Lordenshaws are protected as Scheduled Ancient Monuments, it will be clear from the plan that the area represents an extensive archaeological landscape. It is important to protect the entire area to ensure the survival of the unscheduled remains, thus protecting the context of those sites which are legally protected.

Plate 2. Aerial photograph of the Lordenshaws hillfort. Note the Romano-British settlement overlying the south east ramparts of the fort (refer also Figure 1). Photograph: Stan Beckensall.

Plate 3. The apparently worked *Pinus sylvestris* stake from Caudhole Moss.

The earliest visible archaeological remains on the moor are the Neolithic rock carvings or "cup and ring marks" (Beckensall, 1993) of which several examples can be seen. Most of the more complex carvings are sited at significant points in the landscape which command extensive views and which may have been located along early trackways. Although they must have been of great significance to the people who carved them, probably about 5,000 years ago, the meaning of these motifs remains a mystery to us today.

The recent discovery of a buried layer of Scots pine (*Pinus sylvestris*) at a depth of 4 metres in the side of a gully on Caudhole Moss is of great interest. Some of this wood appeared at first to have been artificially worked (Plate 3), although it is now known that pine can erode naturally to such shapes. The deposit, which has been carbon dated to 6110 ± 60 bp (or about 5,000 calendar years BC), is of considerable palaeoenvironmental interest in view of the fact that the existence of pine within the uplands of the northern Pennines had hitherto not been established (Tipping, pers. comm.). Proposals are currently being drawn up for the investigation and long-term management of the site.

A number of stone cairns are visible on the moor, including one which has been excavated exposing a stone cist which would originally have contained a Bronze Age burial. Although some of the cairns are probably the result of field clearance, many others must also contain burials and these should remain undisturbed so that they can be scientifically examined in due course. Some of the larger cairns, most if not all of which are presumably sepulchral, are located in association with panels of rock carvings (Bradley, 1993) thus suggesting some kind of significant relationship even though the carvings may pre-date the cairns by several centuries. Three particularly large cairns are prominently located on the Simonside ridge to the south west of the RCHME survey area (one of these is just visible towards the top right hand corner of

Plate 1) and these may prove to be of very early date.

About 2,500 years ago, perhaps a thousand years after the last of the cairn burials, a large hillfort was constructed at Lordenshaws (Plate 2). The visible remains of this fort appear to represent at least two phases of construction, and there may also have been a timber palisade on the site before the hillfort was first constructed. The fort ramparts, in which stone facing blocks can still be seen in places, stand as a stark reminder of the need for defended settlements in the centuries prior to the Roman invasion. Although this area is some 30km north of Hadrian's Wall, more peaceful conditions seem to have developed during the Roman period and many hillforts were superseded by smaller, relatively undefended "villages" of stone roundhouses with associated paddocks and fieldsystems. Exactly this type of settlement developed at Lordenshaws, and the remains of several roundhouses can be seen overlying the flattened ramparts in the fort's south east quadrant as well as within its interior (refer Figure 1).

It is not known when this village fell out of use, but documentary research has shown that the area was part of the medieval Forest of Rothbury from early medieval times. The remains of the boundary bank or pale of the 13th century deer park can be seen crossing the moor, as can many areas of rig and furrow which represent medieval fields. The remains of a number of rectangular buildings, presumably medieval sheilings, have also been recorded in the area. By the late 14th century the land was owned by the Percy family, in whose ownership it has remained ever since.

• Previous Land-use Problems

A number of conservation issues were tackled by the management agreement. The overwintering of up to 160 suckler cows and their calves on the moor was

causing depletion of the heather moorland and erosion of fragile archaeological earthworks through overgrazing. Further depletion of the heather moorland was occurring through the rapid and largely uncontrolled colonisation of the moorland by bracken (*Pteridium aquilinum*), which was also causing problems for livestock management, public access and archaeological conservation. The loss of heather was responsible in part for a progressive decline in the numbers of moorland game birds, especially grouse, due to loss of habitat. A reduction in the area of semi-natural deciduous woodland and tree cover due largely to the intensity of livestock grazing, absence of fencing and inadequate replacement planting was

Figure 1. RCHME topographic survey of the Lordenshaws hillfort and its environs. © RCHME Crown copyright.

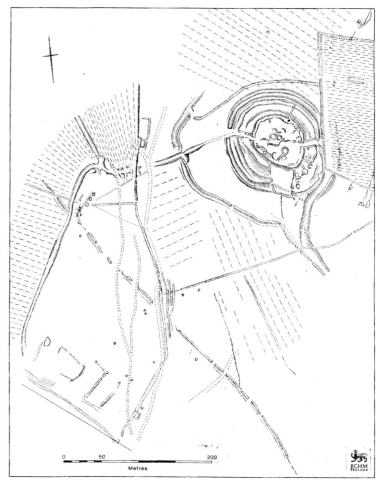

0   50   200
Metres

● The Agreement

The agreement, signed on 20th July 1992, was made under Section 39 of the *Wildlife and Countryside Act 1981* and runs for a period of 25 years. It is not an archaeological management agreement, but covers the archaeology as one important issue within the overall framework of the local landscape. In this respect, it can be seen as a model for many other proposed agreements elsewhere, many of which will not have such a wealth of archaeological remains but all of which will include provision for suitable management of the local archaeological resource.

Some conditions of the Lordenshaws agreement, such as the construction of a car park and the regulation of the rights of way network, were detailed in the agreement, whilst specific details of conservation work were covered by a conservation management plan drawn up by the Park Authority as a condition of the agreement. The Park Authority's financial obligations are to honour the specific commitments outlined below: there is no provision for an annual payment within the terms of the agreement.

● The Provisions

The Park Authority's initial financial outlay was £19,600.00, representing one third of the cost of a new cattle shed to ensure that in future there will be no need for winter or summer grazing of the moorland by cattle. For the duration of the agreement, grazing by sheep will be limited to the existing stocking level of 600 ewes and 125 ewe hoggs. After one year this has already resulted in a noticeable improvement in the quality of the moorland (Plate 4) and trampling of the various earthwork features is no longer a problem. The regeneration of heather moorland will continue to be actively encouraged and monitored with positive management being undertaken to improve its condition and age diversity, for example, by selective rotational burning.

Plate 4. The objective: archaeological remains conserved within healthy heather moorland. A possible prehistoric stone row surrounded by heather one year after the signing of the management agreement. Photograph: André Berry.

another concern addressed by the agreement.

In addition to the conservation work necessary to correct the above problems, public access over the moor was also a major consideration of the management agreement. The network of public rights of way required selective modification and updating to facilitate improved public access and interpretation. There was also a need to regulate car parking to end the practice of random parking at various points over the moor.

Although it is rare for the soil to catch fire during heather burning, it should be noted that no assessment of the possibility of archaeological damage through heather burning has yet been attempted. Possible damage to buried deposits, for example in cairns, or to surface features like rock carvings is an issue of relevance to many areas of the country but does not seem to have been addressed anywhere as yet.

A programme of bracken eradication will be implemented, using both mechanical and chemical means, as appropriate. As is normal policy throughout the Park, the costs of bracken eradication will be grant-aided by the Park Authority where there are proven ecological or archaeological benefits. Other conservation work, for example tree planting and the erection of deer fencing, will take place where appropriate and will be designed so as to cause no damage to the archaeology. The improvements in the quality of heather moorland and woodland resulting from the conservation plan will provide more suitable environments for game birds and is therefore of direct benefit to the landowner.

The conservation plan includes a commitment by the Park Authority to monitor and rectify erosion damage on the hillfort earthworks. A number of erosion scars had developed through the hillfort defences over recent years, and a large cairn had been constructed (using stone from the ramparts and hut circles) at the highest point within the fort. Both of these problems were dealt with in a single day thanks to the pupils of Rothbury Middle School who dismantled the cairn and used the stones to infill the erosion scars (Plate 5). This was an important conservation exercise but was also important in that it involved the children in practical archaeological work as part of their history classes. The infilled erosion scars were subsequently topsoiled and turfed, and should be invisible within a couple of years. The rationalisation of the rights of way network (see below) should ensure

Plate 5. Children from Rothbury Middle School hard at work on the repair of the eroded fort ramparts. This view also shows the attractive location of the site, with views across Coquetdale to the snow-capped Cheviots.

that future damage to the fort is minimal, and where any problems start to develop they will be dealt with at an early stage before any serious damage can occur.

In addition to the conservation work, the provision of public access over the moor is a major aspect of the management agreement. For the duration of the agreement an access zone, extending to 12.5ha and including the Iron Age hillfort and nearby examples of rock carvings, has been defined. The public will have free access at all times over this area, which enjoys spectacular panoramic views of Rothbury, Coquetdale and the Cheviot Hills. The rationalisation of the official rights of way network to better reflect current and future needs of local people, hill walkers and casual visitors has also been undertaken as part of the project. Whilst there is no official bridleway over the top of the moor, the local riding school did ride regularly over the hillfort. However, the school has now agreed voluntarily to bypass the fort and thus further reduce the risk of damage to the ramparts.

As a condition of the agreement, the Park Authority has constructed a new car park to end the widespread practice of informal parking along the roadside and on the moor. This car park (refer Plate 1), is not visually intrusive from ground level and is now merging into the landscape as grass colonises its surrounding banks. Two smaller car parks are planned elsewhere along the road, and these will be carefully designed so as to minimise their impact on the landscape.

Work is in hand on the production of a display panel for the main car park illustrating some of the remains to be seen on the moor. A booklet giving further information is to be published and this will be distributed through National Park visitor centres. The visitor centre at Rothbury is within a couple of miles of Lordenshaws which will figure prominently in the centre's display area when this is redesigned over the next couple of years .

● Conclusion

Since the Agreement was signed there has been much public interest in the site, which has featured in several newspaper articles and on local television and radio. Guided walks in the area have been very well attended, and the new car park is proving popular.

In short, the Lordenshaws management agreement is of benefit to the landowner, the tenant and the general public. It demonstrates what can be achieved through a well thought out integrated approach to conservation, where archaeology, ecology, landscape, land-use and public access are all considered together as part of a single complex. The Lordenshaws agreement is a model which the Park Authority hopes to develop at a number of other historic landscapes in years to come.

● Acknowledgements

Thanks are due first and foremost to Northumberland Estates, and especially to Lord Ralph Percy and Rory Wilson, whose commitment to conservation issues made the management agreement possible. Considerable thanks are also due to RCHME for the provision of the topographic survey of Lordenshaws, and for permission to reproduce Figure 1 within this paper. Thanks also go to Richard Tipping for his provisional work on the Caudhole Moss palaeoenvironmental deposits. Finally, thanks to Stan Beckensall for permission to use Plate 2 and to André Berry for Plate 4.

● References

Beckensall, S. (1992) *Prehistoric Rock Motifs of Northumberland: Volume 2 Beanley to the Tyne.* Hexham: Privately published.

Bradley, R. (1993) *A Field Investigation of the Prehistoric Rock Art of North Northumberland.* University of Reading: Unpublished interim report.

Topping, P. (1993) Lordenshaws Hillfort and Its Environs. A survey by the Royal Commission on the Historical Monuments of England. *Archaeologia Aeliana*, 5th series, XXI.

Wetlands - Integration for Habitat Conservation, Ecology, Sustainable Exploitation and Archaeology: An Overview

Dr. Margaret Cox

Department of Conservation Sciences, Bournemouth University

Plate I. **A corrugated iron peat digger's hut situated in Shapwick Heath (N.G.R. ST 436 401). The Heath is presently a derelict industrial landscape resulting from decades of intensive peat extraction. English Nature are to rehabilitate the area as a minerotrophic mire. The hut which is likely to be destroyed (either through neglect or deliberately) presently houses barn owls (*Tyto alba*) and is itself a valuable habitat.**

● Introduction

Wetland specialists such as ecologists, agronomists, conservationists, soil chemists and hydrologists have years of experience and established methods of managing wetlands and of monitoring the condition of, and change within these complex and valuable ecosystems. Archaeology has been slow to realise this and to make any positive moves to either develop the theory, or facilitate the practice of, integrated holistic wetland management. As such, English Heritage's current *Wetland Management Project* is a welcome measure.

The issue of management of wetlands for archaeology is still in its infancy. Understandably, such work that has been undertaken has concentrated upon known sites. Paradoxically, such sites are usually discovered during the destruction of the resource that has hitherto protected and preserved them. Work is currently underway to monitor the condition of certain sites where there are serious problems of potential degradation. These can reflect a variety of factors such as dewatering due to mineral extraction as at Market Deeping, or degradation due to development such as the Rose Theatre, or sites threatened by pollution and changes to soil biochemistry such as Flag Fen (N.G.R. TL 227 989).

This paper seeks to highlight some extremely difficult questions that must eventually form an essential part of the issue of integrated wetland management with respect to archaeology. It makes no apology for not attempting to answer them - its purpose is to identify important issues, such as sustainability and value, that must be addressed by an informed multi-disciplinary forum of specialists. The term archaeology is used in this paper to include the historic landscape, the industrial landscape (Plate 1), buried archaeology including monuments, artefacts, land surfaces and the palaeoenvironmental record.

The author's experience in wetland management has been primarily in the Somerset Levels and Moors, hence sites within this area will serve as the focus for discussion.

● Catchment - Resource - Site

One of the major problems facing archaeology today is that the outdated importance of "site" rather than "resource" still pervades planning and conservation initiatives and decisions. This is an issue that continues to exist even within the archaeological profession. Despite PPG16,

Plate 2. Alkaline, nutrient rich water being pumped into a series of ditches to maintain a high water level across the site of the Sweet Track.

Plate 3. The Sweet Track lies within the peat substrate, roughly along the line of the ditch. The scheduled site lies within Shapwick Heath National Nature Reserve.

some archaeological curators continue to make planning decisions based upon what is known rather than the potential of the resource, whether it is a dry site or a wetland. As such it is hard to criticise site managers from other agencies such as English Nature, the Royal Society for the Protection of Birds (RSPB), the National Rivers Authority (NRA), the Ministry of Agriculture, Fisheries and Food (MAFF) and the Forestry Commission for taking the view that no known archaeology means no archaeology.

This problem is further complicated in wetlands where it is the catchment area as a whole that affects the resource, that is the raised mire or the river valley, and it is the resource that determines the condition of the site. If one seeks to manage an area for the well-being of a known archaeological monument, for example the Sweet Track in the Somerset Levels, its sustainable management is presently dependent upon the issue of whether the area can be restored to a natural and sustainable wetland. This, in turn, is dependent upon the hydrology of the Brue Valley as a whole (the resource) and this upon factors affecting the water supply and water quality of the run-off from the 200,000ha of upland (the catchment) which drain into the Somerset Levels and Moors (64,000ha). In planning terms, to extend one's area of concern to include the entire catchment area becomes untenable solely on the grounds of archaeology.

The same problem arises where a planning application might affect a healthy wetland, one where no archaeology is known but where the potential for archaeology exists. Is it reasonable to argue that development or agricultural activity should be denied because it might affect the well-being of archaeology which might exist? I think not. However, if archaeology becomes part of the wider conservation lobby, then it can join forces with other agencies concerned to protect wetlands for their wider value. This can include water quality, wildlife, habitat, flood control or fisheries and recreation potential.

Many agencies, such as MAFF with its Environmentally Sensitive Areas scheme, and the NRA with such responsibilities as those of the *Water Resource Act 1991*, have a duty to have regard to archaeology. There can be no doubt that if archaeologists took less of a site-based view of wetlands potentially affected by schemes initiated by either agency (and others), and expanded their perception of the well-being of wetsites to include their capacity to function as natural and sustainable ecosystems, they would not only have the support of habitat conservationists such as English Nature, RSPB and Royal Society for Nature Conservation (RSNC), but would also have a far greater chance of long-term success.

● Sustainability

One issue that has yet to be addressed by the archaeological community is the question as to whether sites which are discovered in severely degraded ecosystems can be managed in a sustainable way. If they cannot, should on-going environmentally-costly methods of preservation, such as the artificial hydration of sites, and subsequent management and monitoring, be undertaken?

Since 1982, efforts have been made to preserve the Sweet Track by the daily pumping of tens of thousands of gallons of nutrient rich alkaline water (Plate 2) onto the perched area of woodland through which the Trackway runs (Plate 3). No criticism of this scheme is intended and it may have prolonged the life expectancy of the monument (for detailed discussion of this scheme see Cox, 1994). There can be no doubt that the site was drying out and degrading prior to this initiative (Coles and Orme, 1983).

The Sweet Track (south from N.G.R. ST 425 410) runs through part of Shapwick Heath, presently a derelict industrial landscape resulting from a century of

intensive peat extraction. English Nature intends to flood the Heath and this may obviate the need for such extensive pumping. However, the level (Ordnance Datum) of the Trackway is above both the potential and optimum flooding horizon of the surrounding Heath, so considerable pumping will still be necessary if the current management regime for the Trackway is to be maintained. The question is, should archaeology undertake non-sustainable management practices? Is the long-term preservation of a monument worth a high environmental cost? If so, for how long?

The worst possible scenario is the present one where the current management regime, which is unlikely to be very effective in the long-term (see Cox et al, 1994), is not being scientifically monitored in terms of its effectiveness. If the present management regime was to be discontinued our science base, in terms of understanding wetland microbiology and soil chemistry in relation to the management of discrete sites, will not have progressed.

A further consideration is that of the ecological effects of such management practice. Hydration of the Sweet Track site has resulted in changes to the flora in the area in question and almost certainly the invertebrate communities dependent upon the habitat. Plate 4 illustrates the herb-rich wet meadows which form part of the scheduled site. The raised water level with its high nutrient levels has almost certainly contributed to the increase of the invasive soft rush (*Juncus effusus*), to the detriment of other species. Who should be responsible for monitoring this? As the "developer", should archaeology bear the costs? If effective methods of sustainably managing wetlands for archaeology were discovered and they were damaging to the ecology of the area, which should take priority? Who should decide?

● Integrated Management

One approach taken to the multi-purpose and multi-disciplinary management of

Plate 4. Herb-rich wet meadows within Shapwick Heath NNR, of regional importance, whose diversity is presently threatened by encroaching soft rush which is thriving as a result of the pumping regime designed to protect the Sweet Track.

wetlands was undertaken by the *Somerset Levels and Moors Project*. The Project was established by Somerset County Council in 1991 (supported by English Heritage and the Countryside Commission) to protect and promote the interests of this internationally important, but fragile and vulnerable, wetland. The Project was pro-active in initiating and participating in schemes designed to restore the wetland; further it commented and informed strategies put forward by diverse agencies which potentially affected the resource.

Until 1993, the Project comprised two officers; an ecologist and an archaeologist. Both officers viewed the area as a wetland ecosystem, a system which must remain healthy and able to function naturally in order to ensure the continued well-being of the resource; thus protecting both archaeological and ecological interests and facilitating sustainable exploitation in such forms as extensive traditional agricultural practice and withy growing.

Unfortunately when the archaeological officer left post, this element of the project was not maintained at a strategic level. This raises doubts about the County's

commitment to what had unquestionably been a successful multi-disciplinary project.

● Value of the Resource

Integrated management implicitly suggests that concern for the well-being of the whole, takes into account specific conservation issues. Wetlands as a resource are valuable in many, diverse respects. These include habitat conservation and water quality/pollution control. They play a part in carbon flux and global warming; the provision of foodstuffs and other resources and, if sensitively managed, they are also a valuable archaeological/landscape repository.

The survival of wetlands into the historic period is (usually) a factor reflecting human inability to drain them in the past. Their survival and functionality depends upon their completeness and the retention of their natural integrity. Both elements can easily be debilitated and consequently their ability to function is degraded. When the functionality of wetlands is impaired their value is degraded and, consequently, their future rehabilitation and management requires scientific and considered evaluation.

In cases where an ombrotrophic mire is so degraded that it can only be rehabilitated as a minerotrophic mire, any surviving archaeology will be put at risk (due to such factors as root and rhizome damage, changes to soil chemistry and microbiology, and erosion). In such circumstances should the *in situ* preservation of archaeology be sacrificed for habitat re-creation? The gut reaction of those archaeologists whose reasoning can be impaired by conformity to the unquestioned application of the *"in situ preservation is best"* ethos is *"no"*. However, this ignores the facts that:

• At present we do not know how to preserve archaeology within degraded wetsites;

• Our application of monitoring regimes is in its infancy;

• Archaeology may not, on a resource level, be more important or even as important as such factors as habitat conservation.

● Conclusion

Integrated, holistic management regimes in wetlands are essential for the well-being and functionality of wetland ecosystems. Archaeology is but one of the valuable attributes of wetlands and, almost certainly, not the most important one. Whatever the prime motive for the restoration and/or management of wetlands, it is considered crucial that in the long-term the functionality of the resource is sustainable and ecologically sound.

In considering the management of wetlands for their archaeological potential, unless it is possible to sustainably re-create the conditions that preserved the resource over past millennia, it is probably best to preserve by record and concentrate upon becoming part of, and a voice in, holistic management strategies for those wetlands that do survive or have the potential to be restored as functioning ecosystems.

● References

Coles, J.M. and Orme, B.J. (1983) Archaeology in the Somerset Levels 1982 in, Coles, J.M. *Somerset Levels Papers* (No 9) Somerset Levels Project.

Cox, M.J. (1994) Archaeology in the Mire: Wetland Archaeology and Nature Conservation in, Swain, H. (ed) *Rescuing the Historic Environment.* Hertford: Rescue. 65-69.

Cox, M.J., Jones, G.E.B. and Hogan, D.I. (in press) Wetland Archaeology: Site Curation and Monitoring in, Barker, K. (ed) *Science and Site.* London: Archetype.

Integrated Management of Archaeology in Coastal Waters

Ben Ferrari

Royal Commission on the Historical Monuments of England

● Introduction

In 1989 *Heritage at Sea* (JNAPC, 1989) was published by the Joint Nautical Archaeology Policy Committee, a group representing a range of archaeological interests and organisations. The document made a number of proposals directed at the better protection of archaeological sites underwater. Whilst it would be quite wrong to date concern for lack of provision for submerged archaeology from this event it did, perhaps, signal a phase of more concerted effort dedicated to improving the situation. Significantly, drafting of the proposals contained in *Heritage at Sea*, and subsequent formulation of the JNAPC Code of Practice for Seabed Developers, involved considerable discussion with nature conservation bodies. Thus, it may be true to say that, in the marine environment, some degree of integration was accepted as desirable from an early stage. However, given this evident awareness of shortcomings, has a coherent approach to the archaeological, let alone integrated, management of archaeology in coastal waters developed in the UK? Whilst there are many factors that can contribute to effective management, this question will be addressed through brief consideration of the extent to which three basic requirements have been met.

● Character and Condition of the Resource

The first is knowledge of the character and condition of the resource. Access to data about the location and character of archaeological deposits in coastal and marine environments has increased with the inclusion of relevant information in databases currently used for policy formulation and development control on land (Firth 1993, 67; RCHME 1993, 48). Data contained in national and local inventories will enable appropriate policies to be developed which could encourage a move away from a reactive mode of management. It may, for example, be possible to identify sea areas which are regarded as having significant archaeological potential and to incorporate appropriate measures to safeguard the known and potential archaeological resource into existing and new management plans.

● Access to Appropriate Strategies for Management

The second basic requirement is access to appropriate strategies for management of the resource including deposit stabilisation. A considerable amount of published information relating to the preservation *in situ* of deposits on land is available including a useful gazetteer of stabilisation techniques (UAE, 1990). Intentional site burial has received considerable attention (Mathewson and Gonzalez, 1988; Mathewson, 1989) and related research has included substantial experimental work (Mathewson *et al.*, 1992). Some information is available from similar sources relating to material submerged in riparian and reservoir environments (Nordby, 1982; Lenihan, 1981) and ship finds on land have been stabilised (Reinders 1984, 109).

Major monitoring programmes have been instigated on large, submerged steel vessels involving efforts at stabilisation (Lenihan, 1989; MacCarthy, 1988; MacLeod, 1987). The process of corrosion, its monitoring and prevention, has been a major focus of attention (for example Brown *et al.*, 1988; Rogers, 1989). In addition, a corpus of observations on processes affecting submerged and semi-submerged archaeological material is developing within the framework of North American cultural resource management reports (e.g. Carrell 1987, 151-7). There is also clear awareness of the need to characterise physical, biological and chemical processes as an element of managing submerged archaeological resources (MacCarthy, 1982; Oxley, 1992; Stephenson 1985, 97-99). Despite this, in the marine environment, there is a disjunction between strident calls for minimal disturbance investigation with conservation *in situ* and knowledge of how this might actually be achieved. In this volume, Dr. Colin Martin describes the management problems posed by a particular shipwreck deposit in the Sound of Mull. His paper illustrates both the progress which is being made towards the development of proven stabilisation techniques and the need to question whether expending effort on stabilisation is necessarily always the most appropriate response.

● Administrative Framework

The third requirement that can be identified is an administrative framework sympathetic to the sensitive treatment of archaeology in coastal waters and which facilitates the implementation of appropriate management strategies. Such a framework can be composed of many different parts - each adding to the options available to archaeological heritage managers or to other managers who wish to include archaeology as a material consideration in their deliberations. Ian Oxley suggests in this volume that a highly specific piece of legislation, the *Protection of Wrecks Act 1973*, can be implemented in a way that embraces wider concerns including the aspirations of those involved in nature conservation. However, an administrative framework need not depend solely on legislation drafted to protect archaeological remains for its strength. Antony Firth, in his paper presented here, indicates that opportunities for integration and sensitive

management can also be identified in developments surrounding the emergence of Coastal Zone Management. His emphasis on the benefits that can flow from careful use of existing and proposed non-statutory provisions is reinforced by Paul Gilman's paper. This provides a welcome case study which illustrates the range of archaeological remains that may be found at the coast and also describes how awareness of the significance of the archaeological resource has been raised through integration of archaeological concerns with other Coastal Zone Management initiatives.

● Opportunities for Co-operation

Although a great deal of work remains to be done, management of submerged and coastal archaeology is developing rapidly. Dialogue with those involved in marine nature conservation has been mutually beneficial. There appears to be very little resistance to the concept of integration. However, as may be expected, actual implementation of an integrated approach is likely to be considerably more difficult than describing the potential benefits that can accrue from such a strategy. This can be illustrated by consideration of opportunities for co-operation between nature conservation, archaeological and fishing interests with regard to limiting the influence of certain types of commercial fishing on sensitive areas of seabed.

Any discussion involving commercial fisheries and the fishing industry is likely to be complex because these general terms encompass a wide range of activities. Fishing gear can be divided into two broad groups within which there is great diversity (c.f., Davis 1958, 5). Mobile gear is towed across the seabed and includes trawls (March 1970, 56-102; Sainsbury, 1986) and dredges (Coombe 1979, 33-48; Strange 1981, 24-26). The term static gear can be used to refer to set nets (Strange 1981, 30-31), baited lines (*ibid.*, 26-29) and traps such as lobster pots (Stewart, 1971). In addition, when considering the fishing community, it may not be appropriate to refer to a single "industry" at all. There has been considerable conflict between those deploying static and mobile gear over the years although some fishermen employ both methods on a seasonal basis. For the purposes of this paper, attention will generally focus on mobile gear deployed within coastal waters. Although fishing activity is isolated here, it is recognised that, in any given location, a number of agents of change to deposits may require mitigation. Attempts to conserve archaeological material *in situ* are therefore likely to involve a number of complementary initiatives.

There is substantial concern amongst nature conservation bodies about the effect of certain types of fishing gear on the seabed and associated biological communities. Some consensus can be detected regarding long-term changes in the benthic community caused by intensive fishing activity; fast-growing species tend to dominate and general diversity is reduced (ICES 1988, 16). There is less agreement about the length of time required for communities to recover or whether complete recovery is actually possible. A species by species breakdown of benthic organisms known to be affected by trawled gear is presented by de Groot (1984, 180-4). He concedes that negative effects can be detected but argues that the industry's role as a major supplier of protein and the fact that such effects are, in theory at least, reversible, make them acceptable. He appears rather more sanguine about the influence of intensive trawling than others who have reviewed the situation (e.g. Fowler, 1989). More general concerns about the nature and sustainability of the present scale of fishing effort have also been expressed (Harrison 1994, 49-50). Indeed, at the Third International North Sea Conference, held in March 1990, it was suggested that the impact of fishing gear should be investigated and dealt with in the same way as pollution of the more conventional variety (Ijlstra 1990, 225).

Comment has not been confined to scientific and official reports. Confrontational tactics employed by Greenpeace activists prompted *Fishing News* (29 July 1990, Editorial) to call for contributions to a fighting fund to combat conservationist propaganda. The national press has also highlighted the issue; for example, the *Daily Telegraph* carried an article entitled *"How Trawlers are Raking the North Sea to Death"* (19 Mar 1990, 16). However, national reportage of the tragic loss of three fishing vessels in accidents during 1991 illustrates something of the dual role of villain and victim which seems to characterise treatment of fishermen in the media (e.g. *The Independent*, 5 October 1991, 8).

Anecdotal evidence relating to damage done to wreck sites by fishing gear is readily available but analysis of the impact of fishing gear on archaeological material is hampered by a lack of quantified data. Despite this, studies undertaken for other purposes can be used to infer the general nature of damage that may occur with some confidence; certain types of gear are likely to cause a reduction in the range, quality and cohesion of material within archaeological deposits. However, other potentially more positive aspects of fishing activity must also be acknowledged. Charts of snags (where nets have encountered obstructions) on fishing grounds have been used as the basis for archaeological survey projects (Redknap and Fleming 1985, 315; fig. 48). Indeed, a number of wrecks currently designated under the *Protection of Wrecks Act 1973* were discovered through investigation of reported snags (see Lavery 1988, vii). In addition, Westerdhal (1980, 312) demonstrates the value of recording and researching the significance of placenames used by the fishing community when investigating maritime landscapes.

It is not in the fisherman's interest to contact an obstruction on the seabed. Real physical danger can attend such an incident and equipment has been modified to lessen the risk of injury to vessel and crew in the event of the gear coming fast (March 1970, 86; *Fishing News*, 29 November 1991, 3). However, due to the known tendency for fish to congregate around wrecks and other obstructions, it is in the fisherman's interest to fish as close as possible to such features. Despite significant advances in position fixing, accidental contacts do occur. It should not be doubted that fishermen will do everything they possibly can to prevent accidents that will lose them time and money but the last word should, perhaps, go to Mr. Price, a trawlerman who gave evidence to a Government inquiry in 1908:

"Putting down a lead will not tell you what obstructions there are in a given five or ten miles, but trawl there with a trawl and you will jolly soon find out."
(ISC 1908, question 1028, 38)

Many of the claims concerning long-term damage to biological communities on the seabed are disputed by the fishing industry. Despite this, recent industry-led initiatives have demonstrated an acceptance that some reduction in effort is necessary and that measures to conserve stocks are also required (NFFO, 1993). The means by which reduction in effort should be achieved, however, are the subject of considerable dispute. A recent editorial in *Fishing News*, (18 January 1991) spoke of *"...fishermen throughout the country who have their backs to the wall and their communities at risk"*. Similar assessments of the state of the industry and phrases such as "raw deal" are occurring with increasing regularity in the fishing press. In such circumstances fishermen may be expected to oppose restrictions on their activities with great energy (see Banks, 1994). Indeed, sectors of the industry have taken steps to develop the ability to influence policy. The Scottish Fishing Federation currently maintains an office in Brussels to facilitate lobbying of the European parliament (*Fishing News*, 6 December 1991, 3). The essential fact is that the fishing industry perceives itself as an industry under intense pressure.

Despite the complexity of the issues alluded to above, some agreement can be detected in terms of possible solutions to recognised problems. Recent proposals stemming from Governmental and Non-Governmental Organisations for Marine Consultation Areas (DoE 1992a, 1992b) superseded by Sensitive Marine Areas (English Nature 1993a, 1993b); and Marine Protected Areas (Warren and Gubbay, 1991; Kellerher and Kenchington, 1993) demonstrate a developing consensus on the need to manage certain activities on an area, rather than site-specific basis. Such an approach may be particularly suited to reducing the impact of certain fisheries on archaeological deposits (Firth and Ferrari, 1992). Restrictions on specific activities within a broad area has the distinctive advantage of offering some degree of protection to currently unlocated and unknown elements of the resource as well as to located sites. Proposals emanating from the fishing industry have also included the option of closing areas to selected types of fishing gear (NFFO, 1993). Thus, an opportunity would appear to exist for the aspirations of several groups, including those perceived as the agents of undesirable change, to be met.

Nature conservation agencies have been relatively active in identifying areas which can be regarded as sensitive from a conservation perspective (English Nature, 1994). The various factors which might contribute to assessment of the archaeological potential of an area are reviewed by Garrison *et al.* (1989, II-9 to II-126). A focus of nature conservation interest on estuaries and associated landscapes seems particularly promising with regard to identification of coincidence of interest in areas proposed for management. Within the fishing community, support for closed areas appears to stem largely from an acceptance that stocks must be conserved and that this can partly be achieved through protection of immature specimens and spawning grounds. Is it possible then, to select an area for protection on the basis of its natural and cultural resources and also serve the interests of stock conservation? Further, does the fact that fishing is not prosecuted within an area mean that, inevitably, target species will become more abundant at that location and that contiguous areas will therefore benefit through subsequent movement out of the protected area?

"Spillover" is the term used to describe enhancement of local fisheries by emigration of adults and large juveniles from a reserve. There is good evidence that this phenomena does occur, although comprehensive data is lacking (Rowley 1992, 26). Species abundance has certainly been shown to increase dramatically within protected areas. Outside such reserves, however, the magnitude of a possible increase in local catches is difficult to predict. What does seem clear is that spillover will probably not increase catches significantly other than very near the reserve boundaries. This has implications for policing. If fishermen are to gain advantage from the reserve, an essential pre-requisite in this context, they must fish very close to the limits of the protected zone. This promotes intensification of impact on a restricted area of seabed. It also increases the chance of accidental infringement through genuine navigational error.

In order to be effective, it would appear that the size, shape and location of closed areas must be determined with care and with full regard to the preferred habitat, behaviour and movement of the target species. It may be very difficult to reconcile these parameters with boundaries based on archaeological priorities. Other problems may be anticipated. Industry proposals have often related to seasonal rather than year-round closures. Such an arrangement offers only limited benefits to archaeological heritage managers. Further, there may be pressing reasons why certain restrictions cannot be accepted. During consultation in advance of establishment of the Kapiti Island reserve in New Zealand (created under the *Marine Reserves Act 1971*) objections were made on the grounds of safety. During bad weather it is necessary to shoot and haul

nets in the lee of the island, within the proposed reserve. This specific requirement was accommodated in the final design of the reserve (Department of Conservation 1990, 10).

It would be quite wrong to suggest that integration of attempts to conserve natural and cultural resources is relatively straightforward while the addition of fishing interests to the equation will cause difficulties. However, promotion of marine protected areas as a *panacea* without full appreciation of the constraints imposed by the need to ensure that such areas do indeed benefit the fishing community, would be pointless. Selection of areas for such treatment will inevitably involve compromise and equal benefit may not accrue to each interest group. For example, voluntary cessation of mobile fisheries within an area initiated solely to protect juvenile stock will still benefit archaeological material whether or not the area is perceived to be of high potential. Despite this, the advantages to resource managers, cultural or natural, that will flow from voluntary compliance with arrangements for planned restrictions on activity are considerable. This is particularly apparent in the light of recent Government discussion papers on coastal management which have emphasised the need to avoid expensive commitments to difficult policing activities (DoE 1993, 3.1).

Accommodation of diverse interests and a wide range of criteria for selection of managed areas inevitably results in a heavy emphasis on liaison between agencies and with local fishing communities; a fact recognised in guidance provided to English Nature project officers (English Nature 1993, 52). However, the situation is complicated by an increase in the number of foreign, particularly Spanish, boats operating in UK waters using licences purchased from British fishermen (*Fishing News*, February 12 1993, 4). Generally, these vessels are not UK based, thus the understanding and co-operation at a local level perceived to be necessary for successful liaison may not develop. Problems associated with such vessels may increase when the various exclusions which currently bar foreign vessels from inshore waters are reviewed in 1995.

● Conclusion

The general concept of marine protected areas offers much to archaeological heritage managers and does represent a means by which integrated management can be achieved. The difficulties highlighted in the preceding paragraphs should serve as a prompt to co-ordination of effort not an excuse for inactivity. Such problems are likely to be more easily solved if identified at an early stage but while considering new approaches it will be essential to maintain the distinction between protection afforded to archaeological material as a by-product of other initiatives and the actual existence of shared objectives.

● References

Banks, R. (1994) *The Sea Fish (Conservation). Act 1992 - A Fishing Industry Perspective* in, Earll, R.C. (ed) *Marine Environmental Management: Review of Events in 1993 and Future Trends.* Candle Cottage, Kempley, Gloucestershire, GL18 2BU. 53-56.

Brown, R., Bump, H., and Muncher, D.A. (1988) An *in situ* Method for Determining Decomposition Rates of Shipwrecks. *International Journal of Nautical Archaeology,* 17. 143-145.

Carrel, T. (ed) (1987) *Charles H. Spencer Mining Operation and Paddle Wheel Steamboat.* Glen Canyon National Recreation Area. *Southwest Cultural Resource Center Professional Report,* 13. Sante Fe, New Mexico.

Coombe, D. (1979) *The Bawleymen: The Fishermen and Dredgermen of the River Medway.* Rainham.

Davis, F.M. (1958) *An Account of the Fishing Gear of England and Wales.* London.

de Groot, S.J. (1984) The Impact of Bottom Trawling on Benthic Fauna of the North Sea. *Ocean Management,* 9. 177-190.

Department of Conservation. (1990) *Kapiti Island Marine Reserve Proposal: A Public Discussion Document.* Conservation Te Papa Atawhai, Department of Conservation, Wellington, New Zealand.

DoE. (1992a) *Marine Consultation Areas.* Department of the Environment and The Welsh Office. February 1992.

DoE. (1992b) *Marine Consultation Areas: A Description.* Department of the Environment and The Welsh Office. February 1992.

DoE. (1993) *Managing the Coast: A Review of Coastal Management Plans in England and Wales and the Powers Supporting Them.* Department of the Environment and the Welsh Office, October 1993.

English Nature. (1993a) *Conserving England's Marine Heritage: A Strategy.* Peterborough: English Nature.

English Nature. (1993b) *Estuary Management Plans: A Co-ordinator's Guide.* Peterborough: English Nature.

English Nature. (1994) *Important Areas for Marine Wildlife Around England.* Peterborough: English Nature.

Firth, A. and Ferrari, B. (1992) Archaeology and Marine Protected Areas. *International Journal of Nautical Archaeology,* 21. 67-70.

Firth, A. (1993) The Management of Archaeology Underwater in, Hunter, J. and Ralston, I. (eds) *Archaeological Resource Management in the UK.* Gloucestershire. 65-76.

Fowler, S.L. (1989) *Nature Conservation Implications of Damage to the Seabed by Commercial Fishing Operations.* Marine Science Branch, Nature Conservancy Council, Report 79.

Garrison, E.G., Giammona, C.P., Kelly, F.J., Tripp, A.R. and Wolff, G.A. (1989) *Historic Shipwrecks and Magnetic Anomalies of the Northern Gulf of Mexico: Reevaluation of Archaeological Resource Management Zone 1. Volume II, Technical Narrative*. US Department of the Interior, Minerals Management Service, Gulf of Mexico OCS Regional Office, New Orleans.

Harrison, N.M. (1994) Fisheries Review: With Emphasis on Nature Conservation - Fisheries Interactions in, Earll, R.C. (ed) *Marine Environmental Management: Review of Events in 1993 and Future Trends*. Candle Cottage, Kempley, Gloucestershire, GL18 2BU. 49-52.

ICES. (1988) *Report of the Study Group on the Effects of Bottom Trawling*. International Council for the Exploration of the Sea, Fish Capture Committee, G & L, C.M. 1988/B:56.

Ijlstra, T. (1990) The Third International North Sea Conference. *Marine Pollution Bulletin*, 21. 223-226.

ISC. (1908) *Injuries to Submarine Cables. Report of the Interdepartmental Committee on Injuries to Submarine Cables with Evidence and Appendices*. 1908 [Cd.4331] XXV.875.

JNAPC. (1989) *Heritage at Sea: Proposals for the Better Protection of Archaeological Sites Underwater*. London: National Maritime Museum, Greenwich.

Kellerher, G., and Kenchington, R. (1991) *Guidelines for Establishing Marine Protected Areas*. International Union for Conservation of Nature and Natural Resources, Gland, Switzerland.

Lavery, B. (1988) *The Royal Navy's First Invincible: The Ship, the Wreck, the Recovery*. Invincible Conservations (1744-1758) Ltd. Hampshire.

Lenihan, D.J. (1981) *The Final Report of the National Reservoir Inundation Study, Vol. I (Summary) & II (Technical Reports)*. National Park Service, Southwest Cultural Resources Centre. Sante Fe, New Mexico.

Lenihan, D.J. (ed) (1989) USS *Arizona* Memorial and Pearl Harbour National Historic Landmark. *Southwest Cultural Resource Center Professional Report*, 23. Sante Fe, New Mexico.

McCarthy, M. (1982) A Wreck Inspection Programme as an Aid to the Co-ordinated Management of a Large Number of Wreck Sites. *International Journal of Nautical Archaeology*, 11. 47-52.

McCarthy, M. (1988) S.S. *Xantho*: The pre-disturbance Assessment, Excavation and Management of an Iron Steam Shipwreck off the Coast of Western Australia. *International Journal of Nautical Archaeology*, 17. 339-347.

MacLeod, I.D. (1987) Conservation of Corroded Iron Artefacts: New Methods for On-site Preservation and Cryogenic Deconcreting. *International Journal of Nautical Archaeology*, 16. 49-56.

March, E.J. (1970) *Sailing Trawlers*. Newton Abbot. (3rd edition)

Mathewson, C.C. (ed) (1989) *Interdisciplinary Workshop on the Physical-Chemical-Biological Processes Affecting Archaeological Sites*. Contract Report EL-89-1. Environmental Laboratory, US Army Engineer Waterways Experiment Station, Vicksburg, Mississippi, USA. US Army Corps of Engineers.

Mathewson, C.C., and Gonzalez, T. (1988) Protection and Preservation of Archaeological Sites Through Burial in, Marinos, P.G. and Koukis, G.C. (eds) *The Engineering Geology of Ancient Works, Monuments and Historical Sites: Preservation and Protection. Vol. 1, Engineering Geology and the Protection of Historical Sites and Monuments*. Rotterdam.

NFFO. (1992) *Conservation: An Alternative Approach*. National Federation of Fishermen's Organisations, Fish Docks, Grimsby.

Nordby, L.V. (1982) Preliminary Experiments in the Structural Preservation of Submerged Anasazi Structures in, Cummings, C.R. (ed) *Underwater Archaeology: The Proceedings of The Eleventh Conference on Underwater Archaeology.* Fathom Eight Special Publication, 4. San Marino. 68-79.

Oxley, I. (1992) The Investigation of the Factors which Affect the Preservation of Underwater Archaeological Sites in, Keith, D.H. and Carrel, T.L. (eds) *Underwater Archaeology Proceedings from the Society for Historical Archaeology Conference, Kingston, Jamaica.* Society for Historical Archaeology. 105-110.

RCHME. (1993) *Recording England's Past: A Review of National and Local Sites and Monuments Records in England.* London: RCHME.

Redknap, M., and Fleming, M. (1985) The Goodwins Archaeological Survey: Towards a Regional Marine Site Register in Britain. *World Archaeology,* 16. 312-328.

Reinders, R. (1984) Excavations on the Former Seabed in, Langley, S.B. and Unger, R.W. (eds) *Nautical Archaeology: Progress and Public Responsibility.* BAR International Series, 220. Oxford. 99-112.

Rogers, B.A. (1989) The Case for Biologically Induced Corrosion at the *Yorktown* Shipwreck Archaeological Site. *International Journal of Nautical Archaeology,* 18. 335-340.

Rowley, R.J. (1992) Impact of Marine Reserves on Fisheries: A Report and Review of the Literature. *Science and Research Series,* 51. Department of Conservation, Wellington, New Zealand.

Sainsbury, J.C. (1986) *Commercial Fishing Methods.* Farnham.

Stephenson, R. (1985) Physical Processes at the CSS *Chattahoochee* Wreck Site in, Johnston, P.F. (ed) *Proceedings of the Sixteenth Conference on Underwater Archaeology.* Special Publications Series, 4. Society for Historical Archaeology. 97-100.

Stewart, R. (1971) *A Living from Lobsters.* London

Strange, E.S. (1981) *An Introduction to Commercial Fishing Gear and Methods Used in Scotland.* Scottish Fisheries Information Pamphlet 1. Marine Laboratory, Aberdeen.

UAE. (1990) *The Archaeological Site Stabilisation Protection and Preservation Notebook.* US Army Corps of Engineers, Environmental Impact Research Programme. US Army Engineers Waterways Experiment Station, Vicksburg, MS.

Warren, L., and Gubbay, S. (1991) *Marine Protected Areas: A Discussion Document.* Godalming: World Wide Fund For Nature.

Westerdhal, C. (1980) On Oral Traditions and Placenames. *International Journal of Nautical Archaeology,* 9. 311-29.

Salt Marsh Loss to Managed Retreat in Essex: An Integrated Approach to the Archaeological Management of a Changing Coastline

P.J. Gilman, D.G. Buckley and S. Wallis

Essex County Council and Dorset County Council

● Introduction

The Essex coast contains a rich and varied archaeological resource, which is under increasing threat from both natural and human agencies. The County Council is in the forefront of efforts to protect the coast and the addition of this paper to the proceedings of the conference was, therefore, considered appropriate, since it could assist other organisations which have not reached the stage achieved in Essex.

The paper describes the initiatives which the Archaeology Section is carrying out to record and manage the coastal archaeological resource. They include close liaison with local and national agencies concerned with the coast, such as English Nature, programmes of survey and recording, and the provision of specialist advice and information to the planning authorities in the coastal areas of the County. This advice includes recommendations concerning individual development proposals as well as provision of archaeological information and policy wordings for inclusion in Local Plans. To illustrate this process in action a specific example, the Blackwater Estuary Management Plan, is discussed in detail. The paper concludes with a brief consideration

of how information and "policy" are being brought together in the furtherance of specific projects such as managed retreat.

● The Essex Coast

Essex has the longest and one of the most important coastlines in the country (English Nature, 1993). Including the many estuaries and creeks, it stretches for over 480km and consists of five basic habitats - mudflats and sandbanks; saltmarshes; shingle spits; grazing marsh; seawalls and grassland. All of these habitats support an abundance of birds and wildlife and the Essex coast is, therefore, of great international importance for nature conservation. There are extensive areas of Sites of Special Scientific Interest (SSSIs), National and Local Nature Reserves (NNRs and LNRs), Special Protection Areas (SPAs) and Ramsar sites. The latter are sites protected under the *Convention on Wetlands of International Importance*, first drafted at Ramsar in Iran in 1971 and ratified by the UK Government in 1976. The Ramsar convention aims to conserve wetlands and promote their sustainable use. Moreover, large tracts of the coast have been declared an Environmentally Sensitive Area (ESA) and it is also possible that sections of the coast may gain Heritage Coast status.

In addition to its significance for wildlife conservation, the Essex coast contains many important archaeological and historic sites. These range in date from the early prehistoric periods through to the very recent past. As well as sites directly associated with the coast, such as wrecks, ports and defences, the intertidal zone in particular contains a rich archaeological resource. This has been preserved as a result of past changes in the coastline (Figure 1 shows the estimated shoreline of the Blackwater Estuary during the Neolithic period), and is now being extensively exposed by modern changes in sea level and other coastal processes. Relatively few of these important archaeological sites are protected as Scheduled Ancient Monuments, although this imbalance is being addressed through English Heritage's Monuments Protection Programme.

● The Sites and Monuments Record

The Archaeology Section maintains the computerised County Sites and Monuments Record (SMR) which is the most complete and up to date source of information about the archaeology of Essex. However, when the SMR was first created, it inherited the biases of the information used to compile it. These sources, such as the Ordnance Survey record cards and the inventories compiled by the Royal Commission on the Historical Monuments of England (RCHME), were largely terrestrially-based in their coverage of the archaeology of the County. Following this initial phase of SMR

Figure 1. The Blackwater Estuary showing the modern and Neolithic shore lines (after Wilkinson and Murphy, forthcoming).

formation, the Archaeology Section has been continually seeking to enhance and extend the coverage of the SMR, principally through programmes of survey and recording. Subject areas where further work is specifically being carried out include post-medieval, Industrial, and maritime archaeology.

● Archaeology of the Essex Coast

The following examples have been chosen to illustrate the range of sites to be found along the Essex coast.

● Cropmarks

The archaeological richness of the Essex coast is demonstrated by the wealth of

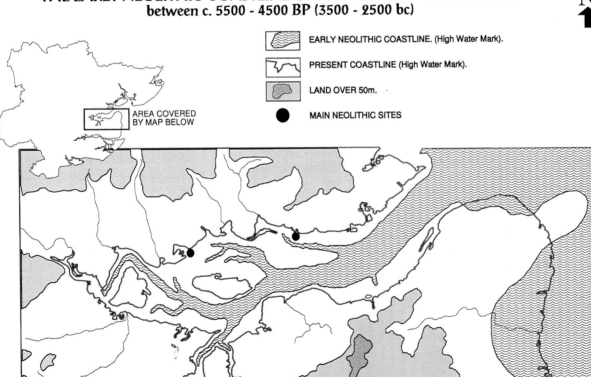

THE EARLY NEOLITHIC COASTLINE OF THE BLACKWATER ESTUARY
between c. 5500 - 4500 BP (3500 - 2500 bc)

N

EARLY NEOLITHIC COASTLINE. (High Water Mark).

PRESENT COASTLINE (High Water Mark).

LAND OVER 50m.

● MAIN NEOLITHIC SITES

AREA COVERED
BY MAP BELOW

0   2km

cropmarks, dating from the Neolithic onwards, which have been discovered, especially from the gravel terraces of the estuaries such as the Blackwater, Chelmer, Crouch and Thames. The cropmark sites are less well-preserved, on the whole, than contemporary features within the intertidal zone. They should, however, be seen as complementary, providing an indication of the extent of past settlement. In particular, it has been possible to build up a picture of the changes in the use of the landscape of the area from the Neolithic period to the present-day.

● Ancient ground surfaces in the intertidal zone

One of the most important aspects of the archaeology of the Essex coast consists of the ancient ground surfaces which are emerging from the eroding mudflats. These surfaces, which often date to the Neolithic and Bronze Age, have intact soil profiles which have been largely removed from inland sites by ploughing. Thus, sites where these surfaces survive contain information that cannot be recovered elsewhere. However, the continuing erosion of the mudflats within the estuary is a double-edged sword for archaeologists. Sites that have been buried beneath the mud for millennia are appearing, but continuing erosion means they may not survive for long.

● Red hills

"Red hills" are a particular feature of the Essex coast. They consist of low mounds of debris from salt extraction, which was a major industry during the late Iron Age and early Roman periods. Their chief constituent is partly-fired clay (briquetage), some of which can be recognised as fragments of vessels used in the salt-extraction process.

Most red hills have been adversely affected in the two thousand years since their use. Many have been lost through coastal erosion, and even more have been damaged by ploughing. Of the latter, many only appear as reddish areas in ploughed

fields, having been flattened and levelled over many years of ploughing. Many red hills were at the edge of dry land and, as a result, were often incorporated into later sea walls. Now that most sea walls have been faced with concrete, these red hills have been obscured.

The most recent study of this subject, published by the Colchester Archaeological Group (Fawn et al, 1990), includes a gazetteer of 341 known and suspected red hill sites. Although red hills are a prominent feature of Essex coastal archaeology, and have attracted much attention (e.g. Rodwell, 1979), only a limited amount is actually known about them. This is in part a consequence of the difficult conditions in which investigation has often to take place. There is a need for further research and the Archaeology Section has presented the case for further survey and investigation (Essex County Council, undated).

● Wrecks

Many wrecks are to be found along the Essex coast and estuaries, notably the remains of sailing barges, which were very important in coastal trade between East Anglia and London for many hundreds of years. However, until the recent work by the Spritsail Barge Society (1993), there had been very little systematic survey of these sites. Similarly, there has been very little investigation of wrecks in deep water off the Essex coast.

● Sea walls

The earliest sea walls date from the Middle Ages or perhaps even earlier. For example, on Foulness Island, a section through a medieval sea wall revealed an internal timber framework dated to the late 15th century (Crump, 1981). Dendrochronology established the most likely felling date of timbers as between AD 1483 and 1489 with a mean calibrated radiocarbon date of 1415-1565 AD (HAR 1689 and 1690). Sea walls were originally built to protect marsh pastures from flooding, though most today are protecting arable areas. In parts of

Essex, early walls survive where later sea walls have been constructed further out. Some are inland counter walls, whilst others have been converted into tracks or roads. In several places, lines of posts next to modern sea walls may represent earlier sea defences. Essex saltmarshes have been reclaimed for grazing or agriculture for at least the past 500 years. One of the most notable examples is Canvey Island which was reclaimed by Dutch engineers in the 17th century (Grieve, 1959).

● Oyster pits

The farming of oysters has been an important coastal industry since at least the Middle Ages (Benham, 1993). It is normally associated with Colchester and the Colne estuary, but it also took place in the Blackwater. The most important legacy of the industry are numbers of disused oyster pits situated along the coast or on offshore islands.

● Coastal defences

Defensive structures have been a feature of the Essex coast since the late Roman period with the Saxon shore fort at Bradwell-on-Sea (N.G.R. TM 031 082). In the medieval period, the defence of the coast was based on the royal castles at Colchester (N.G.R. TL 998 254) and Hadleigh (N.G.R. TQ 810 860). However, most of the surviving defensive sites post-date the introduction of artillery for shore defence in the 16th century, when a number of blockhouses were built in Essex by Henry VIII, for example at East Tilbury (N.G.R. TQ 691 768) and on Mersea Island (N.G.R. TM 0720 1518). In the succeeding centuries, the pattern was generally one of short, intensive phases of construction during invasion scares, followed by longer periods of neglect. Surviving fortifications include Tilbury Fort (N.G.R. TQ 651 754), the most important example of a 17th century fort in the country; the mid-19th century Coalhouse Fort at East Tilbury (N.G.R. TQ 6869 7735); the late Victorian Beacon Fort at Harwich (N.G.R. TM 262 317) and

remains from both the First and, especially, the Second World Wars (see below).

● Coastal Processes

A range of processes are now affecting the Essex coast, causing destruction of both archaeological sites and areas important for nature conservation. As a result, various organisations are concerned about the consequences of these processes which include:

● Sea level rise

The Essex coast is predominantly low-lying and is, therefore, very vulnerable to the rise in sea level as a result of global warming and the isostatic adjustments which have been on-going since the last Ice Age. As a result, the Essex coast is sinking relative to sea level by up to 5mm a year (Essex County Council and Coastal Districts, 1994a).

● Loss of saltmarsh and grazing marsh

This is a particular issue along much of the Essex coast, as there has been a considerable loss, especially in this century. For example, in the Greater Thames Estuary 73% of coastal grazing marshes were lost between 1935 and 1989 (English Nature, 1992). Saltmarshes have been lost as a result of several factors, including the rise in sea level already mentioned; tidal currents; wave action (c. 100ha per year); dredging of channels for shipping in the main estuaries; and especially enwalling for agriculture which, it is estimated, has caused the loss of 48,000ha since the 17th century.

● Maintenance of sea defences

This is also a major issue along the Essex coastline. Until recently, sea defences were mainly constructed with "hard" engineering but now the potential benefits of "soft" engineering are being examined. At national level, the Government has responded to the threat to the coast from natural processes by recommending that where it is not economical or feasible to preserve existing sea defences, a policy of "managed retreat" should apply. This can mean different things in different areas. For example, where cliffs are eroding whole sections of coastline are simply being abandoned. In other areas, consideration is being given to the deliberate breaching of sea defences in an attempt to re-establish saltmarsh, to form a natural sea defence. The latter will, of course, be particularly relevant to the Essex coast. In deciding whether to implement particular strategies of sea defence, the Government are being guided by three criteria - new schemes have to be technologically sound, cost-effective, and environmentally sustaining.

● Man-made Threats

As well as natural processes, threats to archaeological remains are also posed by human activities, which range in scale and effect from large-scale disturbance and development such as dredging, offshore mineral extraction, marinas and caravan parks, through to boating, recreation, bait-digging, and fishing. The increasing demand for coastal water recreation is a particular concern since activities such as jet ski-ing and water ski-ing can cause damage to sensitive ecological and archaeological features as a result of wave action.

● Archaeological Survey

Since its inception in 1971, the Archaeology Section has carried out and co-ordinated various coastal survey programmes. The following are summaries of the most significant of these initiatives.

● Intertidal survey

The importance of the ancient land surfaces in the intertidal zone has long been recognised, at least since the early years of this century, notably by the work of Hazzledine Warren who recorded a number of Neolithic sites on the Essex coast (e.g. Warren et al, 1936). In the 1970s the Blackwater and Crouch estuaries were

systematically searched by two amateur archaeologists (Vincent and George, 1980). More recently, realisation of the need for more systematic survey was prompted by further discoveries in the Crouch estuary, including flint scatters, pottery, human skulls, old land surfaces and peat layers. The Archaeology Section instigated an initial survey project, the Hullbridge Survey, funded by English Heritage. The results of this work were so encouraging that the survey's scope was expanded, eventually covering most of the County's coastline from the Thames estuary in the south to the Stour in the north (Wilkinson and Murphy, forthcoming). The scope of the work was broad, with the project directed

Plate 1. Aerial view of the timber alignments at Collins Creek. Photograph: Caroline Ingle.

**Plate 2. Some of the timber
alignments at Collins Creek.
Photograph: C.P. Clarke.**

by Tony Wilkinson, an archaeologist and
geomorphologist, with Peter Murphy, an
archaeologist and palaeoenvironmentalist.
The survey located numerous sites in the
intertidal zone, many of which dated to the
later prehistoric period, such as several
Bronze and Iron Age sites with surviving
timber-work; a Bronze Age paddle from
Canewdon (N.G.R. TQ 9244 9591); and
numerous red hills. Several of these sites
were investigated, including the excavation
of a Neolithic settlement at the Stumble
(N.G.R. TL 9014 0725), in the Blackwater
Estuary, near Osea Island; The new
information from the survey (over 100
sites) has been incorporated into the SMR,
and has made a significant addition to its
coverage of coastal and intertidal
archaeology.

● Collins Creek

The surveys mentioned above were only
able to examine those parts of the intertidal
zone that could be reached safely on foot.
One of the most exciting recent
developments in the study of the Essex
coast has been the realisation that aerial
survey can make a valuable contribution to
the discovery of sites in the intertidal zone.
This realisation was prompted by the

discovery, by a local boatman, Ron Hall, of
an extensive series of timber structures at
Collins Creek (N.G.R. TL 950 075) in the
Blackwater Estuary (Plate 1). Aerial survey
revealed the true extent of the structures
(some of the alignments are over 1km
long), which are only visible for short
periods at very low tides. Visits were made
to the site and two samples were taken for
radiocarbon dating. The results were
surprising, since one sample dated to the
7th century AD and the other to the 9th
(calibrated dates 640-675 AD [UB-3485]
and 882-957 AD [UB-3486], both to one
standard deviation). The initial work has
been followed by further aerial and
terrestrial survey, with funding from English
Heritage (Plate 2). This included a full
photogrammetric survey carried out by the
Cambridge University Committee for Aerial
Photography and a programme of
dendrochronological dating. Although this
project is still on-going, results so far
indicate that the site contains remains of
several phases of activity, some of which
may be prehistoric. At present, it is thought
that most of the structures represent the
remains of mid/late Saxon fish traps. If this is
correct, there are significant implications for
understanding of the scale and nature of
mid/late Saxon settlement and economic
activity on the coast.

● Aerial survey

As a result of the Collins Creek discovery,
the Archaeology Section, with the aid of a
grant from the Royal Commission on the
Historical Monuments of England, has
carried out a systematic programme of
flights over other areas of the Essex coast.
In 1992, this resulted in the discovery of a
very large fish trap near Mersea Island (Plate
3) (N.G.R. TM 052 122), and the
rediscovery of another fish trap near
Bradwell-on-Sea (N.G.R. TM 0390 0975).
The latter was previously known from the
work of a local archaeologist, Kevin Bruce,
but the flights have revealed much more of
the site. Such fish traps played an important
part in the coastal economy of Essex. They
are frequently referred to in medieval and

later documents, usually referred to as "kiddles" and were even being constructed as recently as 1975 (Wallis and Crump, 1992).

Aerial reconnaissance of the coast has continued in 1993 and 1994, and sites continue to be found, including a fish trap off Pewet Island, near Bradwell-on-Sea (N.G.R. TL 990 083), discovered in 1993. Although this project is still in its infancy, it has already provided encouraging results. It has also shown the problems of this kind of flying. The flights must coincide with the lowest tides and these may occur very early in the day when the light is poor. Also, even at low tides, parts of some structures may still be under water and difficult to see. Even when a structure is found, it may be necessary to observe it from different angles to record it fully and obtain the best photographs. As with land-based survey, the need is for repeated flights over a long period to recover as much detail as possible.

● Second World War defences

In 1940, the Essex coast was considered to be a likely landing site for the German invasion. From here, the invaders could quickly reach London and the industrial Midlands. As an immediate response, a "hard crust" of coastal defences was established. Some of these sites re-used existing fortifications, reinforced by many others constructed at completely new locations. These were mainly pillboxes, but other structures were also set up such as artillery and searchlight emplacements, minefield control towers, and anti-tank obstacles. Many were built under such hurried conditions that no central record of their positions was kept, so that they are now known only to people living in their immediate vicinity. In recent years, there has been increasing interest in these monuments to an important period in 20th century history and attempts are underway to record the structures that survive. The Archaeology Section has carried out pilot surveys of the coast on Mersea Island (N.G.R. TM 01 SW and SE), at Burnham-on-Crouch (N.G.R. TQ 99 NE) and, further to the north, in the Frinton and Walton (N.G.R. TM 22 SW) areas. On average, the pilot surveys have more than doubled the total of sites known from other sources (e.g. Wills, 1985). They have confirmed the variety of sites along the coast (e.g. Plate 4) and also that many have been lost, both to development and to coastal erosion.

Plate 3. Aerial view of fish trap at Mersea Flats. Photograph: Steve Wallis.

Plate 4. Minefield control tower near Burnham-on-Crouch. Photograph: Fred Nash.

● RCHME survey

National archaeological organisations are also becoming concerned with the need to record and protect coastal archaeological sites. The Royal Commission on the Historical Monuments of England (RCHME) is establishing a National Maritime Record. The RCHME's own survey programme is also embracing coastal areas and the Commission's Cambridge office is considering a survey of the ESAs of the East Anglian coast. This will include the intertidal zone and will allow for a check to be made on the condition of those sites which were discovered in the Hullbridge survey. The Archaeology Section is fully involved in the discussions concerning the programme for this survey and its implementation. New information will be integrated into the SMR, according to national agreements between RCHME and the Association of County Archaeological Officers (ACAO).

● Coastal Management Plans

Planning Policy Guidance Note 20 (DoE, 1993), sets out the Government's policy on the coast. The Essex County Council, in fulfilling its strategic role for the coast, has long sought to provide relevant coastal plans and policies, notably in a Coast Protection Subject Plan and in the County Structure Plan (Essex County Council, 1991). Most recently, the County Council and the Essex coastal districts prepared a coastal issues document for consultation. The aim of this report was to provide an overview of the main issues concerning the Essex coast and to raise issues of implementation and coastal management. At the time of writing a draft coastal strategy had been prepared (Essex County Council and Coastal Districts, 1994b), which includes detailed policies for the survey, recording and protection of archaeological sites. At a more local level, district authorities are working to prepare coastal zone management plans, for example Maldon District Council who are currently revising the Blackwater Estuary Management Plan.

● The Blackwater Estuary Management Plan

The recent discoveries in the intertidal zones prompted Maldon District Council, during the preparation of a new Blackwater Estuary Management Plan (BEMP), to fund the Archaeology Section to produce an enhanced section on the archaeology of the estuary. The first version of this Plan, in 1980, had only included one page of text concerning the archaeological importance of the Plan's study area. The revised version of the Plan has been considerably expanded and updated - a reflection of the increased awareness of archaeological remains and their significance. This was highlighted in the planning process by the publication in 1990 of the Department of the Environment's *Planning Policy Guidance Note 16 (Archaeology and Planning)*.

The approach adopted in preparing the archaeological text involved the following:

• Enhancement of particular aspects of the Sites and Monuments Record for the study area;

• Extraction of information from the Sites and Monuments Record;

• Visits to selected parts of the estuary, both on foot and by boat.

A map of the plan area was prepared at 1:25000 scale, with symbols showing the different categories of site (Figure 2). The map is accompanied by a report which gives particular emphasis to various aspects of coastal and maritime archaeology, notably the red hills and intertidal discoveries described above. Other aspects included:

• Cropmarks

North of Maldon and Heybridge, an area 12km long from east to west and up to 2km wide contains one of the largest and most concentrated cropmark complexes in Essex. On its western side, the complex covers both sides of the valley of the rivers Blackwater and Chelmer, in the parishes of Woodham Walter, Ulting and Langford. To the east, it extends along the north bank of the Blackwater estuary through the parishes of Great Totham, Little Totham and Goldhanger. The subsoils of the cropmark complex are largely Pleistocene terrace gravels associated with the rivers Chelmer and Blackwater.

Large areas of this complex have been destroyed by quarrying, although much of this destruction was preceded by archaeological excavation. In the late 1970s and early 1980s, work at Lofts Farm (N.G.R. TL 8689 0935) and Rook Hall (N.G.R. TL 8785 0925) was carried out by members of the Maldon Archaeological Group. The

Figure 2. The Blackwater Estuary Management Plan base map. Drawn by Stewart MacNeill and Roger Massey-Ryan.

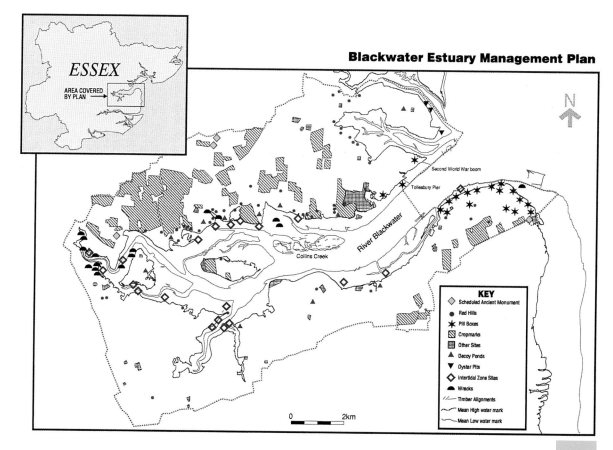

ESSEX

AREA COVERED BY PLAN

Blackwater Estuary Management Plan

Second World War boom

Tollesbury Pier

River Blackwater

Collins Creek

KEY

◇ Scheduled Ancient Monument
● Red Hills
✳ Pill Boxes
▨ Cropmarks
▦ Other Sites
▲ Decoy Ponds
▼ Oyster Pits
◇ Intertidal Zone Sites
◣ Wrecks
//— Timber Alignments
— Mean High water mark
— Mean Low water mark

0   2km

Essex County Council Archaeology Section
excavated a late Bronze Age enclosure at
Lofts Farm in 1985 (Brown, 1988), and,
between 1988 and 1990, carried out large-
scale excavations at Chigborough Farm
(N.G.R. TL 880 081) and Slough House
Farm (N.G.R. TL 873 092) (Wallis and
Waughman, forthcoming).

These excavations produced much
important information. Some of these
discoveries were of significance in
themselves, such as a Neolithic enclosure
and timber-lined Saxon wells at Slough
House Farm; a late Bronze Age enclosure at
Lofts Farm; and a possible Neolithic building
and a series of fenced Bronze Age field
systems at Chigborough Farm.

● Wrecks

Although few sites were recorded on the
SMR prior to the study, it has been possible
to include them in the BEMP, largely as a
result of a survey by the Society for Spritsail
Barge Research (1987). An approach was
also made to RCHME to supply information
from the National Maritime Record on the
Blackwater Estuary. Fortunately, the
Hydrographic Office had supplied data to
RCHME who were able to supply a listing
for inclusion in the Plan.

● Oyster beds

In the study area, there are a group of
examples off Old Hall Marshes, Tollesbury.
Oysters require unpolluted water to survive,
and it is a credit to the estuary's cleanliness
that the industry has recently reappeared in
the Goldhanger area.

● World War defences

During the First World War, the Royal
Navy operated a motor torpedo boat
station on Osea Island (N.G.R. TL 917
059), substantial remains of which still
survive. The map shows known Second
World War sites in the BEMP study area.
This is based on the nationwide survey by
Henry Wills, conducted by correspondence
(Wills, 1985). During visits to the area, six

other pillboxes were recorded - one on
Osea Island, five near Bradwell power
station. The latter were almost certainly
associated with the defence of a wartime
airfield. In addition, it was discovered that a
boom had been laid across the estuary, one
end of which still survives at Tollesbury.

● Results of the assessment

Archaeological assessment of the study area
for the Blackwater Estuary Management
Plan showed that it contains a high density
and wide variety of archaeological remains.
Two groups of sites were found to be
particularly at risk:

● 1. Red hills, several of which are being lost
to coastal erosion, and many others are
being flattened and dispersed by ploughing.

● 2. Timber structures and other sites within
the intertidal zone which are continually
being exposed, then lost soon after, by
erosion.

For both groups, this is of special concern.
Red hills are almost unique to Essex, and
the Study Area contains a large proportion
of them. The timber structures in and
around the Blackwater estuary appear to be
paralleled in Britain only by examples in the
Severn estuary and the Solent.

● Implementation

Following completion of the draft text and
plan for the Subject Plan, Maldon District
Council set up a working party to consider
a number of specific subject areas, one of
which was archaeology. At the time of
writing, discussions were still on-going, but it
is expected that the end result will be a
series of policies and initiatives aimed at
ensuring the future protection of
archaeological sites in the Estuary and
immediately surrounding area. The BEMP
may result in initiatives to encourage
farmers to take some of the surviving
cropmarks out of agriculture under such
schemes as Countryside Stewardship and
the ESA. Maldon District Council are in a
very good position to influence the use of

the Blackwater Estuary, as a result of a 12th century charter which granted ownership of much of the river west of Osea Island.

● Managed Retreat

The Archaeology Section's work on coastal archaeology is still on-going. However, as a result of the progress which has already been made with survey, assessment, and coastal policies, the Section is well-placed to respond to specific coastal initiatives such as "managed retreat".

In Essex, a research project has already been carried out on Northey Island and English Nature are currently planning a second experiment at Tollesbury (N.G.R. TL 960 114). In addition, the National Rivers Authority is proposing to establish two managed retreat sites, on the north and south banks of the Blackwater Estuary respectively. These experimental projects will be carefully studied to assess their effectiveness and to help formulate strategies for future, larger scale projects. Managed retreat will have significant implications for the archaeology of the Essex coast. Although the long-term survival of much coastal archaeology may be improved, particular sites may be damaged or destroyed by construction of new sea defences and the creation of new beaches, creek systems, and saltmarshes.

Although managed retreat in Essex is at a very early stage, the Archaeology Section is already closely involved in the assessment of the implications for archaeological sites. At English Nature's proposed experimental site at Tollesbury, the route of a new sea wall was evaluated by geophysical prospection and trial trenching (Germany, 1994). An important middle Iron Age red hill (N.G.R. TL 9592 1130) was found, which will be preserved in situ, by altering the course of the sea wall. Following discussions with English Nature and English Heritage, the area of the managed retreat itself will be evaluated by English Heritage's Ancient Monuments Laboratory. At the time of writing, the Archaeology Section was in

discussion with the National Rivers Authority concerning the appropriate archaeological response for the two sites proposed by this organisation. It is anticipated that this will include prior evaluation and also close monitoring of the establishment of a new beach and saltmarsh.

● Conclusion

Coastal and maritime archaeological sites are increasingly threatened by natural erosion and pressure from development proposals. Government planning guidance emphasises the role of local authorities in the protection and management of this important archaeological resource. In carrying out this role, local authorities need to have access to specialist archaeological advice based on up to date and accurate records. The archaeological input provided to the Blackwater Estuary Management Plan shows how the Archaeology Section has been able to ensure that full consideration is given to archaeological issues in drawing up policies. This paper also demonstrates the way in which the Section is working with other organisations, such as the NRA, RCHME, English Heritage and English Nature, to conserve the coast, with its environment, both natural and human-made. By carrying out programmes of archaeological survey and recording, and by liaising closely with these organisations, the Archaeology Section has enabled archaeological requirements to be properly integrated with such initiatives as managed retreat. Moreover, it has been possible to achieve integration at an early stage. Much remains to be done, but the work which has been carried out to date has provided a firm basis for the future protection and management of the important archaeological remains of the Essex coast.

● Acknowledgements

Acknowledgement is made to Essex County Council for its financial support for the publication of this article.

● References

Benham, H. (1993) *Essex Gold*. Essex County Council.

Brown, N. (1988) A Late Bronze Age Enclosure at Lofts Farm, Essex. *Proceedings of the Prehistoric Society*, 54. 249-302.

Crump, R. and Wallis, S. (1992) Kiddles and the Foulness Fishing Industry. *Essex Journal*, 27 (2). 38-42.

Crump, R. (1981) Excavation of a Buried Wooden Structure at Foulness. *Essex Archaeological History*, 13. 69-71.

Department of the Environment. (1990) *Planning Policy Guidance Note 16, Archaeology and Planning*.

Department of the Environment. (1992) *Planning Policy Guidance Note 20, Coastal Planning*.

English Nature. (1992) *Erosion and Vegetation Change on Saltmarshes of Essex and North Kent Between 1973 and 1988*. Peterborough: English Nature.

English Nature. (1993) *Wildlife and Conservation of the Essex Coast*. Peterborough: English Nature.

Essex County Council. (1991) *Essex Structure Plan - Approved First Alteration (July 1991)*.

Essex County Council and Coastal Districts. (1994a) *The Essex Coast: Issues Report*.

Essex County Council and Coastal Districts. (1994b) *The Essex Coast: Consultation Draft Essex Coastal Strategy*.

Essex County Council. (undated) *Red Hills Survey*. Limited circulation document.

Fawn, A.J., Evans, K.A., McMaster, I. and Davies, G.M.R. (1990) *The Red Hills of Essex - Salt-making in Antiquity*. Colchester Archaeological Group.

Germany, M. (1994) *Tollesbury Creek, Tollesbury, Essex. Archaeological Evaluation, Trial Trenching*. Essex County Council, limited circulation document.

Grieve, H. (1959) *The Great Flood*.

Rodwell, W.J. (1979) Iron Age and Roman Salt-winning on the Essex Coast in, Burnham, B.C. and Johnson, H.B. (eds), *Invasion and Response*. British Archaeological Reports Supplement, 11. 181-367.

Society for Spritsail Barge Research. (1987) *The Last Berth of the Sailorman*. Privately published.

Vincent, S.W. and George, W.H. (1980) *Some Mesolithic Sites along the Rivers Blackwater and Crouch, Essex*. Privately published.

Wallis, S. (1993) Aerial survey of the Essex Coast in, Bennett, A. (ed.), Work of the ECC Archaeology Section. *Essex Archaeological History*, 24. 193-194.

Wallis, S. and Waughman, M. (forthcoming) Archaeology and the Landscape in the Lower Blackwater Valley. *East Anglian Archaeology*.

Warren, S.H., Piggot, H.S., Clark, J.G.D., Burkitt, M.C., Godwin H. and Godwin, M.E. (1936) Archaeology of the Submerged Landsurface of the Essex Coast. *Proceedings of the Prehistoric Society*, 2. 178-210.

Wilkinson, T.J. and Murphy, P. (forthcoming) Archaeology of the Essex Coast: Volumes I and II. *East Anglian Archaeology*.

Wills, H. (1985) *Pillboxes*. Leo Cooper/Secker and Warburg.

Archaeology and Coastal Zone Management

Antony Firth

Faculty of Law, University of Southampton

● Introduction

This paper is intended to bring Coastal Zone Management (CZM) to the attention of archaeologists, to give a brief account of recent developments in England (and, to some extent, Wales), and to consider how CZM may contribute to the integrated management of monuments in coastal areas. The paper focuses on the use of non-statutory management plans because such plans seem likely to play a central role in CZM and, consequently, in establishing the climate necessary for integrated management of monuments at the coast. The paper indicates some ways in which guidance relating to management plans can be read creatively to facilitate policies for integrated management of monuments. It also considers some policies which have already been introduced which present useful precedents from which to progress.

CZM has been defined as:

"A process by which a co-ordinated strategy is developed and implemented for the allocation of environmental, socio-cultural and institutional resources to achieve the conservation and sustainable multiple use of the coastal zone".
(CAMPNET, quoted in House of Commons Environment Committee 1992, para. 116)

CZM is of considerable relevance to the management of monuments at the coast because of the holistic outlook of CZM, the focus on integration, the appreciation of the dynamic interaction between natural and cultural processes, and the explicit concern for sustainability. Although CZM is not a new concept it has had an escalating impact on the way that individuals, agencies, developers and authorities are involved in the treatment of the coast.

Spatially, this paper adopts the understanding of the coast expressed by the House of Commons Environment Committee:

"We agree that the coastline should not be seen as a physical or administrative boundary, but that the coastal zone should be treated as one integrated unit, embracing inshore water, intertidal areas and maritime land".
(House of Commons Environment Committee 1992, para. 17)

It is worth noting that the range of archaeological material found in inshore waters, intertidal areas and maritime land is not limited to the remains of maritime activities. Although a predominance of material which had some connection with the sea might be expected, material which has no apparent connection with the sea may now be found in or close to the coast as a result of sea level change (see Darvill, 1987: 54-59). CZM applies equally to maritime and non-maritime monuments.

The recent increase of interest in CZM coincides with, and has contributed to, the re-emergence of coastal and underwater archaeology as matters of interest to the wider archaeological community. Other factors which appear to be contributing to increasing interest in coastal archaeology among both archaeologists and non-archaeologists include recognition of specific pressures affecting coastal archaeology, realisation that a focus on the coast may facilitate integration of the archaeology of the sea with the archaeology of terrestrial communities which made use of the sea, and an awareness of the contribution that archaeology can make to other disciplines and debates concerned with the interaction between human activity and coastal environments.

Although a holistic philosophy is apparent in many practitioners, the impetus behind

CZM lies largely with nature conservation, recreation, engineering and oceanographic interests. Invisibility of archaeology in early discussion of CZM has not resulted in a total absence of provision for the subject, but interest in archaeology is still relatively marginal to other concerns. Consequently, agreeable interpretations conjured from ambiguous guidance and oblique precedents are not in themselves guaranteed to further the incorporation of archaeology within CZM. It appears that a change in perspective is required among planners, councillors, civil servants and ministers so that they recognise that integrated management of monuments is, on the one hand, a manifestation of the complexity of coastal environments in which humanity has played a major role in the past and, on the other, an opportunity to enhance understanding and appreciation of the coast in the present and in the future. The assumption underlying this paper is that such a change in perspective is most likely to be achieved by archaeologists co-operating with coastal managers to demonstrate practically the benefits that can be gained through the integrated management of monuments.

● Recent Developments in CZM

It is convenient to date the recent interest in CZM to the deliberations of the House of Commons Environment Committee which presented its report, *Coastal Zone Protection and Planning*, in March 1992. However, the pressures which led to the Committee's consideration of this topic had been accumulating for some time, not least among Non-Governmental Organisations. Research and reports presented by the Marine Conservation Society (MCS) and the World Wide Fund for Nature (WWFN) (Gubbay, 1990) and by the Royal Society for the Protection of Birds (RSPB) (Rothwell and Housden, 1990) appear to have been particularly influential. Equally, Government agencies such as the Nature Conservancy Council (now English Nature)

and the Countryside Commission had already engaged in a reappraisal of estuaries (Davidson *et al*, 1991) and Heritage Coasts (Countryside Commission, 1990) respectively. The Heritage Coast initiative emphasised the role of archaeology, which it recognised among its main objectives in the following terms:

"to conserve, protect and enhance the natural beauty of the coasts, including their terrestrial, littoral and marine flora and fauna, and their heritage features of architectural, historical and archaeological interest".
(Countryside Commission, 1991: 3)

These initiatives took place in the context of growing European Community interest in CZM, manifested in a Council Resolution on future Community policy concerning the European coastal zone (Council of the European Communities 1992 59/01) which referred to the cultural heritage as an integral element of the coastal environment (Firth, 1992: 113-114). Additionally, at a local level a number of local authorities were already introducing their own policies, strategies and management plans for the coast. Such policies appear to have had a considerable influence on the Environment Committee's deliberations (House of Commons Environment Committee 1992, para. 121).

The House of Commons Environment Committee Report set out approximately 50 conclusions and recommendations (House of Commons Environment Committee 1992, para. 7), including the formation of a National Coastal Zone Unit and of regional Coastal Zone Management Groups (House of Commons Environment Committee 1992, para. 35, 42, 131). It also suggested that the Government should try to harmonise landward and seaward planning control as far as the 12 nautical mile limit of territorial waters (House of Commons Environment Committee 1992, para. 52). The Committee also proposed that CZM be based on natural coastal cells of sediment transport (House of Commons Environment Committee 1992, para. 131) and that there should be a hierarchy of Coastal Zone Management Plans from the national to regional and local levels (House of Commons Environment Committee 1992, para. 125). The subordinate position of archaeology in CZM is apparent in the House of Commons Environment Committee Report as although the Committee received over 80 submissions of written evidence and heard oral evidence from 15 groups of witnesses (House of Commons Environment Committee 1992, para. 9), none of the evidence is identifiable as being principally concerned with archaeology.

The Government responded to the House of Commons Environment Committee Report in July 1992 (Department of the Environment, 1992b), stating that it was not persuaded that the extension of local authority planning powers below low water was *"necessarily the most effective approach"* (Department of the Environment 1992b, para. 38). The Response placed considerable emphasis on preparation of coastal management plans, particularly for estuaries, but the Government did not accept that management plans should be prepared as a hierarchy from national to local plans (Department of the Environment 1992b, para. 44-47). Similarly, the Government did not accept that there was a need for a national coastal unit, or for increased competence for existing regional coastal groups (Department of the Environment 1992b, para. 79). Instead, the Government proposed that local planning authorities should take the lead in preparing management plans, in conjunction with other interests (Department of the Environment 1992b, para. 45). Notwithstanding the lack of reference to archaeology in the House of Commons Environment Committee Report, the Government's Response identified damage to archaeological conservation interests as an important theme for coastal management plans (Department of the Environment 1992b, para. 46). The Government also accepted the need for consistent application of consent

procedures for marine industries and for improved application of Environmental Assessment (EA) in coastal areas, raising the possibility of more consistent consideration of archaeology in advance of marine developments (Department of the Environment 1992b, para. 71).

Shortly afterwards, new planning guidance was set out in *PPG 20: Coastal Planning* (DoE/WO, 1992), following a draft available for consultation in the spring of 1992. The final version included consistent reference to historic landscapes, and it acknowledged that the coastal zone has a rich heritage both above **and below** low water mark (DoE/WO 1992, para. 2.8). PPG 20 included references to PPG 16 but the implication of this juxtaposition was unclear, as PPG 16 sets out the Secretary of State's policy for archaeology **on land** (DoE 1990, para. 1). PPG 20 indicates that development plans are to include policies for all elements of the coastal zone, as well as policies for the protection of historic landscapes and archaeological sites and monuments (DoE/WO 1992, para. 4.5). While PPG 20 confirms that decisions on development proposals are generally outside the scope of the planning process, local planning authorities are required to take the offshore impacts of onshore developments into account when making planning decisions (DoE/WO 1992, para. 1.8-1.9).

The autumn of 1993 saw a renewed burst of publication relating to CZM. The Ministry of Agriculture, Fisheries and Food published guidance on flooding and coastal defence in September 1993 (MAFF, 1993). In October 1993 English Nature produced detailed guidance relating to the preparation of Estuary Management Plans (English Nature 1993d, 1993e) as part of a wider strategy under the heading *"Campaign for a Living Coast"*, which also included initiatives on coastal and marine conservation (English Nature 1992, 1993a, 1993b). In early October, the Department of the Environment and Welsh Office published a consultation paper on implementation of the Habitats Directive, of particular relevance to the designation of areas below low water mark (DoE/WO, 1993a). Two further discussion documents were published jointly by the Department of the Environment and the Welsh Office to satisfy commitments made in the Government's Response to the House of Commons Environment Committee Report of July 1992, namely *Managing the Coast* (DoE/WO, 1993b) and *Development Below Low Water Mark* (DoE/WO, 1993c). In addition, research commissioned from Rendell Geotechnics by the Department of the Environment into Planning Policy for the Coast was published in late November 1993 (DoE, 1993a), presenting important background information on current management of the coast. The progressive role of a number of local authorities in CZM was also made clear in the course of 1993 by the publication of *Coastal Planning and Management: A Good Practice Guide* by the National Coastal and Estuaries Advisory Group (NCEAG, 1993). The implications of these recent publications are considered below.

● Management Plans

Management plans have been defined in relation to Areas of Outstanding Natural Beauty (AONBs) as:

"an advisory document that is prepared by, or on behalf of, all those organisations or individuals with a management role within the AONB, which establishes common aims and objectives of management based on a strategic view of the whole area within a wider planning context, and which recommends area-based proposals that will guide and stimulate management actions towards the achievement of these objectives".
(Countryside Commission/Countryside Commission for Wales, 1992: 4)

The definition has relevance more generally if "AONB" is replaced by "coast", "estuary" or "Heritage Coast", as appropriate. In addition, there are other types of management plans which are relevant to the coast, but which are not discussed here.

For example, Shoreline Management Plans address erosion and flooding (DoE, 1993: 34-35), and Catchment Management Plans are being developed by the National Rivers Authority (NRA) for rivers, their estuaries and adjacent coastal waters (DoE/WO 1993b, para. 3.17).

Managing the Coast gives further details of the intention of coastal management plans:

"Coastal management plans need to build on, complement and inform existing strategic initiatives to plan and manage the coastal zone. They should not replace the statutory powers and rights of existing bodies. Rather they provide a framework for improved co-operation and understanding. Used constructively, they have the potential to improve the speed and effectiveness of existing decision-making procedures".
(DoE/WO 1993b, para. 3.8)

It appears that coastal management plans are expected to serve as a milieu within which existing authorities may continue to carry out their traditional responsibilities. Coastal management plans can be expected to shape results by refining decision-making, by encouraging a strategic outlook and by facilitating concerted use of a wide range of coastal management tools. Consequently, coastal management plans present an appropriate means of deliberating and pursuing policies for the integrated management of monuments.

● Coastal Management Plans and Statutory Development Plans

The relationship between coastal management plans and statutory plans is indicated in PPG 20, which states:

"For estuaries and parts of the open coast, local planning authorities and other agencies and interest groups may co-operate to prepare estuary or coastal management plans... The management plan should be taken into account in preparing and reviewing

development plans".
(DoE/WO 1992, para. 4.17)

The incorporation of coastal management plan policies for archaeology in statutory development plans is supported by PPG 12 which refers to *"sustaining the character and diversity of... undeveloped coasts"* and *"giving high priority to conserving the built and archaeological heritage"* as priorities indicating the range of environmental issues that need to be taken into account in development plan preparation (DoE 1992a, para 6.5-6.6). The joint Countryside Commission/English Heritage/English Nature publication *Conservation Issues in Strategic Plans* provides tacit support for integration of archaeology with other coastal conservation issues by discussing the coast as a specific environment in relation to strategic integration, regional and structure plans (Countryside Commission/English Heritage/English Nature, 1993: 22, 33, 59).

Overall, there are strong grounds for translating policies in coastal management plans into development plan policies where they will acquire statutory force. Northumberland presents an example of such translation in Policy L6 of the *Northumberland County Structure Plan: Draft for Consultation* which states:

"Development within the coastal zone should be consistent with the management objectives and policies contained in the Northumberland Coast Management Plan".
(Northumberland County Council, 1992: 12)

Although the majority of such policies may focus on development control, there is scope for introducing general policies relating to management of monuments. The draft *Strategy for the East Sussex Coast* illustrates a relationship between management plans and statutory plans which is not limited to development control, as the purpose of the Strategy is stated as follows:

"to present the views of the County Council on many pressing issues and, following discussions

and consultations among all coastal interests, to provide a comprehensive framework for the planning and management of the East Sussex coast and an input into the review of the Structure Plan and more detailed local plans and management plans".
(East Sussex County Council, 1992: 1)

East Sussex County Council also states its intention to adopt Heritage Coast objectives in the planning and management of the undeveloped coast, to complete the review of the existing Heritage Coast Management Plan, and to consult and work with District Councils in preparing management plans and in carrying out their proposals (East Sussex County Council, 1992: 24), indicating strongly that Heritage Coast and other coastal management plans will play a significant role in informing the County Council's statutory plans on a range of issues additional to development control.

Although coastal management plans are linked to statutory plans, the link is not binding, which is both a strength and a weakness. On the positive side, management plans are not limited to the planning process; the Northumberland Coast Plan, for example, is free to state a plan policy which falls outside the definition of development and largely beyond the boundaries of planning jurisdiction: *"It is Plan policy to... formulate guidelines on correct conservation practice relating to underwater historic remains"* (Northumberland County Council, 1991: 28-29). On the negative side, implementation of non-development policies lacks statutory support, as highlighted in the Department of the Environment/Rendell Geotechnics publication of November 1993:

"...management plans can be complemented by appropriate land use policies within development plans... [but] There is... no statutory equivalent to the development control process for ensuring that coastal

activities are in accordance with management plan policies".
(DoE, 1993a: 167-168)

This deficiency may be countered to some extent through the application of coastal management plan policies to sectoral consent procedures, through reform of coastal bye-law powers, and through self-regulation.

● Sectoral control of marine development

The Government confirmed that it would not extend the terrestrial planning system seawards in the document *Development Below Low Water*, where it stated a clear preference for sectoral (industry-by-industry) control of marine development by licensing authorities in central Government (notably MAFF, Department of Transport, Department of Trade and Industry, and the Welsh Office) and, in some cases, by harbour authorities. These central and local authorities often have environmental duties, including duties with respect to archaeology, in carrying out their marine functions, but it is not clear whether they will take account of coastal management plans in considering licences for activities in or adjacent to areas of coast for which management plans have been prepared. The Government's stated commitment to environmental protection and to consultation with conservation agencies and local authorities in sectoral consent procedures (DoE/WO 1993c, para. 2.3) suggests that coastal management plans will be taken into account, but there appears to have been no explicit undertaking to this effect.

Consultation in the course of a licence application is, like other forms of development control, quite a reactive approach to monument management. Hampshire County Council presented an example of a more pro-active approach to managing maritime archaeological sites when it stated its intention to *"seek the assistance of harbour authorities in ensuring that important sites are not damaged"*

(Hampshire County Council, 1991: 42). Coastal management plans may provide an appropriate means of addressing similar policies to central Government departments. For example, a policy might be phrased as follows: *"the County Council will seek the assistance of the Department of Transport, the Department of the Environment and MAFF in ensuring that the present and future management of important coastal sites receives adequate consideration".* Such a policy could be used to initiate a dialogue with the licensing authorities which might result in early avoidance of sensitive areas or the adoption of specific arrangements for licence applications in the area of the coastal management plan.

● Reform of coastal bye-law making powers

The Government, in its Response to the Report of the House of Commons Environment Committee, accepted that the benefits of coastal management plans may be undermined by lack of statutory support, noting that:

"...the Government recognises that there is a case for considering whether the effective management of the coastal zone would be enhanced by some extension of local authority powers".
(DoE/WO 1993b, para. 49)

The meaning of this comment was made clear in *Managing the Coast* where the Government indicated that it would reform local authority bye-law making powers. The document suggests that coastal bye-law powers could in future be used for environmental purposes *"such as the conservation of flora, fauna, landscape and heritage features"* (DoE/WO 1993b, para. 8.5). The need to standardise the area over which bye-laws can be applied was considered and the distance of 1000 metres seaward of the local authority boundary was suggested for discussion. The Government stated that bye-law powers would not apply where they duplicate existing legislation, but one implication is that bye-laws could be used to bring the level of control over various conservation interests up to a common level, which might be expected to facilitate integrated management of monuments. The reform of bye-law making powers is still under discussion but it would appear that bye-laws could play a significant role in implementing coastal management plan policies concerned with matters outside of the planning system.

● Self-regulation

In certain respects the use of management plans represents a more discursive approach to management compared to the use of statutes and development control, placing considerable emphasis on co-operation between all relevant parties at all stages of plan preparation and implementation. Increased communication and understanding might be expected to lead to greater voluntary compliance, so the weaknesses in the powers available to support coastal management plan policies need not limit the effectiveness of implementation. In *Managing the Coast*, the Government makes it clear that it considers voluntary compliance to be a vital element of coastal management (DoE/WO 1993b, para. 6.8.-6.11) and coastal management plans are considered to play an important role in establishing the necessary framework:

"The Government emphasises the importance of management plans being developed where they are needed, at a scale where they can best address real problems and in ways which build cost-effectively on existing structures and responsibilities. One of the key benefits of coastal management plans can be the development of networks linking different parts of the public and private sectors, or different interests on the coast. Improved understanding and communication is in many cases as important as the development of formal policies, enabling an effective continuing response to changing circumstances and new issues".
(DoE/WO 1993b, para. 3.23)

"The Government believes it must be for those locally responsible for the preparation of management plans to settle the details of their content. The key must be that content reflects issues and problems relevant to the area covered and the interests of the many users of the coastal zone..."
(DoE/WO 1993b, para. 4.1)

The *Position Statement of Issues for the Heritage Coast Management Plan of North Yorkshire and Cleveland* indicates how the matter of voluntary compliance can be introduced in practice:

"These issues need to be supported by the promotion of public awareness of the importance and vulnerability of the coast's archaeological resource and the part that everyone needs to play in its preservation. There still remains much scope for the dissemination of the conservation message supported by interpretation of a representative sample of monuments".
(North Yorkshire and Cleveland Heritage Coast Steering Group, 1993: 25)

In this case the promotion of public awareness through interpretation, which is a desirable aim in itself, is seen to play an integral role in supporting the implementation of the management plan.

● The Process of Coastal Management Plan Preparation

The reflexive character of coastal management plans evident in the quotations from *Managing the Coast* requires that their use be regarded as a process rather than as preparation of a final product. English Nature's guidance on Estuary Management Plans (EMPs) supports this perspective as the *Co-ordinator's Guide* (English Nature, 1993e) takes the reader step-by-step from plan initiation, through production of a preparatory document, repeated consultation and decision-making to implementation, monitoring and review. The document goes into considerable detail and might usefully be adopted as a model for other forms of coastal management plans.

The *Co-ordinator's Guide* emphasises the role of the organisational structure which underlies the EMP process, presenting some insight into how integrated management of monuments might be encouraged at an institutional level. Identification of management agencies and the formation of committees, including "Topic Groups" are among the early steps of initiating the Estuary Management Plan process (English Nature, 1993e: 17-21). Local authorities and agencies such as the National Rivers Authority, MAFF and English Nature are identified among the organisations likely to have an active interest in the management plan, but neither English Heritage nor any bodies with specifically archaeological or historical interests are mentioned in the *Co-ordinator's Guide* at this stage. "Archaeology and Heritage" is, however, identified as a specific Topic Group, along with "Landscape" and "Nature Conservation". Topic Groups are defined as activity-related committees comprising representatives of organisations, clubs, societies and so on, presenting these bodies with a formalised channel for representation and consultation (English Nature, 1993e: 20). Regular contact between Topic Groups is to be conducted in an Estuary Forum, which would seem to be an appropriate venue at which to pursue questions of integrated management of monuments.

Identification of issues and resolution of conflicts are seen as integral components of the EMP process. The *Co-ordinator's Guide* emphasises the use of matrices to recognise conflicts between different activities, and to identify the impact of estuarine activities on the environment (English Nature, 1993e: 44-45). Although the emphasis of the *Co-ordinator's Guide* is on identifying conflicts between various issues, it also points out that matrices can be used to identify positive or beneficial interactions. The use of matrices is pursued in more detail in *Environmental Appraisal of Development*

Plans (DoE, 1993b). Both documents focus the use of matrices on interactions between conservation and potentially damaging activities; little attention is given to the use of matrices in analysing interactions among conservation topics (for example, between archaeology and landscape), or between conservation and related use (for example, between archaeology and public access). It would appear that matrix analyses could be applied to identify unanticipated conflicts as well as beneficial interactions within conservation, greatly facilitating the development of policies for integrated management of monuments.

● Sources of Poor Integration

The use of tools to encourage integration is necessary because although CZM attempts to be integrative by virtue of its holistic character, clear integration is not always apparent in either guidance or the management plans themselves. Although archaeological monuments will benefit unintentionally from some coastal conservation policies, such as presumptions against development in areas of "unspoilt" coast, other conservation policies relating to managed retreat, to redevelopment of derelict coastal land and to removal of "eyesores", for example, may generate conflict between landscape, wildlife and archaeological interests. In addition to conflicts, poor appreciation of the human temporal dimension of the coast among those responsible for CZM is likely to lead to missed opportunities for appreciation and understanding.

In many cases the language of guidance relating to CZM is inimical to integrated management; there are many references to the coast as having a predominantly natural and physical character, with references to the influence of humanity only in terms of **current** impacts and risks. PPG 20, for example, frequently implies that the coastal environment of England and Wales is essentially "natural", and repeats the visual preoccupations which often characterise planning documents (e.g. DoE/WO 1992, para. 2.22-2.25, 3.3-3.4). Other documents, such as *Development Below Low Water*, militate against integration by maintaining an ambiguity as to whether archaeology is considered to be an integral (rather than an optional) component of the coastal environment (e.g. DoE/WO 1993c, para. 9).

In coastal management plans, archaeology often appears to be treated as a parallel consideration to other conservation concerns, notably wildlife and landscape, running along side and never touching. For example, documents such as a *Strategy for Hampshire's Coast* (Hampshire County Council, 1991), the *Position Statement of Issues of the North Yorkshire and Cleveland Heritage Coast Management Plan* (North Yorkshire and Cleveland Heritage Coast Steering Group, 1993) and the *Northumberland Coast Management Plan* (Northumberland County Council, 1991) have separate sub-sections under the general heading of conservation for archaeology/historic sites and for landscape, wildlife, woodlands, geology and so on. Although in many cases the policies described are similar or mutually supportive, or there are integrated site-specific policies (see below), there is no immediate and general attempt to deal with them collectively, as befits a unitary environment.

The *Sussex Heritage Coast Management Plan* (in contrast to the draft *Strategy for the East Sussex Coast*, see below) presents an example of apparent lack of integration between conservation and related interests in that "Conservation" is considered under a separate heading to "Recreation and Visitor Services" and to "Information and Interpretation" (East Sussex County Council [County Planning Officer]/The Sussex Downs Officer, 1993). Recreation, visitor services, information and interpretation are of obvious importance to integrated management of monuments, so it is unfortunate that they are held apart by the structure of the plan.

● Improving Integration

Separation of environmental concerns in coastal management plan policies is, to some extent, a requirement of the level of analysis that management plans require, and it might be argued that the various interests are integrated when programmes and projects are formulated. This cannot be assumed, however, so it might be suggested that the approach to integration should be stated explicitly within the coastal management plan. The following examples illustrate a number of ways in which integration has been pursued.

The *North Kent Marshes Study* presents a good example of how disintegration arises from analysis, and of how it can be dealt with. The Study involved assessment of 11 topics, including "Landscape" and "Nature Conservation" as well as "Historic and Cultural Resources", which were studied in relative isolation to produce topic papers. The topic papers were integrated through the Consultants' Final Report which noted that *"the integration of issues and recommendations to resolve.. conflicts is fundamental to this study"* (Kent County Council/AERC Ltd., 1992: 6). The apparent success of this process is evident in one of the proposals of the Consultants' Final Report:

"Liaison should be established to identify sites with both archaeological and wildlife interest, which could be designated as 'reserves' where active management policies should be pursued".
(Kent County Council/AERC Ltd., 1992: 105)

A different approach to integration in the course of implementation is apparent in the *Northumberland Coast Plan*. The approach used is to complement the separate consideration of each relevant topic, noted as a source of poor integration above, with Area Proposals in which the various topics are considered together. For instance, a management priority for the area from

Beadnell Bay to Seaton Point is stated as follows:

"Develop information and interpretation facilities in the south of the zone to provide an introduction to the geological features of the area, to the history of the whinstone industry and to its natural variety".
(Northumberland County Council, 1991: 52)

The draft *Strategy for the East Sussex Coast* also focuses integration through reference to specific areas, but this is in support of a more general policy which recognises the importance of integration among conservation interests and of integration between conservation and related interests, namely training, education and recreation. In the draft Strategy, the County Council states that it will:

"Work with public and other organisations to develop means of protecting, interpreting and managing underwater archaeological sites, including training and education, and to link these with recreational and wildlife interests. Priority will be given to the existing Voluntary Marine Conservation Area off Seven Sisters and the Rye Bay area from Hastings eastwards".
(East Sussex County Council, 1992: 16)

English Nature's proposed management plan for Lundy encourages integration by addressing it as a principle consideration. The plan also demonstrates how integration can be pursued in the cascade from objectives to projects:

*"**Objective 9:** To integrate the nature conservation and archaeological interests".*

*"**Rationale:** The conservation of the island's archaeological resource is a high priority. There is a need to assess the conflict and common ground between archaeological and nature conservation interests and manage these accordingly".*

*"**Policy Development:** English Nature will liaise with relevant archaeological bodies, and*

other interested bodies, to discuss relevant issues".
(English Nature, 1993c: 40)

*"**Policy 9.1:** To consider an integrated policy towards nature conservation and archaeological features".*

*"**Project 9.1.1:** Investigate the importance of the wrecks around Lundy to nature conservation".*

*"**Project 9.1.2:** Establish contact with relevant archaeologists to discuss reconciling the management of both nature conservation and archaeological features both in the MNR (wrecks) and SSSI (monuments)".*
(English Nature, 1993c: 50)

MAFF's *Strategy for Flood and Coastal Defence in England and Wales* approaches integration at the level of definition. In contrast to the ambiguity of some of the Government's guidance, the Strategy presents a model of inherent integration of conservation issues by referring to the environment in the glossary as follows:

"where environmental issues are referred to this term is used to encompass landscape/natural beauty, flora, fauna or geomorphological features and buildings, sites and objects of archaeological, architectural or historic interest".
(MAFF, 1993: 35)

Explicit reference in strategies, plans and guidance to the approach to integration which will be adopted is important because it demonstrates the presence of an integrative perspective. This perspective might be expected to persist within an institution, facilitating an integrative approach to matters beyond the document in which the approach is set out. The initiative of the Government's conservation agencies on *Conservation Issues in Strategic Plans* (Countryside Commission, English Heritage and English Nature, 1993) might be expected to increase the incidence of this type of perspective in future.

Conclusion

The development of CZM presents considerable opportunities for dealing with monuments as an integral element of the coastal environment. The holistic approach of CZM suggests frameworks for monument management which allow for integration on several planes, including the inter-relationship between humanity and its environment in the past, the combination of cultural and natural factors in the preservation of monuments, the contribution of monuments to habitats and the countryside, appreciation of the complexities of today's environment and its dynamics, and public enjoyment of the coast.

This paper has surveyed recent developments and documentation relating to CZM. Although archaeology has not received uniform or unambiguous attention so far, neither has it been omitted entirely and the indications are that it will be included consistently in future. Several examples of coastal management plans which refer to archaeology were considered in the paper, presenting models which might be adopted in encouraging further integrated management of monuments. Currently, coastal management plans have little statutory support, but a combination of development plan policies, consultation in the course of sectoral licensing, self-regulation and bye-laws can be expected to contribute to the implementation of coastal management plan policies.

One area of difficulty is where the analytical structure of coastal management plans divides archaeology from other aspects of conservation, and conservation from other topics, notably recreation and education. Techniques for examining interactions between coastal interests, including various types of matrix analysis, present opportunities to isolate unanticipated conflicts between archaeology and other conservation interests. Matrices may also be of use in recognising and encouraging positive interactions among conservation interests, and between conservation and other topics.

It is important that coastal management plans should be considered in terms of the process through which they are prepared, rather than as isolated documents. Such processes have organisational consequences, reflecting the departure from traditional approaches to terrestrial and marine management that CZM represents. Although the Government rejected most suggestions for changing the structure of coastal management, the dynamics of CZM are such that conceptual and institutional frameworks will have to evolve to cope with changes that are already occurring. Archaeology must have a role in such changes, not for its own sake but because CZM's approach to the coastal environment will be flawed if archaeology is not included. Although we might expect all those involved in CZM, irrespective of their principal discipline, to collaborate in the inclusion of archaeology, archaeologists bear much of the responsibility for encouraging and directing the integration which is required.

Acknowledgements

The author would like to thank David O'Regan for collating many of the management plans used in the preparation of this paper, and for his comments on earlier drafts. The paper was prepared in the course of doctoral research into the management of archaeology underwater in the Faculty of Law and the Department of Archaeology of the University of Southampton, supported by a studentship from the Economic and Social Research Council.

References

Coastal Area Management and Planning Network (CAMPNET). (1989) *The Status of Integrated Coastal Zone Management.* Rosential School of Marine Science, University of Miami, Florida. Quoted in,

House of Commons Environment Committee, March 1992, *Coastal Zone Protection and Planning*. 1, para. 116.

Countryside Commission. (1990) *Heritage Coast Policies and Priorities: Draft Policy Statement*. Cheltenham: Countryside Commission.

Countryside Commission. (1991) *Heritage Coasts in England: Policies and Priorities 1991*. CCP 305. Cheltenham: Countryside Commission.

Countryside Commission/Countryside Council for Wales. (1992) *AONB Management Plans: Advice on their Format and Content*. CCP 352. Cheltenham: Countryside Commission.

Countryside Commission/English Heritage/English Nature. (1993) *Conservation Issues in Strategic Plans*. CCP 420. Northampton: Countryside Commission.

Council of the European Communities. (1992) *Council Resolution of 25 February 1992 on the Future Community Policy Concerning the European Coastal Zone*. OJ 92/C 59/01. Brussels: Commission of the European Communities.

Darvill, T. (1987) *Ancient Monuments in the Countryside: An Archaeological Management Review*. Archaeological Report No.5. London: Historic Monuments and Buildings Commission for England.

Davidson, N.C., Laffoley, D., Doody, J.P., Way, L.S., Gordon, J., Key, R., Drake, C.M., Pienkowski, M.W., Mitchell, R. and Duff, K.L. (1991) *Nature Conservation and Estuaries in Great Britain*. Peterborough: Nature Conservancy Council.

Department of the Environment. (1990) *Planning Policy Guidance: Archaeology and Planning (PPG 16)*. London: HMSO.

Department of the Environment. (1992) *Planning Policy Guidance: Development Plans and Regional Planning Guidance (PPG 12)*. London: HMSO.

Department of the Environment. (1992) *Coastal Zone Protection and Planning: The Government's Response to the Second Report from the House of Commons Select Committee on the Environment*. London: HMSO.

Department of the Environment/Welsh Office (1992) *Planning Policy Guidance: Coastal Planning (PPG 20)*. London: HMSO.

Department of the Environment. (1993a) *Coastal Planning and Management: A Review*. London: HMSO.

Department of the Environment, (1993b), *Environmental Appraisal of Development Plans: A Good Practice Guide*. London: HMSO.

Department of the Environment/Welsh Office. (1993a) *Implementation in Great Britain of the Council Directive on the Conservation of Natural Habitats and of Wild Fauna and Flora (92/43/EEC) - "The Habitats Directive": Consultation Paper*. Bristol: Department of the Environment (Directorate of Rural Affairs).

Department of the Environment/Welsh Office. (1993b) *Managing the Coast: A Review of Coastal Management Plans in England and Wales and the Powers Supporting them*. Bristol: Department of the Environment (Directorate of Rural Affairs).

Department of the Environment/Welsh Office. (1993c) *Development Below Low Water Mark: A Review of Regulation in England and Wales*. Bristol: Department of the Environment (Directorate of Rural Affairs).

East Sussex County Council, County Planning Department. (1992) *A Strategy for the East Sussex Coast: Draft*. Lewes: East Sussex County Council.

East Sussex County Council (County Planning Officer)/The Sussex Downs Officer. (1993) *Sussex Heritage Coast Management Plan: Report*. Lewes: East Sussex County Council.

English Nature (1992) *Coastal Zone Conservation: English Nature's Rationale. Objectives and Practical Recommendations.* Peterborough: English Nature.

English Nature. (1993a) *Conserving England's Marine Heritage: A Strategy.* Peterborough: English Nature.

English Nature. (1993b) *Managing England's Marine Wildlife: Draft.* Peterborough: English Nature.

English Nature. (1993c) *Managing Lundy's Wildlife: A Management Plan for the Marine Nature Reserve and Site of Special Scientific Interest - Consultation Draft.* Okehampton: English Nature.

English Nature. (1993d) *Strategy for the Sustainable Use of England's Estuaries.* Peterborough: English Nature.

English Nature. (1993e) *Estuary Management Plans: A Co-ordinator's Guide.* Peterborough: English Nature.

Firth, A. J. (1992) The Past in the Coastal Environment: European Perspectives. *Papers and Proceedings: The Regional Coastal Groups - After the House of Commons Report* Newport (Isle of Wight): Standing Conference on Problems Associated with the Coastline (SCOPAC).

Gubbay, S. (1990) *A Future for the Coast? Proposals for a UK Coastal Zone Management Plan.* Ross-on-Wye: Marine Conservation Society, World Wildlife Fund.

Hampshire County Council. (1992) *A Strategy for Hampshire's Coast.* Winchester: Hampshire County Council.

House of Commons Environment Committee. (1992) *Coastal Zone Protection and Planning.* 1. London: HMSO.

Kent County Council/Applied Environmental Research Centre Ltd. (1992) *North Kent Marshes Study Consultants Final Report.* Maidstone: Kent County Council Planning Department.

Ministry of Agriculture Fisheries and Food/Welsh Office. (1993) *Strategy for Flood and Coastal Defence in England and Wales.* London: MAFF.

National Coasts and Estuaries Advisory Group. (1993) *Coastal Planning and Management: A Good Practice Guide.* London: NCEAG (ACC - ADC - AMA).

Northumberland County Council. (1991) *Northumberland Coast Management Plan: Consultation Draft.* Morpeth: Northumberland County Council.

Northumberland County Council. (1992) *Northumberland County Structure Plan: Draft for Consultation.* Morpeth: Northumberland County Council.

North Yorkshire and Cleveland Heritage Coast Steering Group. (1993) *Management Plan Second Review: Position Statement of Issues, 2nd Draft.* Helmsley: North Yorkshire and Cleveland Heritage Coast Steering Group.

Rothwell, P. I., and Housden, S. D. (1990) *Turning the Tide: A Future for Estuaries.* Sandy: RSPB.

Royal Society for the Protection of Birds. (1993) *A Shore Future: RSPB Vision for the Coast.* Sandy: RSPB

Royal Society for the Protection of Birds. (1993) *Making the Coast Count: Strategic Planning and Management on the North-west Coast.* Sandy: RSPB.

The Role of the *Protection of Wrecks Act 1973* in Integrated Management of the Marine Archaeological Heritage: A Personal View

Ian Oxley

Archaeological Diving Unit, University of St. Andrews

● Introduction

This paper examines the role of the *Protection of Wrecks Act 1973*, one of the mechanisms available to protect and conserve one part of the archaeological resource, namely shipwrecks. 1993 saw the twentieth year of the implementation of the Act and it is useful to examine its success, or otherwise, against a background of the protection and conservation of the underwater cultural heritage of the UK as a whole. There is no specific system for managing and protecting all of the underwater cultural heritage so it is appropriate to discuss the ways in which the various statutory and voluntary measures which are available can be effectively combined.

Although the 1973 Act can be seen to have shortcomings (both in coverage and implementation) it does encompass provisions that could be of importance to cultural and natural heritage managers responsible for marine environments. These possibilities will be discussed in this paper using examples of integrated cultural resource management initiatives from overseas. It is appropriate to stress that the views expressed here are solely those of the author and not the Archaeological Diving Unit or any other organisation involved in the current or past implementation of the 1973 Act.

● Background

The management of the underwater cultural heritage is undergoing a period of rapid change and the current situation could be characterised by limited knowledge of the overall resource set against a background of increasing exploitation and increasing threat. Archaeological sites submerged under UK territorial waters can quite legally be disturbed or destroyed unless they are specifically protected. Not only do we not know what sites are out there, we do not know their significance, or the nature of potential threats against them. In addition, in comparison with their terrestrial equivalents, relatively little is known about underwater ecosystems and habitats and the ways in which archaeological remains interact with them.

The two most significant pieces of legislation affecting archaeology underwater in the UK are the *Protection of Wrecks Act 1973* (which concerns the protection of sites) and Part IX of the *Merchant Shipping Acts of 1894* (which deals with the ownership of wreck material). To date no completely submerged sites have been scheduled under the *Ancient Monuments and Archaeological Areas Act 1979* although there is provision to do so.

● *The Protection of Wrecks Act 1973*

The objectives of the 1973 Act have been defined by the Government as:

"...to ensure that wrecks of historical, archaeological or artistic importance in United Kingdom territorial waters are protected from unauthorised interference and that only competent and properly equipped people

survey and excavate such sites" (Department of Transport, 1986).

The 1973 Act applies to United Kingdom waters and the seabed submerged at high water of ordinary spring tides. UK waters are defined as any part of the sea (including estuaries, "arms of the sea" and any part of a river within the ebb and flow of ordinary spring tides) within the seaward limit of territorial waters (normally 12 nautical miles) (Firth, 1993: 69). Government is empowered to make designation orders which identify the site of the wrecked vessel and the extent of the "restricted area" around it. Within this area it is an offence to carry out activities which can be broadly defined as diving or salvage operations; or to deposit anything which will obliterate or obstruct access to the site, or damage the wreck; or tampering with, damaging or removing any part of the wrecked vessel or anything contained in it, unless under licence.

The 1973 Act owes its origins to improvements in diving equipment in the late 1960s and early 1970s which led to a rapid growth of sport diving and a consequent increase in underwater exploration and the discovery of many new wreck sites. Many of these wrecks were exploited for "treasure" and salvors fought over the right to exploit them at the expense of their historical and archaeological value. The ensuing widespread destruction caused archaeologists, historians and sympathetic divers to lobby for a change in the *Merchant Shipping Act of 1894*. Its provisions were unsuitable for dealing with the problem of increasing public access to historic wrecks, in fact it was encouraging destructive activity by requiring wreck material to be raised for reporting (Dromgoole, 1989). The outcry resulted in the *Protection of Wrecks Act 1973* which was introduced as a temporary measure to prevent the destruction of a small number of sites whilst the more general legal problems were solved. However, because laws generally take a long time to introduce, amend or repeal, no

improvement in the legislative coverage of the marine archaeological resource (and in particular shipwrecks) was forthcoming and the 1973 Act was allowed to become the central, and virtually the only, active component of this area of territorial responsibility throughout the following decades (A. Firth, pers. comm.).

● Relationship of the 1973 and 1894 Acts

Inadequacies of the 1894 Act in the management of the cultural heritage included:

● Problems with the control of access to historic wrecks as no restrictions were imposed on salvors recovering what they could, using whatever methods they chose;

● Receivers of Wreck had no resources to store materials recovered from the sea in a way which prevented deterioration;

● Salvors were not obliged to keep records (other than a list of recoveries) which clearly encouraged the loss of potentially valuable archaeological and historical data as well as objects (i.e. those considered by the salvors to be unworthy of preservation);

● The disposal of material was required in order to raise funds to cover the Receiver's costs;

● There were no controls to prevent objects of great historical/archaeological value being sold off indiscriminately;

● The museum/archaeological community had no prior knowledge of what was being found and lacked resources to take any responsibility for historic wreck sites.

The Government's view, however, was given as:

"In order to encourage the recovery and disclosure of items of historic interest, the present practice it (sic) *to dispose of items in such a way as to leave a reasonable amount*

Table 1. List of designated Historic Shipwreck Sites as of November 1994. Numbers relate to Figure 1.

Number	Name	Date	Type	Location
1	Cattewater wreck	1500-1550	armed merchantman?	Plymouth
2	*Mary Rose*	1545	warship	Solent
3	*Grace Dieu*	1439	warship	Hamble River
4	*Amsterdam*	1749	Dutch East Indiaman	Hastings
5	*Mary*	1675	Royal Yacht	Anglesey
6	*Assurance/Pomone*	1738/1811	warships	Isle of Wight
7	*Anne*	1690	warship	Near Hastings
8	Tearing Ledge	1707	warship	Isles of Scilly
9	Rill Cove	early 17th C	armed merchantman?	Lizard
10	South Edinburgh Channel	late 18th C	merchantman	Thames Estuary
11	Church Rocks	16th C	warship?	Teignmouth
12	Pwll Fanog	medieval	slate carrier?	Menai Strait
13	Moor Sand	c. 1000BC	artefact scatter	Salcombe
14	*Coronation* (inshore)	1691	warship	Plymouth
15	*Kennemerland*	1664	Dutch East Indiaman	Shetland
16	Langdon Bay	c.1100BC	artefact scatter	Dover
17	Tal-y-Bont	1600-1650	armed merchantman?	Barmouth
18	*Stirling Castle*	1703	warship	Kent
19	*Invincible*	1758	warship	Solent
20	Bartholomew Ledge	16th C	armed merchantman	Isles of Scilly
21	*Northumberland*	1703	warship	Kent
22	*Restoration*	1703	warship	Kent
23	*St. Anthony*	1527	merchantman	Lizard
24	*Schiedam*	1684	merchantman	Lizard
25	Brighton Marina	c.1600	warship?	Brighton
26	Yarmouth Roads	c.1600	armed merchantman	Isle of Wight
27	Studland Bay	c.1500	armed merchantman	Dorset
28	*Admiral Gardner*	1809	English East Indiaman	Kent
29	*Hazardous*	1706	warship	Bracklesham
30	*Coronation* (offshore)	1691	warship	Plymouth
31	*Iona II*	1864	paddle steamer	Lundy
32	Gull Rock	15/16th C	artefact scatter	Lundy
33	*Wrangels Palais*	1687	warship	Shetland
34	Erme Estuary	17-18th C	armed vessel	South Devon
35	The Smalls	c.1100AD	sword guard findspot	South Wales
36	Duart Point	1653	warship	Sound of Mull
37	*Dartmouth*	1690	warship	Sound of Mull
38	*Girona*	1588	warship	Ulster
39	*Royal Anne*	1721	warship	Lizard
40	Erme Ingot Site	unknown	artefact scatter	South Devon
41	Dunwich Bank	17th C	warship	Suffolk

for salvage" (Department of Transport, in Dean, 1988: 43).

Both Acts were at one time the responsibility of the Department of Trade (later the Department of Transport) because of their interests in navigation and shipping, rather than the Department of the Environment as an aspect of archaeology. Hence implementation of the Acts remained distant from the management of archaeology on land and from the Government's general archaeological policies (A. Firth, pers. comm.).

● Limitations of the 1973 Act

The 1973 Act provides a level of protection for one particular type of archaeological site, namely shipwrecks, and there are a number of factors to be considered relating to the history of the implementation of the Act and its interpretation which have significant bearing on its effectiveness as a protection measure:

● The scope of the 1973 Act is defined in terms of adequately assessing the archaeological, historical and artistic importance of **individual** wreck sites, and it is not restricted to sites dating to before any particular cut-off date;

● There are no established criteria for the assessment of importance, along the lines of those published by English Heritage to assist the management of the Monuments Protection Programme (Darvill et al, 1987); selection depends upon the reaction of the relevant Secretary of State to the advice or opinions of the Advisory Committee on Historic Wreck Sites and the Archaeological Diving Unit;

● There has been no provision (until recently) to assess the resource as a whole in order to manage it more effectively;

● The 1973 Act can only apply to specific sites with a known position because it relies upon the precise definition of a discrete

area of seabed (typically 50 - 300m) around this position to be protected. There is no provision for the designation of archaeological areas;

● Most of the wrecks protected under the 1973 Act are post-medieval warships or armed merchantmen (Table 1), and the distribution is biased towards frequently dived areas of the south and south-western coasts (Figure 1). The wrecks represent the more easily located sites containing readily recognised cannon or anchors, or are sites for which there were existing documentary records of location and significance;

● The 1973 Act has principally relied upon recreational divers and other finders choosing to come forward with their discoveries. Subsequently, (until 1986 and the advent of the Archaeological Diving Unit) they were largely left to their own devices and the archaeological standards that they were able to attain were often low;

● There have been difficulties in enforcement of the 1973 Act (which were recognised at its inception) but it was felt that the vigilance of the locally based Receivers of Wreck, the diving fraternity and the local community would provide a reliable safeguard (Dromgoole, 1989a). However, the diving community has remained largely ignorant of the 1973 Act and at a local level there is a widespread lack of awareness of its existence and provisions;

● Until recently no resources were provided for locating new sites and no assistance is available to help licensees satisfy licence conditions (e.g. support for acquiring access to archaeological expertise or advice).

The effectiveness of the 1973 Act can be assessed in the light of the number and nature of sites which are currently protected under the Act. After more than twenty years there are only 41 designated Historic Shipwreck Sites (4 in the territorial waters of Scotland, 4 in Wales, 32 in England and 1 in Northern Ireland) (refer

Figure 1). The relationship of their
distribution to actual ship losses in these
countries, or the levels of maritime activity
in the past, is unclear but evidence suggests
that the correlation is poor. The true extent
of the archaeological resource is largely
unknown but the current situation can be
extrapolated from documentary sources
such as fishermen's data on net fastenings,
wreck maps and recreational diver guides to
wreck sites. It has been estimated that up to
500,000 wreck sites lie within British waters
and the Royal Commission on the Historical
Monuments of England initiative to record
maritime sites is expected to include
between 30,000 and 50,000 sites in the
territorial waters of England alone in its first
three years (B. Ferrari, pers. comm.).

● The Advisory Committee on Historic Wreck Sites

Throughout the implementation of the
1973 Act the Government sought the
opinions of the Advisory Committee on
Historic Wreck Sites (ACHWS), a non-
statutory body with a membership made up
of individuals belonging to interest groups
such as museums, the Hydrographic Office
of the Ministry of Defence, and the British
Sub Aqua Club. Only in 1986, with the
contracting of the Archaeological Diving
Unit, did the Government gain access to
consistent professional advice based directly
upon archaeological evaluations of
protected sites and licensed investigations.
Confidence in the 1973 Act and the
ACHWS has not been encouraged by the
lack of change of membership of the
Committee in more than twenty years
(particularly in the representation of
archaeological interests) and that all its
dealings are confidential. In addition, it has
been common (and the situation still exists)
for members of the ACHWS to be issued
licences to investigate designated sites, and
to be appointed archaeological
advisors/directors of designated sites,
thereby creating potential conflicts of
interest.

Figure 1. Map of UK designated
Historic Shipwreck Sites as of
November 1994, also showing the
limit of UK Territorial Waters.

● The Archaeological Diving Unit

In 1986, the Department of Transport and
the Secretary of State's Advisory
Committee on Historic Wreck Sites had
recognised that for the past thirteen years
they had been relying solely on the
evidence produced by prospective licensees

when considering applications for designation. In addition, when assessing the work of existing licensees they had been limited to considering the submitted reports of those licensees. There was no independent, objective assessment available.

The ADU currently provides field archaeological data on the existing designated Historic Wreck Sites and new sites proposed for designation to the ACHWS. The ADU can also provide informed archaeological advice on any aspect of archaeological work in the marine zone and the Unit has taken on an increasing role in commenting on development proposals in the marine zone (e.g. Environmental Statements and scoping documents). In addition the ADU is co-operating with the Institute of Field Archaeologists in the production of guidelines on the assessment of the marine archaeological resource (Oxley, 1995). The ADU has consistently maintained a role in the development of archaeology underwater from being involved in the production of guidelines (Dean, 1988; NAS, 1992), through participation in development of training schemes in nautical archaeology (such as the Nautical Archaeology Society Certification Scheme as described in NAS 1992), to promoting an integrated approach to heritage management, whether natural or cultural. Developments in archaeological diving procedures have also benefited from the ADU's position as the only archaeologists working within the full *Diving Operations at Work Regulations 1981* (as amended) without the benefit of exemption certificates.

● The Role of Government

In 1989, the Department of Transport was the only Ministry with responsibilities for archaeology underwater. A transfer of responsibility to the Department of Environment, which had general responsibility for archaeology and also the planning process in England, was a principal recommendation of *Heritage at Sea* - a

review of the situation, and a series of recommendations to Government, produced by the Joint Nautical Archaeology Policy Committee in 1989 (JNAPC, 1989). In April 1991, responsibility for the *Protection of Wrecks Act 1973* was transferred to the Department of the Environment and its administration in Scotland, Wales and Northern Ireland was devolved simultaneously to Historic Scotland, to Cadw: Welsh Historic Monuments, and to the Historic Monuments and Buildings Branch (DoE, NI) respectively. Significantly, responsibility for the *Merchant Shipping Act 1894* remained with the Department of Transport, and responsibility for the 1973 Act in England remained within the Department of the Environment, rather than being transferred to English Heritage. This meant that whilst in Scotland, Wales and Northern Ireland archaeology underwater was administered by professional archaeologists, and effectively integrated with the management of archaeology on land, in England the situation was much as before. This has continued through a further reorganisation in April 1992 when the Department of National Heritage was formed from elements of the Department of the Environment. Further discussion of the development of legislation relating to wrecks and other underwater archaeological remains can be found in a number of sources (Dromgoole, 1989a and 1989b; Firth, 1993; Spoerry, 1993).

● The Role of the 1973 Act in Integrated Management

The 1973 Act contains some very useful provisions which could be used to considerable effect within an overall scheme of archaeological management, particularly as the extent of the restricted area is whatever the Secretary of State deems appropriate to ensure protection of the wreck and to facilitate enforcement. On designated sites all investigation is prohibited except under the authority of a licence issued by the statutory heritage body of the country concerned on behalf of the appropriate Secretary of State. Such licences are granted (subject to annual renewal) to named individuals and they can include specific conditions. Application procedures for licences require information about research design, resources and equipment, conservation, archiving and publication, and the submission of an annual report to the Advisory Committee on Historic Wreck Sites (ACHWS). Licensees must arrange for an archaeological advisor or director to oversee work on the site unless they are judged as being qualified to carry out this role themselves.

A further potential advantage is that although the Secretary of State is charged with consulting with such persons as he/she considers appropriate before making a designation order, this consultation may be dispensed with in a case of urgency. The 1973 Act can therefore be effective in providing emergency protection to a threatened site.

● Integrated Resource Management

The nature of the burial environment of a site clearly plays a fundamental role in determining what evidence survives, in what form and in what position. In this respect the interests of the archaeological community coincide with those of natural heritage managers. Certain specific conditions will promote the survival of particular material types. Studying the nature and impact of the environment on a site is vital to understanding the quality of the evidence that is eventually recovered. The physical environment of a site also dictates the techniques and methods that will be most effective throughout the archaeological investigation, from the initial survey stage to the post-excavation analysis and the determination of the most effective conservation treatments for any archaeological materials that may be recovered (Oxley, 1992).

In recent years, site environmental studies have been recognised as a fundamental part of effective management of the underwater cultural resource in many parts of the world. However, the inclusion of an assessment of the natural and burial environment in underwater archaeological investigation has not been adopted universally in the United Kingdom and it is in this area that co-operation with natural resource managers could be most beneficial. The factors which have caused archaeological materials to be generally better preserved in underwater environments (the effects of anaerobic organisms as opposed to the influence of the aerobic fungi, bacteria and insects of land archaeological environments) need to be better understood (Oxley, 1994).

Site environmental assessments should form a fundamental part of any cultural resource management (CRM) scheme, as such evaluations provide the basis for achieving a better understanding of the site and its formation, and indicate ways in which it can be better managed and preserved for the benefit of future generations. Strategies such as the taking of baseline information, followed by periodic monitoring, form a fundamental part of the management plans for underwater heritage parks in many parts of the world.

The policy enshrined in the *Guidelines for the Management of Archaeological Resources in the Canadian Parks Service* produced by the Canadian parks authorities to deal with archaeological remains within their park boundaries, is a good example of integrated CRM:

"The first step in applying CRM Policy to archaeological resources is to undertake surveys of lands and waters under CPS (Canadian Parks Service) administration to inventory and record in situ resources.... Beyond this stage, other stages of treatment of the archaeological resource will be determined by a weighting of such factors as national/regional/local importance, research significance, interpretative potential,

accessibility, vulnerability to natural or human impacts and the presence of valued ecosystem elements and valued natural resources"(Environment Canada, 1993: 3)

One of the reasons for the poor and uneven record of considering the environment of underwater archaeological sites is the lack of clear and tested methodologies in evaluation techniques, particularly the identification of actual or potential threats. For example, which physical, chemical or biological factors should be measured and how often? What are the important individual environmental parameters (the single characteristic of the total environment that can be measured by an objective methodology such as pH or temperature)? What are the important interactions between parameters or components (such as degradation or preservative processes)?

CRM strategies from overseas can provide pointers. One example is the investigation of the USS *Arizona*, one of the battleships sunk at Pearl Harbour, which represents a major landmark in site assessment studies as no-one had previously confronted the problem of developing a long-term preservation program for a whole ship *in situ*. The United States' National Parks Service (NPS) programme for the site included collecting a baseline inventory of biological communities on the structure of the 600 foot battleship which would help determine the particular biochemical processes causing an impact on the vessel's fabric. Stations around the vessel were also established to enable quantified measurements of the state of deterioration of structural elements to be collected at periodic intervals (Lenihan *et al*, 1989).

A second example from the National Parks Service demonstrates the benefits of comprehensive, multi-disciplinary assessments of the underwater cultural resource on an area basis. The National Parks system contains 356 areas of which at least 60 have significant submerged resources. The publication of the *Dry Tortugas National Park Submerged Cultural Resources Assessment* demonstrates a commitment by the NPS to provide a firm foundation for the future research and stewardship of the archaeological resources of the park. In addition, as the Foreword points out (Lenihan in Murphy, 1993: xxiii), the study demonstrates the information returns from site descriptions and analyses undertaken without impact on the resources. These benefits can be compared to the meagre data returned by highly invasive treasure hunting activities conducted in the same area, thus helping to clarify the rationale behind the adamant rejection in NPS policy of the practice of antiquity harvesting for profit on public lands. The fieldwork strategy for the area was designed to produce a database which will aid long-term resource management decision-making. It is also stated that management should not be limited to site specific concerns, it should be cumulative to be cost-effective; should involve questions and scientists of numerous disciplines; and should be carried out with as little negative site and environmental impact as possible (Murphy, 1993).

In the UK important advances have been made in developing a management plan for the Marine Nature Reserve situated around the island of Lundy in the Bristol Channel (N.G.R. SS 140 460). The plan was produced by English Nature in co-operation with The Landmark Trust (who manage the island and the marine reserve) and Devon Sea Fisheries Committee (who regulate fisheries in the surrounding waters). Two sites designated under the *Protection of Wrecks Act 1973* lie within the Marine Nature Reserve boundaries and English Nature acknowledge the importance of integrating the management of the archaeological heritage with that of other heritage interests (English Nature, 1993a). Within the Lundy Marine Nature Reserve a zoning scheme has been adopted to show people where they can undertake activities with minimal impact on the wildlife or conflict with other users of the Reserve (English Nature, 1993b). The brochure detailing the scheme includes the restrictions for the two designated sites required under the 1973 Act.

Documents produced as part of the process of developing a management plan for the North Yorkshire and Cleveland Heritage Coast, published by the North Yorkshire and Cleveland Heritage Coast Steering Group, also give equal coverage to the archaeological heritage (North Yorkshire and Cleveland Heritage Coast Steering Group, 1993) and Issue 10 of *Heritage Coast* was devoted to coastal archaeology (Heritage Coast Forum, 1993).

● Preservation *in situ*

In recent years it has become apparent that particular attention needs to be paid to the management of wreck sites from the iron/steel era. These sites are relatively less well-preserved than wooden wrecks because of the deterioration of metals in seawater and they are more prone to impacts (they are larger and, as far as we know, more numerous; and better documentation exists about their nature and location). Therefore they are at greater risk from irresponsible divers, the impact of commercial fishing and developments such as mineral extraction. Again, the strong prohibitive provisions of the 1973 Act could be useful in this respect for suitable sites.

It is well known that artefact deterioration on site can be lessened by action based on an understanding of the chemical and physical processes of the marine environment (McCarthy, 1982). Significant work has been carried out in Australia on the measurement of the factors on which the corrosion of iron objects is dependent. On-site measurement of corrosion potentials together with the use of sacrificial anodes (to continually "treat" metal objects) has demonstrated the link between studies of the burial environments of wreck sites and the benefits of *in situ* conservation methods in cultural resource management (MacLeod, 1987; Brown *et al*, 1988; McCarthy, 1988).

An interesting aspect of assessing impact on the site of HMS *Pandora*, on the Great Barrier Reef in Australia, is the proposal to study the effects of any prior, archaeological "excavation-backfilling" cycles on the (deeper lying) hull remains and artefact assemblages of the wreck. The work would determine if such activities have altered the bacterial communities in the sediment leading to increased or decreased metabolic activity or changes in species composition. Additional studies are aimed at assessing whether the *status quo* is reached within a specific number of years after excavation/backfilling (Gesner, 1992).

● Site Stabilisation

Site stabilisation techniques are increasingly necessary to mitigate a threat which is unavoidable. Typical strategies employed on land, riverbanks or foreshores (for example the use of filter fabrics, mattresses and barrier layers) may be appropriate underwater, but little or no research or applications exist apart from protective measures applied to oilfield pipelines. It is salutary to note that in a major bibliography on site stabilisation references, there are virtually no references relating to underwater archaeological sites (Thorne, undated).

In underwater parks in Florida, site stabilisation strategies have been developed to encourage the deposition of protective sediment through the placement of artificial and natural seagrasses (Wild, 1984). Artificial seagrass has also been used successfully to inhibit sediment movement on the *William Salthouse* wreck in Victoria, Australia (Elliget and Breidahl, 1991).

● Encouraging Access to Underwater Sites

One of the most important aspects of any cultural resource management strategy must be that of encouraging the public to visit and have access to heritage sites, wherever possible. A number of innovative schemes have been established overseas, particularly under the auspices of national or state park authorities

In Israel, at Caesarea (the remains of the city and harbour built by King Herod the Great), an underwater park has been established together with procedures which enable visiting divers to explore much of the presently submerged site by following clearly marked guidelines made of plastic covered steel cables which run about half a metre above the seabed. Divers are issued with plasticised illustrated and annotated guidebooks and the scheme is managed with the co-operation of local dive shops. The dive shop, which assists in maintaining the lines and accompanying signs, also offers boat services and diving instructors (Raban, 1992: 27).

A pilot study was carried out in Western Australia at Rottnest Island which involved the marking of wrecks underwater with plaques, the placement of information panels on land close to the location of the site, and the provision of pamphlets describing the historical background to the sinking of the ships. There is an associated land trail, local museum exhibition and visits to some of the wrecks by glass-bottomed boat and lately by a semi-submersible. The ideas embedded in the Rottnest study influenced the addition of criteria for the protection of sites with educational and recreational value into the *Australian Historic Shipwreck Act 1976* (McCarthy, 1986: 136).

• Recent Improvements in the Implementation of the *Protection of Wrecks Act 1973*

In the UK, in recent years (particularly since the introduction of the Archaeological Diving Unit) there have been significant changes in the way in which sites designated under the *Protection of Wrecks Act 1973* have been managed, involving:

• Allowing controlled access to designated Historic Wreck Sites for survey work for purposes other than archaeological (e.g. marine biological studies on the *Coronation* site);

• The testing of procedures that may allow controlled access for recreational visits (e.g. on the Duart Point site: see Martin - this volume);

• Raising the standard of archaeological work through encouraging licenced teams to undertake training courses, in particular the Nautical Archaeology Society Certification Scheme (as described in NAS, 1992);

• The allowing of area survey and site prospection to be carried out by the Archaeological Diving Unit as part of their contractual duties to the Department of National Heritage.

One fundamental factor in the development of these initiatives has been the increasing involvement of the individual statutory heritage bodies for the separate countries of the UK (e.g. Historic Scotland, Cadw and DoE(NI)) in the implementation of the 1973 Act in their respective territorial waters.

• Conclusion

In the UK, the trend appears to be one of increasing development and exploitation of underwater environments and this clearly represents an increasingly, unquantified danger to the submerged archaeological heritage. Since there is little likelihood of a change in the 1973 Act until such time as there is a comprehensive overhaul of heritage legislation, our aim must be for more effective management of the marine archaeological heritage across all environments (and across all historically-derived boundaries). We must encourage a move away from underwater archaeology's preoccupation with wrecks at the expense of other types of archaeological site and we need to continue to lobby for reform of portable antiquities legislation to include material recovered from Territorial Waters, thus removing the treatment of archaeological finds from nineteenth century salvage laws. It is clearly anomalous that even finds from designated Historic Wreck Sites are still dealt with under such legislation.

Successful cultural resource management depends upon a combination of routine pre-disturbance survey and analysis of sites, widespread yet controlled public involvement and access to heritage sites, and increased public awareness and education. There is a great deal to be gained from encouraging the trend towards increasing the involvement of Non-Governmental Organisations (e.g. English Nature and the National Trust) and the voluntary sector (e.g. the Nautical Archaeology Society).

We need to lobby for a reappraisal of the anomalous situation with regard to English Heritage's position in relation to the marine archaeological heritage, and for a review of the administration of the 1973 Act to include increased involvement of other natural heritage interests and agencies. The effective management of the shipwreck heritage of the United Kingdom must be integrated with other heritage initiatives, whether related to the natural heritage, terrestrial archaeology or other cultural remains found underwater. Sustainable management of the marine archaeological resource for the benefit of present and future generations will rely on the co-operation and co-ordination of a wide range of institutions and organisations rather than proscriptive legislation which rapidly becomes dated and inappropriate.

● References

Brown, R., Bump, H., and Muncher, D.A. (1988) An *in situ* Method for Determining Decomposition Rates of Shipwrecks. *The International Journal of Nautical Archaeology*, 17.2. 143-145.

Darvill, T., Saunders, A. and Startin, D.W. (1987) A Question of National Importance: Approaches to the Evaluation of Ancient Monuments for the Monuments Protection Programme of England. *Antiquity*, 61. 393-408.

Dean, M. (1988) *Guidelines on Acceptable Standards in Underwater Archaeology*. Scottish Institute of Maritime Studies Development Association, University of St. Andrews.

Department of Transport (1986) *Historic Wrecks Guidance Note*. Department of Transport, Marine Directorate.

Dromgoole, S. (1989a) Protection of Historic Wreck: The UK approach. Part I: The Present Legal Framework. *International Journal of Estuarine and Coastal Law*, 4.1. 26-51.

Dromgoole, S. (1989b) Protection of Historic Wreck: The UK approach. Part II: Towards Reform. *International Journal of Estuarine and Coastal Law*, 4.2. 95-116.

Elliget, M. and Breidahl, H. (1993) *A Guide to the Wreck of the Barque* William Salthouse. Melbourne: Victoria Archaeological Survey.

English Nature (1993a) *Managing Lundy's Wildlife*. Consultation draft. Peterborough: English Nature.

English Nature (1993b) *Managing Lundy's Wildlife - Have Your Say! Management Proposals for the Marine Nature Reserve and Site of Special Scientific Interest*. Peterborough: English Nature.

Environment Canada. (1993) *Guidelines for the Management of Archaeological Resources in the Canadian Parks Service*. Ottawa: Environment Canada Parks Service.

Firth, A. (1993) The Management of Archaeology Underwater in, Hunter, J and Ralston, I. (eds) *Archaeological Resource Management in the UK: An Introduction*. Stroud: Alan Sutton Publishing and the Institute of Field Archaeologists.

Gesner, P. (1992) Raine Island Area
Shipwrecks Programme (Great Barrier Reef)
HMS *Pandora* (1791). *The International
Journal of Nautical Archaeology*, 21.3. 269-
270.

Heritage Coast Forum (1993) *Heritage
Coast, Coastal Archaeology*. Issue 10.
Heritage Coast Forum, The Manchester
Metropolitan University, St Augustine's,
Lower Chatham Street, Manchester M15
6BY.

JNAPC. (1989) *Heritage at Sea: Proposals for
the Better Protection of Archaeological Sites
Underwater*. Greenwich: Joint Nautical
Archaeology Society, National Maritime
Museum.

Lenihan, D.J., *et al.* (1989) *USS Arizona.
Memorial and Pearl Harbour National
Historic Landmark. Submerged Cultural
Resources Study*. Santa Fe, New Mexico:
South-west Cultural Resources Center
Professional Papers No.23.

MacLeod, I.D. (1987) Conservation of
Corroded Iron Artefacts - New Methods
for on-site Preservation and Cryogenic
Deconcreting. *The International Journal of
Nautical Archaeology*, 16.1. 49-56.

McCarthy, M. (1986) Protection of
Australia's Underwater Sites in, ICCROM,
1986 *Preventive Measures During Excavation
and Site Protection*. Rome: Proceedings of
the Ghent Conference 6-8/11/1985.
ICCROM.

McCarthy, M. (1988) SS *Xantho*: The pre-
disturbance Assessment, Excavation and
Management of an Iron Steam Shipwreck
off the Coast of Western Australia. *The
International Journal of Nautical Archaeology*
17.4. 339-347.

Murphy, L.E. (1993) *Dry Tortugas National
Park Submerged Cultural Resources
Assessment*. Santa Fe: Submerged Cultural
Resources Unit, National Parks Service. US
Department of the Interior.

NAS. (1992) *Archaeology Underwater: the
NAS Guide to Principles and Practice*. London:
Nautical Archaeology Society and
Archetype Press.

North Yorkshire and Cleveland Heritage
Coast Steering Group. (1993) *North
Yorkshire and Cleveland Heritage Coast
Management Plan: Second Review, Position
Statement of Issues*. North Yorkshire and
Cleveland Heritage Coast Steering Group,
c/o North York Moors National Park,
North Yorkshire County Council, The Old
Vicarage, Bondgate, Helmsley, York YO6
5BP.

Oxley, I. (1992) The Investigation of the
Factors Which Affect the Preservation of
Underwater Archaeological Sites in, Keith,
D.L. and Carrell, T.L. (eds) *Underwater
Archaeology Proceedings from the Society of
Historical Archaeology Conference*, Kingston,
Jamaica 1992. Tucson: The Society for
Historical Archaeology. 105-110.

Oxley, I. (1994) The Assessment of the
Environment of Archaeological Sites
Underwater in, *Science and Site*.
Bournemouth: Bournemouth University and
Archetype Press. In press.

Oxley, I. (1995) *The Marine Archaeological
Resource*. Birmingham: Institute of Field
Archaeologists. Technical Paper. In press

Raban, A. (1992) Archaeological Park for
Divers at Sebastos and Other Submerged
Remnants in Caesarea Maritima, Israel. *The
International Journal of Nautical Archaeology*,
21.1. 27-35.

Spoerry, P. (1993) *Archaeology and
Legislation in Britain*. Hertford: RESCUE, The
British Archaeological Trust.

Thorne, R.M. (undated) *Archaeological Site
Stabilisation Bibliography*. University, MS:
National Clearing House for Archaeological
Site Stabilisation, University of Mississippi.

Wild, K.S. (1984) The Legare Anchorage
Shipwreck Project: Data Retrieval and Site
Preservation in, Bream, J.W., *et al.* (eds) *In
Search of our Maritime Past: Proceedings of
the Fifteenth Conference on Underwater
Archaeology*, Williamsburg. Greenville, NC:
East Carolina University, .158-159.

Assessment, Stabilisation and Management of an Environmentally Threatened Seventeenth Century Shipwreck off Duart Point, Mull

Colin J.M. Martin

Scottish Institute of Maritime Studies, University of St. Andrews

● Introduction

Environments are the products of a wide range of interactive factors and inputs - physical, chemical, and biological. They normally function in a state of overall balance which, unless the mix of influences undergoes modification, tends to sustain itself. Change, if it occurs, is often a gradual response to shifts in the inputs. Whilst the cumulative effect on an environment of, say, a shifting climatic regime may be considerable, the environment will generally tend to undergo progressive alteration as the new inputs harmonise with the old. At no point will the underlying balance be lost, and such a situation may be characterised as change by continuous adjustment.

Environmental change can also, however, be precipitated by a cataclysmic re-ordering of the inputs, as might (for instance) be the consequence of a major seismic event. By its nature such change is dynamic and unbalanced, and whilst the disrupted environment will once again trend towards harmony the new balance may be very different from the old, and the move from the one to the other is likely to be characterised by complex and often violent processes of adjustment.

A shipwreck tends to be cataclysmic both for the human beings involved in the disaster and for the seabed environment within which it takes place. The ordered entity which a ship represents, with its watertight and stable hull, means of propulsion and direction, management regimes, social structures, and specialist functions, normally begins an irreversible progression of disordering at the moment of wrecking. The seabed upon which the ship has impacted will, at the same time, have received a destabilising anomaly likely to trigger a range of responses as the disrupted environment seeks to regain its former state of balance.

In a simplistic sense it is the wreck and not its surroundings that are of consequence to the archaeologist who is, after all, primarily interested in the ship and its contents as expressions of the human past. But unless he/she takes account of the environment within which it lies, and seeks to understand the mechanisms of destruction, dispersal, integration and stabilisation with which the relevant area of sea floor has reacted to the intrusion of the wreck, he/she will be unable to interpret the observed remains in archaeological terms. It will be impossible to work backwards, as it were, through the wrecking process, and so draw conclusions about the ship before it became a wreck. For this reason alone the archaeological residues of a shipwreck cannot be separated from their environmental matrices: on the contrary the two elements must be regarded as inextricably related phenomena or, to use Frederic Dumas's felicitous phrase (Dumas, 1962: 29), as a single *"wreck formation"*.

No two wreck formations are identical, because the variables presented by the environment itself, the nature of the wrecked ship, and the circumstances of its loss, can lead to a virtually limitless number of consequences. At one end of the scale a vessel may survive almost intact, with most of its contents complete and *in situ*. At the other a ship may be broken up and dispersed, and its component parts reduced by mechanical, chemical, and biological degradation, to a point at which all trace of it effectively ceases to exist. In a majority of cases, however, wreck formations lie somewhere between these extremes, and in reaching a state of environmental balance they usually undergo two distinct evolutionary phases, the one dynamic and frequently very destructive and the other (more or less) static and benign.

The dynamic phase may be extremely violent and short-lived, as may happen when a ship strikes a reef in heavy seas and disintegrates in a matter of seconds. The wreck of the Dutch East Indiaman *Adelaar*, lost off the Outer Hebrides in 1728, is an instance of this (Martin, 1992). On the other hand it may, as in the case of a hull which has settled into a relatively benign environment, continue for many years or even centuries. Such a situation is illustrated by the disintegration and encapsulation of the *Mary Rose* in the Solent (Rule, 1982: 44-5). In both cases, however, the dynamic or unstable phase is characterised by the wreck's status as an environmental anomaly; it is unstable, it lacks integration with its surroundings, and it is prone to disintegration and dispersal by a variety of external influences.

Some of its components and contents, by virtue of their buoyancy, may simply float away. Tides, surge, currents, and wave action can induce movement which may result in the break-up of structures and the transport elsewhere of their fabric and contents. These effects will be enhanced or minimised by the geology and sedimentary covering of the sea bed on which the wreck lies, and its depth below the surface. The chemical composition and physical properties of the water, especially of sea water, and the amount of dissolved oxygen it contains, will cause reactions of various kinds, particularly to metals. Organic materials will be susceptible to the effects of water penetration, temperature, light, and biological attack. Seabed movement may cause mechanical degradation, while rock falls, the laying down and shifting of

sediments, and other processes of geomorphological evolution may further influence the dynamic phases of a wreck formation's development. Biological eco-systems will also play their parts - protectively, destructively, or both. Human activity focused on the wreck, such as salvage or intrusive archaeology, may be regarded as dynamic influences in the evolution of its formation, whilst the effects of constructional work, mineral extraction, the impact of fishing gear, dumping or even the intrusion of a later wreck are other possibilities to be taken into account. Finally, sea level change, geological upheaval, or land reclamation may in various ways influence the environment and hence the wreck formation.

Once the dynamic phase of a wreck's integration with the sea bed has been completed a static, or stabilised, state will normally follow. This can happen quickly, and perhaps with little change to the ship's status as an organised entity, as for example when a vessel sinks into and is encapsulated by a semi-fluid environment such as soft mud, which will provide stable anaerobic conditions. A broadly similar situation may obtain when a ship founders in mid ocean and arrives more or less intact on a deep sea floor where there is effectively no water movement, oxygen, or light (Bascom, 1976).

On the other hand the dynamic phase may be short-lived but so violent that much of the vessel's substance and most of its coherence is lost by the time stability is achieved. The structure of the hull may disintegrate rapidly, releasing its contents, which either fall to the sea bed or float away according to buoyancy. Pieces of the hull, if of wood, are also prone to dispersal and loss by flotation. If, as is likely in such circumstances, the sea bed is uneven, the distribution of heavy objects which fall upon it may further be influenced by its topography and drawn towards gully bottoms where they may become trapped and stabilised. Such a wreck formation will almost invariably be fragmentary, jumbled up, and perhaps dispersed over a wide area.

The situation may be complicated further if the ship, or parts of it, moves over considerable distances whilst breaking up; here a number of apparently disparate sub-formations, each perhaps further dispersed by subsequent influences, may be encountered.

When a static or balanced environmental stage is reached the processes of wreck formation are complete and the remains of the ship, however much they may have been reduced, spread about, and scrambled during the dynamic phase, now lie in harmony with their surroundings and resist further change. Such, at any rate, is the theory; in practice, of course, the processes of decay and change never entirely cease. But, given a state of relatively stable environmental balance, the rate and degree of change can slow down to an extent at which, in human terms at any rate, it has

effectively stopped. The violent dislocation and dispersal which may have occurred within a matter of seconds during the dynamic phase are replaced in the static one by gradual and often scarcely perceptible changes over a time scale to be measured in centuries or even millennia. However difficult it may be to determine in a philosophical sense the precise moment at which this metamorphosis takes place, the distinction between the two phases is, so far as the archaeologist is concerned, clear enough. An environmentally balanced wreck site may therefore, unless it is threatened by external interference such as excavation or gravel extraction, be regarded as archaeologically secure. The best management option for such a site would normally be to leave it alone. Only compelling cultural imperatives, backed by a full suite of appropriate archaeological, conservational, curatorial, and financial

Figure 1. The Duart Point shipwreck: general site plan, 1994.

base of cliff

0   10

metres

resources, would justify intrusive archaeology of any kind.

In many cases, however, a static wreck formation can revert to the dynamic state, and indeed the phases often fluctuate according to the shifting balance of environmental factors which affect a particular site, or discrete areas within it. Such reversions, by their nature, are likely to have a destructive effect on the archaeological content, and therefore give rise to complex management problems. How can the destabilising factors be recognised and quantified, and their likely effects assessed? Can the instability be reversed or mitigated? Under what circumstances might rescue excavation be regarded as a management option? And, if excavation does take place, what effects might this have on adjacent stable areas?

• The Wreck off Duart Point

All of these problems have arisen in the management of an historic wreck in the Sound of Mull, off the west coast of Scotland. The site was discovered close to Duart Point (N.G.R. NM 748 355) in 1979 by John Dadd, a naval diving instructor whose duties had brought him to the area. Dadd made some recoveries during this and subsequent visits, but was unable to undertake extensive work. In 1991, anxious that his discovery should be investigated more thoroughly, he reported it to the Archaeological Diving Unit (ADU) at St. Andrews University, whose contractual duties to the Government in connection with the *1973 Protection of Wrecks Act* include the support of Historic Scotland (the national regulatory authority) in matters relating to historic shipwrecks in Scottish waters. A visit to the site that summer confirmed the presence of an historic wreck, and evidence was obtained which, together with Dadd's finds, suggested a mid-seventeenth century date. On this basis the ADU recommended that the site should be designated as a Protected Wreck.

Subsequent research has convincingly identified the ship concerned as one of three lost in a storm on 13 September 1653 during an expedition to Mull by a small Cromwellian task-force (Martin, 1994).

The site lies at the base of a rock face which slopes at about 45 degrees from the Point, and the wreck material lies on and is contained within a seabed of gravely sand, silts, and some intrusive rocks, at depths ranging (at low water) from *c.* 8m to *c.* 9.5m (Figure 1). There is a maximum tidal range of *c.* 4.5m. The general environment of the site, as indicated by its biological regimes, may be categorised as including mid-energy and moderately high-energy zones (Erwin and Picton, 1987: 13-15). A tidal set of up to 1.5 knots, which runs only on the ebb, flows from west to east across the site.

The visible remains comprise seven heavily concreted cast-iron guns of up to 2.5m in length, a small iron anchor, various iron concretions and concretion complexes, two distinct piles of stone ballast, and considerable quantities of wholly or partially exposed organic material, including elements of articulated structure. A number of human bones were noted. A further monitoring visit by the ADU in 1992 revealed extensive destabilisation of the site, exacerbated by (though evidently not caused by) its independent discovery a few weeks earlier by members of the Dumfries and Galloway Branch of the Scottish Sub-Aqua Club, shortly before the designation order came into effect. The Club had raised a number of exposed artefacts, including elements of carved wooden decoration, a badly-corroded hoard of silver coins, a grindstone, various organic objects, and the brass lock-plate of a snaphaunce pistol. This material was subsequently deposited with the National Museum of Scotland in Edinburgh, where it is currently undergoing conservation treatment.

In the opinion of the ADU's director, Martin Dean, the destabilised material demanded immediate rescue action if it was not to be degraded or lost. A rapid survey assessment

Plate 1. Organic material exposed on the wreck site in 1992. Elements of ship structure appear on the right, whilst the partially unburied cherub shows barnacle infestation indicative of progressive exposure from the upper right. In the centre foreground is a small stave-built vessel, whilst between it and the cherub lies a human ulna. Photograph: ADU/Kit Watson

was therefore made, and the positions of 83 items recorded before they were packaged and raised. This operation was carried out with the support of staff and students from the Scottish Institute of Maritime Studies, with archaeologists and conservators from the National Museum of Scotland in attendance. The material has been declared in favour of the National Museum, in whose care it now rests.

The cause of the site's destabilisation, and its future prognosis, is still unclear. Various suggestions have been considered: the introduction of larger ferries on the Oban-Craignure run, which pass close to the site hourly during the summer months; seismic activity (the site lies directly on the Great Glen Fault, and there have been significant episodes in its immediate proximity during recent years); and intrusion by divers. All are possibilities, individually or in concert.

A programme is now in hand to investigate environmental factors affecting the site, mitigate potentially destructive processes, and set in place an effective management strategy. This is being conducted by the writer under licence from Historic Scotland. Occasional visits over the winter of 1992-3 revealed the exposure of rich but vulnerable organic deposits which were consolidated, on a temporary basis, by laying down gravel aggregate. A four-week season in August 1993 saw the beginnings of a full survey of the site and its environs. This involves contouring of the sea bed at 0.25m intervals, a detailed mapping of both natural and archaeological features, and a biological zoning which should indicate water energy levels at different parts of the site. Geological, sedimentological, and water-movement data are being collected, whilst biological and chemical effects on various classes of material are being examined by David Gregory of Leicester University as part of a Ph.D investigation (Gregory, 1995).

In 1994 a study of the corrosion potential of *in situ* iron objects was conducted by Dr Ian MacLeod of the Western Australian Maritime Museum (MacLeod, 1995). Observation at a fairly basic level has already shown biological activity to have a wide range of effects on the degradation of those parts of the wreck that have recently been uncovered. Boring macro-fauna quickly attack exposed organic material, particularly wood. This activity, exacerbated by mechanical abrasion caused by water-transported sediments, is extremely destructive. Such infestation, however, halts if the affected material becomes re-buried,

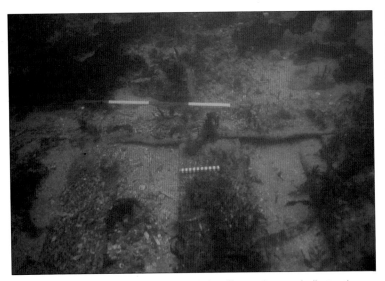

Plate 2. Abraded ship's timbers showing, on the right, colonisation by young *Laminaria hyperboria*. The longer scale is 1m.

from its upper edge, and the age of the oldest individuals (six months), gives a progressive and chronologically quantifiable record of sediment removal at this part of the site.

An area of exposed remains of timber hull structure provided firm evidence of cyclical uncovering and re-burial (Plate 2). Extensive abrasion and biological activity had removed much of the upper substance of the wood - a process which indicates a cumulative exposure of many years, or even centuries. A similar process was noted on the hull remains of the *Dartmouth*, a small warship lost only some 5km from the Duart wreck in 1690 (Martin, 1978). It was clear that these abraded remains had been in a buried state during the comparatively recent past, since their surfaces were in the process of being colonised by juvenile plants of *Laminaria hyperboria*, for which the degraded but hard surface of the wood provided good adhesion for holdfasts. No adult plants were present. The under-parts of the exposed timbers were being actively exploited by scavenging fauna, mainly crabs,

though its effect and extent indicates the cycle of destabilisation that has taken place. Another sensitive indicator, this time of exposure in active commission, was provided by the carving of a cherub which was progressively being colonised by barnacles (*Balanus crenatus*) as the silts in which it had been encapsulated were removed (Plate 1). The differential intensity of colonisation across the object advancing

Plate 3. A hand-built Hebridean pot of *craggan* type to which a kelp plant has attached its holdfast. Scale in cm.

which found among them rich opportunities for burrowing.

Timber objects, once displaced, move freely across the site, trending eastwards with the run of the tide. The recognition of abraded fragments of wood as far as 250m downtide of the wreck suggests that a considerable quantity of material has recently been lost in this way. Heavier objects are less prone to such displacement, but not immune from it. An example is provided by a large piece of pottery, representing about half a complete vessel, which had been dragged off the site by the fronds of a kelp plant which had become established on its surface (Plate 3). Differential infestation by barnacles on the pot's surface indicates that it had emerged relatively recently from a buried context, so exposing itself to colonisation by the kelp plant which, when its fronds reached sufficient size, acted as water-sails in the running tide.

A further indication of complex dislocating and re-burial mechanisms operating on this site was provided by the following sequence of observations. In October 1992, an eroded area which contained exposed organic material was consolidated by the application of sterile gravel. A month later a clay pipe of mid seventeenth century date was noted partially buried within the gravel. This demonstrated that wreck material is capable not only of displacement and transport, but also of integration into fresh environmental contexts. It follows that contextual associations and stratigraphical sequences underwater may not always be what they seem.

Random observations of the kind noted above indicate the effects, not the causes, of localised destabilisation. An opportunity to observe a specific destabilising event occurred during the second highest spring tide of the year (tidal range at Oban = 4.2m) on 20 August 1993, and the three days that followed. The high tidal range, with its concomitant increase of tidal flow during the ebb, coincided with a north to north-westerly wind which rarely dropped

below Force 4 and frequently reached Force 5 or 6 for the next three days. By p.m. on the 23rd it was gusting occasionally to 7. During Low Water on 21 August it was observed that waves breaking on the shallow western end of Duart Bay, west of the site, were displacing considerable quantities of sand, which discoloured the water up to 500m from the shore. At the start of the ebb tide this discoloured water

moved eastwards in a distinctive line, reaching the wreck site about an hour after slack water.

Divers on site at the time noted a sudden and severe drop in visibility, from c. 8m to c. 2m, coupled with observable surface transport of sand across the site. They also commented on the exposure of previously unseen organic material on the up-slope (i.e. shoreward) side of the wreck, particularly towards its eastern end. The next pair of divers found that a substantial area of organic wreckage, about 4 square metres, had been uncovered. The material, which included fine panelling and part of a wooden lantern, was generally of a condition which suggested that this was its first exposure since incorporation within its

Plate 4. Freshly exposed organic material photographed on 22 August 1993. The eroded timber at the top left has evidently been exposed for some time, but the pieces of edge-moulded panelling below it, and the partially obscured circular object (probably part of a wooden lantern), are in a condition which indicates that they have been buried since their primary deposition shortly after the wrecking event. Note, however, the faunal infestation on the left-hand timber, and the clearly defined line at which it stops, which is indicative of the limit of a previous exposure episode. Scale in cm.

Plate 5. A single skin of sandbags in place over the eroding organic deposits.

contained within. The main deposit appears to cover some 4 by 6 metres, though there are some indications that it continues **under** the rock tumble, which suggests that the latter derives from a post-depositional episode. General observation suggests that the deposit may be of considerable depth, possibly in excess of 1m in places, although because of the fragile nature of what it probably contains probing was not attempted.

environmental matrix, although some areas close to the pre-exposure surface supported colonies of juvenile barnacles which indicated previous, though probably quite recent, exposure (Plate 4).

These observations confirm that the greatest area of instability lies within a broad gully which runs up towards the shore at the eastern end of the site. It is filled, in its upper part, with large tumbled boulders. At the foot of this tumble is a steep sandy deposit, and it is this deposit which is shifting to reveal the organic material

The morphology of this gully, with its natural sediment slope, may have been responsible for the initial deposition, subsequent preservation, and current erosion of the organic deposit. The northerly wind of 23 August generated a considerable swell which, no doubt, caused a strong surge when the weight of piled-up water is forced down into the gully (the adverse conditions precluded diving to investigate). This effect may have been exacerbated by the unusually strong tidal stream, as discussed above. In turn this may have influenced sediment transportation, removal, and deposition. A comparable situation, though on a larger scale, has been observed on the wreck site of *El Gran Grifon*, the Armada ship wrecked off Fair Isle (Martin, 1983: 176-81).

Plate 6. A turned wooden bowl (diameter = 12cm) from an exposed organic context which shows four distinct episodes of partial uncovering and damage. The latest, represented by a clean break and the fresh colour of the granular structure, is evidently very recent.

The nature of this deposit, and the active environmental threat to its integrity and survival which has now been demonstrated, gives considerable cause for concern. As an interim measure a single skin of sandbags, covering some 30 square metres, has been laid on top of it (Plate 5), and similar protection has been applied to the abraded areas of hull structure described above. Monitoring visits over the winter of 1993-4 have, up to the time of writing (January 1994), indicated that the measure has generally been successful, although the sandbags themselves are tending to trigger new erosion beyond their downtide edges. On one occasion this revealed a small organic deposit, from which some rescue recoveries were made before it was consolidated with further sandbagging. One of the recovered objects, a turned wooden bowl, shows biological and mechanical damage which indicated that it had undergone at least four distinct episodes of partial destabilisation since its primary deposition (Plate 6).

It may be that the only realistic response to the active instability of this deposit's environment is rescue excavation, though at the time of writing no firm decision on the matter had been reached. However, the established viability of techniques to control erosion in the short term means that excavation, if considered appropriate, can be managed in such a way as to ensure that it is conducted to full research standards. This wreck may indeed provide a test-bed for the development of management strategies which may be of value in similar cases.

● Conclusion

The value of the site as an indicator of wreck formation processes in a dynamic phase of activity has already been stressed. This will have implications for a more general understanding of shipwreck archaeology as well as being crucial to the interpretation of this particular example. Its historical and cultural importance is also considerable. The Cromwellian period in

Scotland is not richly represented in the material heritage, and the site undoubtedly represents a major archaeological discovery of relevance to naval, military, technological and social studies. On any reckoning the Duart shipwreck is a significant, if vulnerable, resource.

● References

Bascom, W. (1976) *Deep Water, Ancient Ships*. London.

Dumas, F. (1962) *Deep-water Archaeology*. London.

Erwin, D. and Picton, B. (1987) *Guide to Inshore Marine Life*. London.

Gregory, D. (1995). Experiments into the Deterioration Characteristics of Materials on the Duart Point Wreck Site: An Interim Report. *International journal of Nautical Archaeology, 24*.

MacLeod, I.D. (1995). *In Situ* Corrosion Studies on the Duart Point Wreck, 1994. *International Journal of Nautical Archaeology, 24*.

Martin, C.J.M. (1978) The *Dartmouth*, a British Frigate Wrecked off Mull, 1690. 5. The Ship. *International Journal of Nautical Archaeology, 7*. 1: 29-58.

Martin, C.J.M. (1983) *The Equipment and Fighting Potential of the Spanish Armada*. Unpublished Ph.D thesis, University of St. Andrews.

Martin, C.J.M. (1992) The Wreck of the Dutch East Indiaman *Adelaar* off Barra in 1728. In, Mason, R. and Macdougall, N. (eds.), *People and Power in Scotland: Essays in Honour of T.C. Smout*. Edinburgh.145-169.

Martin, C.J.M. (1995) A Cromwellian Shipwreck off Duart Point, Mull: An Interim Report. *International Journal of Nautical Archaeology, 24*.

Rule, M. (1982) *The Mary Rose: The Excavation and Raising of Henry VIII's Flagship*. London.

Who's Who in the Environment?

© The Environment Council

Based on listings of the same name compiled by:

**The Environment Council
21 Elizabeth Street,
London.
SW1W 9RP.
Tel: 0171 824 8411
Fax: 0171 730 9941**

The Environment Council is a dedicated, independent charity. Through building awareness, dialogue, understanding and effective action The Environment Council strives to improve the quality and diversity of Britain's environment for present and future generations. Their independence means that they can serve as a fair and unbiased forum where different environment charities, Government and business interests can develop practical solutions to complex issues.

Their initiatives include:

Environmental Resolve: brings people together from communities, business, the voluntary sector and Government to find practical solutions that prevent and resolve environmental conflicts, using concensus building. As well as providing this mediatory service, Environmental Resolve runs a series of highly successful training courses in environmental dispute resolution and concensus building for decision makers in Government, business and the voluntary sector.

Business and Environment Schemes: help people at all levels in their workplace to understand environment and reduce the environmental impact of their activities. Through the **Business and Environment Programme** The Environment Council runs the largest network of professional Environment Managers in the world. The programme handbook and the range of fascinating leading edge seminars help managers to introduce sound environment policies and reduce the impact of their business on the environment. **Conservers at Work** helps people in the workplace to reduce the environmental impact of their daily work and make cost savings. There are already over 1000 Conservers at Work throughout Britain in commerce, Government and industry.

The Information Programme: The Environment Council's **Who's Who in the Environment** series is the definitive guide to British environment organisations. The directories are available for England, Scotland, Wales and Northern Ireland and are regularly updated. The directory for England is now available from The Environment Council, on subscription, on low density 3.5in, double-sided diskette in dBase III Plus format for IBM compatible PC (XT or above) and is recognised by many programs including dBase IV, FoxPro, Paradox and WordPerfect. The directory comes complete with its own reader program, enabling access and search facilities for those without use of the above-named databases.

● Acknowledgements

The editors gratefully acknowledge the enormous assistance provided by Rachel Adatia and Kate Aldous of The Environment Council in enabling the use of this listing and Sue Haygarth of the Heritage Group, Clwyd County Council for support in compilation and checking of the information contained therein.

● Disclaimer

Whilst the information contained within the following directory has been compiled from the range of Who's Who in the Environment directories provided by The Environment Council, any errors are those of the editors of this volume. Every effort has been taken to ensure that the information in this directory is correct. However, neither The Environment Council, the editors of this volume, nor Clwyd Archaeology Service, Clwyd County Council accept any responsibility for errors, nor any liability arising from the use of this directory. The listing of an organisation in this directory does not imply acceptance or endorsement of it or its activities by The Environment Council, the editors of this volume nor Clwyd Archaeology Service, Clwyd County Council.

● Cross-referencing

The directory has been partially cross-referenced to enable ease of use, using key subjects e.g. amphibians/reptiles, birds, caving, deer, etc. In such cases the cross-referencing leads users to all specialist bodies concerned with the key subject, but does not access those other agencies or statutory bodies with broad remits, for which the key subject is only one of many functions.

• Advisory Committee on Protection of the Sea

11 Dartmouth Street,
London.
SW1H 9BN.

Tel: 0171 799 3033
Fax: 0171 799 2933

The Committee promotes the preservation of the seas of the world from pollution by human activities; promotes and conducts research into the causes and effects of pollution of the seas including research into means whereby the injurious effects of such pollution may be affected or reduced. Skills training and consultancy service available.

• **Algae** SEE: British Phycological Society, The

• Amateur Entomologists' Society

4 Steep Close,
Green Street Green,
Orpington.
Kent.
BR6 6DS.

The Society is dedicated to the study and of practice of entomology by the junior and the amateur through publications, correspondence, field meetings and conservation work.

• **Amphibians/Reptiles** SEE:
British Herpetological Society
Herpetological Conservation Trust
Reptile Protection Trust

• Aquatic Sciences and Fisheries Information System

UK National Co-ordinating Input Centre,
MBA Laboratory,
Plymouth Marine Laboratory,
Citadel Hill,
Plymouth.
Devon.
PL1 2PB.
Tel: 01752 222772
Fax: 01752 226865

ASFIS is a UN system dealing with information relevant to the science, technology and management of the marine and freshwater environments, including their socio-economic and legal aspects.

• Association for the Protection of Rural Scotland

Gladstone's Land (3rd Floor),
483 Lawnmarket,
Edinburgh.
EH1 2NT.

Tel: 0131 225 7012/7013
Fax: 0131 225 6592

A voluntary body concerned with the protection of the countryside (including country towns and villages) in Scotland from unnecessary disfigurement or damage. Its main aims are to stimulate and guide public opinion regarding the need for action to safeguard the welfare of the countryside and encourage appropriate development in rural areas. In pursuit of this it acts as a source of information and advice on all matters relating to the preservation of the rural scenery and amenities.

A

• Association of Garden Trusts, The

Oaklea,
Smalls Hill Road,
Leigh,
Reigate.
Surrey.
RH2 8PF.

Tel: 01306 611268 (9.30a.m.-
2.30p.m. Mon-Fri)

The Association is an educational charity whose objectives are to promote and co-ordinate the work of County Garden Trusts (CGTs) and through them the interest, education and involvement of the public in matters connected with the arts and sciences of historic gardens; to assist CGTs in their work of conservation, restoration or creation of historic gardens in the British Isles for the education, enjoyment and/or benefit of the public; and, mainly, to act as a catalyst for the 21 CGTs in their work of education, promotion and co-operation with related interest groups including the involvement of volunteers at local, regional and national level. Volunteers are involved in the conservation, management, maintenance and provision of designed landscape in the general field of conservation and preservation of historic gardens.

• Association of Sea Fisheries Committees of England

Buckrose House,
Commercial Street,
Norton,
Malton.
North Yorkshire.
YO17 9HX.

Tel: 01653 698219
Fax: 01653 695953

The object of the Association is to assist Sea Fisheries Committees in their regulatory management and development functions and where appropriate to co-ordinate their activities and promote their interests with Government and other organisations.

B

• **Badgers** SEE: National Federation of Badger Groups

• Barn Owl Trust

Waterleat,
Ashburton.
Devon.
TQ13 7HU.

Tel: 01364 653026 (Tues and Thurs)
Fax: 01364 654392

The aims of the Trust are to conserve the barn owl and its environment; to make available free information on barn owl conservation including habitat, nest boxes and barn conversions. Consultancy service available.

• Bat Conservation Trust, The

The London Ecology Centre,
45 Shelton Street,
London.
WC2H 9HJ.

Tel: 0171 240 0933
Fax: 0171 240 4525

The Trust exists to conserve bats, their roosts and their feeding habitats. It aims to prevent further population declines and to encourage the growth of threatened populations. It acts as a source of information on the biology and conservation of bats; as a liaison, co-ordination and resource centre for bat conservation and develops conservation projects and policies. Co-ordinates the work of the County Bat Groups. Enquiry and consultancy service available.

● **Bees** SEE: British Beekeeping Association

● Belfast Naturalists' Field Club

12 Woodland Avenue,
Helens Bay,
Bangor.
BT19 1TX.

Tel: 01247 852276

The club focuses on the practical study of natural sciences and archaeology in Ireland, with membership a mix of professionals, amateurs and enthusiasts.

● **Bibliographic Services** SEE:
Libraries

● Biological Recording in Scotland Campaign

c/o Scottish Wildlife Trust,
Cramond House,
Kirk Cramond,
Cramond Glebe Road,
Edinburgh.
EH4 6NS.

Tel: 0131 312 7765
Fax: 0131 312 8705

BRISC aims to promote and co-ordinate biological recording in Scotland by designing and running its own surveys and those of other organisations working in Scotland. In general, BRISC operates as a central intelligence body developing and linking a comprehensive network of records, record centres, recorders, scientific, environmental and conservation groups covering the whole of Scotland.

● BirdLife International

Wellbrook Court,
Girton Road,
Cambridge.
CB3 0NA.

Tel: 01223 277318
Fax: 01223 277200

BirdLife International is a world-wide partnership of organisations, working for the diversity of all life through the conservation of birds and their habitats. It is the leading authority on the status of the world's birds and their habitats.

● **Birds** SEE:
Barn Owl Trust
BirdLife International
British Association for Shooting and Conservation
British Ornithologists' Club
British Ornithologists' Union
British Trust for Ornithology
Falconaide
Game Conservancy Trust
Game Conservancy Trust (Scotland)
Hawk and Owl Trust
International Waterfowl and Wetlands Research Bureau
National Birds of Prey Centre, The
Royal Society for the Protection of Birds (England) (Northern Ireland) (Scotland) (Wales)
Scottish Ornithologists' Club
Wildfowl and Wetlands Trust, The

● Botanical Society of Scotland

Royal Botanic Garden,
20A Inverleith Row,
Edinburgh.
EH3 5LR.

Tel: 0131 552 7171
Fax: 0131 552 0382

The Society aims to promote botany in Scotland.

● Botanical Society of the British Isles

**c/o Department of Botany,
Natural History Museum,
Cromwell Road,
London.
SW7 5BD.**

The Society is an association of amateur and professional botanists whose common interest lies in the study of British and Irish flowering plants and ferns. Amongst other activities the Society organises plant distribution surveys and publishes plant atlases.

● Botanical Society of the British Isles (Ireland)

**c/o Department of Botany,
Ulster Museum,
Belfast.
BT9 5AB.**

**Tel: 01232 381251 Ext.256
Fax: 01232 665510**

● British Agricultural History Society

**c/o Rural History Centre,
University of Reading,
Whiteknights,
P.O. Box 229,
Reading.
Berkshire.
RG6 2AG.**

Tel: 01734 318660

The aim of the Society is to disseminate knowledge and encourage research in rural and agricultural history. This is achieved principally by publication of research articles, current lists and bibliographies, surveys of work in progress and conferences.

● British Association for Shooting and Conservation

**Marford Mill,
Rossett,
Wrexham.
Clwyd.
LL12 0HL.**

**Tel: 01244 570881
Fax: 01244 571678**

BASC is the national representative body for sporting shooting. The Association seeks to foster a practical interest in the countryside, wildlife management and conservation.

● British Association of Nature Conservationists

**c/o The Nature Conservation Bureau Limited,
48 Main Street,
Woodnewton,
Peterborough.
PE8 5EB.**

**Tel: 01635 550380
Fax: 01635 550230**

BANC provides accurate and reliable information for professionals and amateurs in the field of nature conservation and aims to advance nature conservation in the UK. It addresses philosophy, policy and practice affecting the natural environment and brings forward new views and perspectives. It provides opportunities and resources for individuals working together to influence current thinking and decision making.

● British Beekeepers Association

**National Agriculture Centre,
Stoneleigh Park.
Warwickshire.
CV8 2LZ.**

**Tel: 01203 696679
Fax: 01203 690682**

The aim of the Association is to further the craft of beekeeping.

● British Bryological Society

**Botany Department,
Liverpool Museum,
William Brown Street,
Liverpool.
L3 8EN.**

The aims of the Society are to promote and advance all branches of bryology (the study of mosses and liverworts) throughout the world and especially in relation to bryophytes in the UK.

● British Cave Research Association

**20 Woodland Avenue,
Westonzoyland,
Bridgwater.
Somerset.
TA7 0LQ.**

Tel: 01278 691539

The Association co-ordinates all aspects of the discovery, exploration, description and conservation of caves and similar natural features and their environment.

● British Deer Society

**Beale Centre,
Lower Basildon,
Reading.
RG8 9NH.**

**Tel: 01734 844094
Fax: 01734 844094**

The Society studies deer and disseminates information about them.

● British Deer Society (Scotland)

**Elcho Park,
Rhynd,
Perth.
PH2 8QG.**

**Tel: 01738 21822
Fax: 01738 21822**

● British Dragonfly Society

**1 Haydn Avenue,
Purley.
Surrey.
CR8 4AG.**

Tel: 0181 668 5859

The aims of the Society are to promote and encourage the study and conservation of dragonflies and their natural habitats. Members make themselves available for consultation on conservation matters when and where required.

● British Ecological Society, The

**26 Blades Court,
Deodar Road,
Putney,
London.
SW15 2NU.**

**Tel: 0181 871 9797
Fax: 0181 871 9779**

The aim of the Society is to promote the study of ecology as a science. Increasingly, it aids interpretation of ecology through its Ecological Affairs and Education and Careers Committees.

● British Geological Survey

**Kingsley Dunham Centre,
Keyworth,
Nottingham.
NG12 5GG.**

**Tel: 0115 936 3100
Fax: 0115 936 3200**

The principal aims of the Survey are to undertake geoscience surveying, monitoring and related research and development and to provide advice in these areas. The Survey conducts and maintains systematic geological, geophysical, geochemical and hydrogeological surveys of the UK landmass, coastal and offshore areas, and interprets the results. Central to the work of the Survey is the National Geosciences Information Service which enables the survey to provide an information and advisory service on geological and related matters.

● British Geological Survey (Scotland)

**Murchison House,
West Mains Road,
Edinburgh.
EH9 3LA.**

**Tel: 0131 667 1000
Fax: 0131 668 2683**

● British Geomorphological Research Group

**School of Geography,
University of Oxford,
Oxford.
OX1 3TB.**

**Tel: 01865 271919
Fax: 01865 271929**

The Group aims to foster research in geomorphology, which encompasses processes and changes in landscapes as well as understanding of landforms and their evolution. It provides a forum for exchange of ideas and discussion of research.

● British Hedgehog Preservation Society

**Knowbury House,
Knowbury,
Ludlow.
Shropshire.
SY8 3LQ.**

Tel: 01584 890287

The Society's aims are to encourage and give advice to the public about the care of hedgehogs (particularly when injured, sick, etc.); to supply information and fund research into the behavioural habits of hedgehogs and to ascertain the best methods of assisting their survival.

• British Herpetological Society

**c/o Zoological Society of London,
Regent's Park,
London.
NW1 4RY.**

Tel: 0181 452 9578

The Society was founded with the broad aim of catering for all aspects of interest in reptiles and amphibians. There are four active sub-committees covering research, education, captive breeding and conservation. The Conservation Committee is actively engaged in field study, conservation management and political lobbying with a view to improving the status and future prospects of our native British species. Enquiry and consultancy services available.

• British Horse Loggers' Association, The

**2 Hollington Cottages,
Holme Lacy,
Hereford.
HR2 6LY.**

Tel: 01432 870316

The Association was formed to promote and develop the role of the draught horse in UK forestry through: the development of a register of contractors; the establishment of a technical advisory panel; promotion and demonstration; collection and distribution of information and the promotion of training.

• British Library Environmental Information Service

**25 Southampton Buildings,
London.
WC2A 1AW.**

**Tel: 0171 323 7955
Fax: 0171 323 7954**

The Service undertakes research on behalf of its clients using the British Library's major literature collections covering all environmental issues, together with links to other key libraries and on-line databases. The collection and service is open to anyone.

• British Lichen Society

**Department of Botany,
Natural History Museum,
Cromwell Road,
London.
SW7 5BD.**

**Tel: 0171 938 8852
Fax: 0171 938 9260**

The Society was formed to stimulate and advance interest in all branches of lichenology.

• British Marine Life Study Society

**Glaucus House,
14 Corbyn Crescent,
Shoreham-by-Sea.
Sussex.
BN43 6PQ.**

Tel: 01273 465433

The Society was formed to study the marine fauna and flora of the shore and seas surrounding the British Isles; to publish and distribute information on the same; and, to promote ideas and projects concerning the conservation of the British marine environment.

● British Naturalists' Association

48 Russell Way,
Higham Ferrers.
Northamptonshire.
NN10 8EJ.

Tel: 01933 314672
Fax: 01933 314672

The association supports schemes and legislation for the protection of wildlife; the preservation of natural beauty and the promotion and maintenance of national parks, nature reserves, conservation areas and sanctuaries. It organises information services and observational work, and publishes literature on natural history subjects. Enquiry and consultancy services available.

● British Ornithologists' Club

c/o British Ornithologists' Union,
Tring.
Hertfordshire.
HP23 6AP.

Tel: 01572 722788

The Club promotes discussion between ornithologists and publishes scientific information in connection with ornithology.

● British Ornithologists' Union

c/o Natural History Museum,
Tring.
Hertfordshire.
HP23 6AP.

Tel: 01442 890080
Fax: 01442 890693

The Union advances ornithology, maintaining it as an important branch of Zoology and actively encourages research and awards research grants.

● British Phycological Society, The

Department of Botany,
The Natural History Museum,
Cromwell Road,
London.
SW7 5BD.

Tel: 0171 938 9001
Fax: 0171 938 9260

The Society promotes the study of algae.

● British Pteridological Society

c/o Natural History Museum,
Cromwell Road,
London.
SW7 5BD.

Tel: 01203 715690

The objects of the Society are to promote the growing, study and conservation of ferns and fern allies, both of wild species and cultivated varieties, and to encourage interest in their taxonomy, distribution and ecology.

● British Trust for Conservation Volunteers

36 St. Mary's Street,
Wallingford.
Oxfordshire.
OX10 0EU.

Tel: 01491 839766
Fax: 01491 839646

BTCV is the UK's largest practical conservation charity and each year supports the activities of over 84,000 volunteers in positive steps to improve their environment. A network of 90 local offices throughout the UK organise a wide range of environmental projects and offer training courses to provide hands-on experience in a range of conservation skills.

● British Trust for Ornithology

The National Centre for
Ornithology,
The Nunnery,
Thetford.
Norfolk.
IP24 2PU.

Tel: 01842 750050
Fax: 01842 750030

The BTO exists to conduct and promote research on Britain's birds and their habitats. It provides independent scientific data to a range of agencies and undertakes a wide range of investigations. Consultancy service available.

● British Waterways

Willow Grange,
Church Road,
Watford.
Hertfordshire.
WD1 3QA.

Tel: 01923 226422
Fax: 01923 226081

British Waterways own or manage 3218km of inland waterways in England, Scotland and Wales which are being sensitively developed for leisure, tourism, recreation and, where appropriate, the carriage of freight.

● British Waterways (Scotland)

Canal House,
Applecross Street,
Glasgow.
G4 9SP.

Tel: 0141 332 6936
Fax: 0141 331 1688

● Butterfly Conservation

P.O. Box 222,
Dedham.
Essex.
CO7 6EY.

Tel: 01206 322342
Fax: 01206 322739

Butterfly Conservation is dedicated to the conservation of wild butterflies and their habitats. By making people aware of their declining numbers, funding research into their life needs and by setting up reserves for the rarer species, the aim is to preserve these insects for future generations to enjoy.

● Butterfly Conservation
(Ireland)

**13 Enniscrone Park,
Portadown.
Belfast.
BT63 5DQ.**

Tel: 01762 333927

C

● Cambrian Caving
Council

**White Lion House,
Ynys Uchaf,
Ystradgynlais,
Swansea.
SA9 1RW.**

Tel: 01639 849519

The Council is the national association for caving in Wales, for caving clubs and similar organisations, representing their interests in Wales, The Marches and the Forest of Dean. Amongst its aims are: to encourage the exchange of information between clubs and other regional and national bodies; to encourage the recording of information on sites of speleological interest in the Cambrian Cave Registry or similar body and to encourage conservation.

● Campaign for the
Protection of Rural Wales

**Ty Gwyn,
31 High Street,
Welshpool.
Powys.
SY21 7JP.**

**Tel: 01938 552525/556212
Fax: 01938 552741**

CPRW is Wales' countryside watchdog group, working to protect the countryside and the coast whilst encouraging sustainable rural development.

● **Canals** SEE: **Inland Waterways**

● Caretakers for the
Environment International

**3 High Street,
Banwell.
Avon.
BS24 6AA.**

**Tel: 01934 822415
Fax: 01934 852020**

Caretakers is developing a world-wide network of secondary schools to share environmental concerns and to face environmental challenges. It shares successful innovative environmental education programmes, facilitates joint educational projects and promotes international data exchange and interdisciplinary activities.

● Carnivore Wildlife Trust

**35 Church Street,
Kidlington.
Oxford.
OX5 2BA.**

**Tel: 01865 373241
Fax: 01865 373241**

The purpose of the Trust is to promote the world-wide protection of wildlife, in particular, to conserve carnivore species threatened with extinction and to protect carnivores from human mistreatment.

● Cat Survival Trust

The Centre,
Codicote Road,
Welwyn.
Hertfordshire.
AL6 9TU.

Tel: 01438 716873/716478
Fax: 01438 717535

The Trust is concerned with the conservation of endangered species of cat (not *Felis domesticus*) through captive breeding, habitat protection and environmental awareness and collects and disseminates information in order to create greater public and educational awareness. Enquiry and consultancy service available.

● Caving SEE:
British Cave Research Association
Cambrian Caving Council
National Caving Association
Speleological Union of Ireland

● Centre for Agricultural Strategy

University of Reading,
1 Earley Gate,
Reading.
RG6 2AT.

Tel: 01734 318150/1/2
Fax: 01734 353423

The Centre aims to provide independent and continuing assessments of agricultural and countryside developments and their implications for the balanced use of land, its expanding field of work and influence now extending over a range of farming and countryside issues in the UK, EC and world-wide. The Centre's purposes are: to monitor present policies and identify major issues for discussion; to provide a forum for such discussion; to encapsulate the results of discussions and studies in reports designed to inform and influence; and, to identify and formulate agreed objectives and strategies to achieve their implementation.

● Centre for Marine and Coastal Studies

University of Liverpool,
P.O. Box 147,
Liverpool.
L69 3BX.

Tel: 0151 794 3653
Fax: 0151 794 3646

The aims of the Centre are the encouragement of interdisciplinary research in marine and coastal matters within the University; to act as an umbrella organisation for the preparation and submission of interdisciplinary research projects; to provide a focal point within the University for approaches by industrial, scientific and statutory agencies wanting assistance with marine and coastal projects.

● Centre for the Conservation of Historic Parks and Gardens

University of York,
The King's Manor,
York.
YO1 2EP.

Tel: 01904 433966
Fax: 01904 433949

The aim of the Centre is to promote the study of historic parks, gardens and landscapes by acting as an exchange for information and by providing guidance and education. It has an annual educational programme and undertakes research and consultancy. The Centre is engaged in the preparation of an inventory of historic parks and gardens in England and Wales.

• Church and Conservation Project

**The Arthur Rank Centre,
National Agricultural Centre,
Stoneleigh Park.
Warwickshire.
CV8 2LZ.**

**Tel: 01203 696969 ext. 339
Fax: 01203 696900**

The Project was established to look at ways in which the principles and practices of nature conservation could be applied to the land management, teaching and ministerial training of the churches (ecumenical) working in the wider rural environment.

• **Coastal** SEE: **Marine**

• Coed Cymru

**The Old Sawmill,
Tregynon,
Newtown.
Powys.
SY16 3PL.**

**Tel: 01686 650777
Fax: 01686 650696**

An initiative to promote the use, protection and enhancement of Wales native, broadleaved woodland, bringing together farmers, foresters, conservationists and wood users to bring such woodland back into sound, sustainable management. It provides free help and advice on all aspects of woodland management, tree planting and timber marketing and use. There is a Coed

Cymru Officer based with each County and National Park in Wales.

• Common Ground

**41 Shelton Street,
Covent Garden,
London.
WC2H 9HJ.**

**Tel: 0171 379 3109
Fax: 0171 836 5741**

Common Ground is working to encourage people to value and enjoy their own familiar surroundings, regardless of whether they are rare or unusual. Its strategy for change is to forge links between the practice and enjoyment of the arts and the conservation of landscapes and nature.

• **Common Land** SEE: Open Spaces Society

• Conservation Foundation

**1 Kensington Gore,
London.
SW7 2AR.**

**Tel: 0171 823 8842
Fax: 0171 823 8791**

The Foundation was formed to create and manage sponsorship schemes involving all environmental interests. Referral service, funding and consultancy service available.

● Conservation Volunteers (Northern Ireland)

**Dendron Lodge,
Clandeboye Estate,
Bangor.
BT19 1RN.**

**Tel: 01247 853778
Fax: 01247 853776**

Conservation Volunteers NI is a part of the British Trust for Conservation Volunteers (see separate entry).

● Council for Environmental Education

**University of Reading,
London Road,
Reading.
RG1 5AQ.**

**Tel: 01734 756061
Fax: 01734 756264**

The Council is the national body for the co-ordination and promotion of environmental education, acting as a forum for the exchange of ideas and information and encouraging its development through various projects.

● Council for Nature Conservation and the Countryside (Northern Ireland)

**Commonwealth House,
35 Castle Street,
Belfast.
BT1 1GU.**

**Tel: 01232 251477
Fax: 01232 315717**

The function of the Council is to advise DoE(NI) on the exercise of its nature conservation and countryside functions.

● Council for the Protection of Rural England

**Warwick House,
25 Buckingham Palace Road,
London.
SW1W 0PP.**

**Tel: 0171 976 6433
Fax: 0171 976 6373**

CPRE works for a living and beautiful countryside. It is active locally, through coverage of county branches and district committees, nationally and internationally.

● Country Trust, The

**Stratford Grange,
Stratford St. Andrew,
Saxmundham.
Suffolk.
IP17 1LF.**

Tel: 01728 604818

The Trust is a national educational charity organising and conducting educational expeditions for urban people, particularly children from the most deprived inner city areas, to see the English countryside at work.

● Countryside Commission

**John Dower House,
Crescent Place,
Cheltenham.
Gloucestershire.
GL50 3RA.**

**Tel: 01242 521381
Fax: 01242 584270**

The Commission is a statutory agency which works to conserve and enhance the beauty of the English countryside and to help people enjoy it. The Commission is an advisory and promotional body working in partnership with others and providing grants and advice for projects which conserve the natural beauty of the countryside and make it more accessible for public enjoyment. The Commission acts as the Government's adviser on countryside matters and has special responsibility for designating National Parks and Areas of Outstanding Natural Beauty, defining Heritage Coasts and establishing national trails. There are seven regional offices for England:

Northern: Warwick House, Grantham Road, Newcastle-upon-Tyne. NE2 1QF. Tel: 0191 232 8252.

North West: 7th Floor, Bridgewater House, Whitworth Street, Manchester. M1 6LT. Tel: 0161 237 1061

Yorkshire and Humberside: 2nd Floor, Victoria Wharf, Embankment IV, Sovereign Street, Leeds. LS1 4BA. Tel: 0113 246 9222.

Midlands: Cumberland House, Broad Street, Birmingham. B15 1TD. Tel: 0121 632 6503.

Eastern: Ortona House, 110 Hills Road, Cambridge. CB2 1LQ. Tel: 01223 354462.

South West: Bridge House, Sion Place, Clifton Down, Bristol. BS8 4AS. Tel: 0117 973 9966.

South East: 4th Floor, 71 Kingsway, Holborn. London. WC2B 6ST. Tel: 0171 831 3510.

● Countryside Council for Wales

Plas Penrhos,
Ffordd Penrhos,
Bangor.
Gwynedd.
LL57 2LQ.

Tel: 01248 370444
Fax: 01248 355782

CCW is the Government's statutory adviser on wildlife, countryside and maritime conservation matters in Wales. It is the executive authority for the conservation of habitats and wildlife. There are five regional offices - details from address above.

● Countryside Education Trust

John Montagu Building,
Beaulieu,
Brockenhurst.
Hampshire.
SO24 7ZN.

Tel: 01590 612340
Fax: 01590 612624

The aims of the Trust are: to provide facilities and services which make access to the countryside educational and enjoyable for all; to encourage a concerned and caring attitude towards the environment; to be involved in the practical conservation of the natural environment and its sites of historic significance. Over 7000 schoolchildren visit the Trust each year, with a wide range of environmental activities provided to suit all ages. A wide range of adult courses, etc. are also arranged.

● Countryside Trust, The

John Dower House,
Crescent Place,
Cheltenham.
Gloucestershire.
GL50 3RA.

Tel: 01242 521381
Fax: 01242 584270

Set up by the Countryside Commission, the Trust object is to promote the conservation, preservation and restoration of the natural beauty of the countryside of England for public benefit. It offers "seed corn" grants to community or voluntary bodies concerned with the care of the local countryside, specifically to support the costs of fund-raising appeals intended to benefit practical conservation projects of local rather than national significance. The Trustees give priority to projects which envisage the provision of public access to the area or site concerned and which provide for conservation education.

● Crown Estate, The

16 Carlton House Terrace,
London.
SW1Y 5AH.

Tel: 0171 210 4377
Fax: 0171 930 8259

Responsible for the management of Crown Estate interests in England and Wales including over 72,850ha of agriculture and forestry, commercial and housing properties in London and other urban areas, foreshore and seabed. The estate which is vested in the Sovereign in Right of the Crown is managed by the Crown Estate Commissioners under the provisions of the *Crown Estate Act 1961*.

● Crown Estate Commissioners (Scotland)

Crown Estate Office,
10 Charlotte Square,
Edinburgh.
EH2 4DR.

Tel: 0131 226 7241
Fax: 0131 220 1366

Responsible for the management of almost 40,500ha of agricultural and forestry estates, most of the foreshore and all of the seabed to the twelve mile territorial limit, and property investments in Glasgow and Edinburgh.

● CSW Countryside Trust

Hillhouseridge,
Shottskirk Road,
Shotts.
Lanarkshire.
ML7 4JS.

Tel: 01501 822015
Fax: 01501 823919

CSWCT is leading the Central Scotland Woodlands initiative, the primary aim of which is to continue and extend the transformation of the Central Belt landscape with one which is well-wooded. Other objectives are: to enhance the nature conservation value of the area; to improve opportunities for access and recreation; to develop people's awareness of the local environment and a sense of community pride and to contribute to and foster economic and human resource development opportunities.

D

● **Deer** SEE:
British Deer Society
British Deer Society (Scotland)
Northern Ireland Deer Society
Red Deer Commission

● Department of the Environment

**2 Marsham Street,
London.
SW1P 3EB.**

**Tel: 0171 276 3000
Fax: 0171 276 0818**

The Department's responsibilities include local government structure and finance; land-use planning; housing and construction; conservation of the built and natural heritage; environmental protection and water. The DoE library is the UK National Focal Point for the UN Environment Programme's International Environmental Information System (INFOTERRA), the subject area comprising the entire environmental field. INFOTERRA is intended to assist governments and decision makers at all levels to obtain information to ensure that environmental considerations are incorporated into all development activities. INFOTERRA operates as a referral service (Tel: 0171 276 5672; Fax: 0171 276 5713).

● DoE Environment Service (Northern Ireland)

**Commonwealth House,
35 Castle Street,
Belfast.
BT1 1GU.**

**Tel: 01232 251477
Fax: 01232 315717**

The Environment Service comprises Environmental Protection, Countryside and Wildlife and Historic Monuments and Buildings groups and was set up in 1990. The Countryside and Wildlife group aims to conserve and enhance the natural environment of NI through site protection by designation as Areas of Special Scientific Interest (ASSIs), NNRs, Marine Nature Reserves and AONBs; and by encouraging others to conserve the countryside and its wildlife, providing facilities to help people to enjoy the countryside.

● **Dolphins** SEE:
International Dolphin Watch
Whale and Dolphin Conservation Society

● **Dragonflies** SEE: British Dragonfly Society

● Dry Stone Walling Association of Great Britain

**c/o YFC Centre,
National Agricultural Centre,
Kenilworth.
Warwickshire.
CV8 2LG.**

**Tel: 0121 378 0493
Fax: 0121 378 0493**

The Association is an organisation which seeks to ensure that the best dry stone walling craftsmanship of the past is preserved and that the craft has a thriving future. The Association supports the working waller; provides opportunities for the public to learn the craft; and publishes and provides technical data and information on all aspects of the craft. DSWA has two branches for Wales:

North Wales: 12 Percy Road, Wrexham. Clwyd. LL13 7EE. Tel: 01978 263148.

South Wales: Cwm-y-Gwengad, Llangadog. Dyfed. SA19 9DR. Tel: 01550 777653; Fax: 01550 777653

● Dunstaffnage Marine Laboratory

P.O. Box 3,
Oban.
Argyll.
PA34 4AD.

Tel: 01631 62244
Fax: 01631 65518

Part of the Natural Environment Research Council (NERC), the Laboratory conducts a programme of basic, strategic and applied research into marine organisms and the sea of Scotland

● Ecology Research Group

Science Department,
Canterbury Christ Church College,
North Holmes Road,
Canterbury.
Kent.
CT1 1QU.

Tel: 01227 767700
Fax: 01227 470442

The Group is concerned with all forms of ecological research, consultancy and environmental management; having considerable experience in the areas of malacology, pollution, avian biology and freshwater and estuarine ecology.

● English Nature

Northminster House,
Peterborough.
PE1 1UA.

Tel: 01733 340345
Fax: 01733 68834

English Nature was established by Act of Parliament and is responsible for advising Government on nature conservation in England. It promotes, directly and through others, the conservation of England's wildlife and natural features; selects, establishes and manages National Nature Reserves and

identifies and notifies Sites of Special Scientific Interest; provides advice and information about nature conservation and supports and conducts research relevant to these functions. Through the Joint Nature Conservation Committee (see separate entry) it works with its sister organisations in Wales and Scotland on UK and international nature conservation issues.

There are 21 regional teams:

Northumbria - Tel: 0191 281 6316; Fax: 0191 281 6305
Cumbria - Tel: 015394 45286; Fax: 015394 88432
North West - Tel: 01942 820342; Fax: 01942 820364
North and East Yorkshire - (York) 01904 432700; Fax: 01904 432705; (Leyburn) Tel: 01969 23447; Fax: 01969 24190
Humber to Pennines - Tel: 01924 387010; Fax: 01924 201507
East Midlands - Tel: 01476 68431; Fax: 01476 70927
Peak District and Derbyshire - Tel: 01629 815095; Fax: 01629 815091
West Midlands - (Shrewsbury) Tel: 01743 709611; Fax: 01743 709303; (Banbury) Tel: 01295 257601
Three Counties at Malvern - Tel: 01684 560616/7/8; Fax: 01684 893435
Bedfordshire, Cambridgeshire, Northamptonshire - Tel: 01733 391100; Fax: 01733 394093
Norfolk - Tel: 01603 620558; Fax: 01603 762552

E

Suffolk - Tel: 01284 762218; Fax: 01284 764318

Essex, Hertfordshire and London - (Colchester) Tel: 01206 796666; Fax: 01206 794466; (London) Tel: 0171 831 6922; Fax: 0171 404 3369

Kent - Tel: 01233 812525; Fax: 01233 812520

Sussex and Surrey - Tel: 01273 476595; Fax: 01273 483063

Thames and Chiltern - Tel: 01635 268881; Fax: 01635 268940

Hampshire and Isle of Wight - Tel: 01703 283944; Fax: 01703 283834

Wiltshire - Tel: 01380 726344; Fax: 01380 721411

Dorset - Tel: 01929 556688; Fax: 01929 554752

Somerset and Avon - Tel: 01823 283211; Fax: 01823 272978

Devon and Cornwall - (Okehampton) Tel: 01837 55045; Fax: 01837 55046; (Trelissick) Tel: 01872 865261; Fax: 01872 865534

● **Entomology** SEE: **Invertebrates**

● Environment Council, The

21 Elizabeth Street,
London.
SW1W 9RP.

Tel: 0171 824 8411
Fax: 0171 730 9941

See descriptor at head of this directory.

● Environmental Change Unit

University of Oxford,
1a Mansfield Road,
Oxford.
OX1 3TB.

Tel: 01865 281180
Fax: 01865 281181

The Unit is an interdisciplinary unit dedicated to the collaborative research on the nature, causes and impacts of environmental change, and to the development of management strategies for coping with future changes. The Unit focuses on five major research themes: modelling and forecasting impacts of future climatic changes; geological and archaeological evidence for long-term changes; energy and the environment, land-use change; monitoring of contemporary environmental changes; information retrieval and collation.

● Environmental Information Centre

Institute of Terrestrial Ecology,
Monks Wood,
Abbots Ripton,
Huntingdon.
Cambridgeshire.
PE17 2LS.

Tel: 0148 73381
Fax: 0148 73467

The Centre is part of the Natural Environment Research Council. Its overall objective is to encourage the use of digital information processing techniques, including remote sensing and geographical information systems, in order to maximise the utility of the Institute's ecological and environmental databases for scientific research and for practical applications in environmental survey, monitoring and in the development of predictive models of ecological processes. Enquiry and consultancy services available.

● Environmental
Information Service

P.O. Box 197,
Cawston,
Norwich.
Norfolk.
NR10 4BH.

Tel: 01603 871048
Fax: 01603 871048

The Service provides a central contact point
for all enquirers to assist them in locating
groups, organisations and individuals
involved with the environment. It acts as a
signpost for environmental organisations
and groups both in the UK and world-wide.
EIS also runs an environmental employment
register and agency. Enquiry and
consultancy service available.

● **Estuarine** SEE: **Marine**

● Falconaide

Slackwood Farmhouse,
Silverdale,
Carnforth.
Lancashire.
LA5 0UF.

Tel: 01524 701353

Falconaide is concerned with the care and
rehabilitation of injured birds of prey and
the conservation of their environment; it
seeks to educate the public in an awareness
of and respect for birds of prey and to act
as a pressure group for effective and
improved legislation protecting birds of
prey. Gives flying and static displays.

● Farming and Wildlife
Advisory Group

National Agricultural Centre,
Stoneleigh,
Kenilworth.
Warwickshire.
CV8 2RX.

Tel: 01203 696699
Fax: 01203 696760

The mission of FWAG is to unite wildlife
and landscape conservation with farming
and forestry. It employs approximately 50

Farm Conservation Advisers, based across
the UK and supported by 65 local voluntary
county-based groups. Skills training and
consultancy service for landowners and
farmers.

● Farming and Wildlife
Advisory Group
(Scotland)

Rural Centre,
Ingliston,
Newbridge.
Midlothian.
EH28 8NZ.

Tel: 0131 335 3982
Fax: 0131 333 2926

● **Ferns** SEE: British Pteridological Society

● Field Studies Council

Central Services,
Preston Montford,
Montford Bridge,
Shrewsbury.
SY4 1HW.

Tel: 01743 850674
Fax: 01743 850178

The Council is an educational charity providing environmental understanding for all through training, education, publications, research and consultancy. It manages a network of 11 field centres in England and Wales providing both day and residential fieldwork courses on all aspects of the environment. FSC courses are designed for schools, colleges and universities with an emphasis on practical activity in the environment. There are also a wide range of adult courses.

● Fieldfare Trust

**67a The Wicker,
Sheffield.
S3 8HT.**

**Tel: 0114 270 1668
Fax: 0114 276 7900**

The Trust promotes enjoyment and education in the countryside for all sections of the community, especially those who by reason of disability or disadvantage are handicapped in pursuing opportunities. Enquiry service available, skills training offered, consultancy service to landowners.

● Forestry SEE:
British Horse Loggers' Association
Campaign for the Future of the Border Hills
Coed Cymru
CSW Countryside Trust
Forestry Authority
Forestry Commission
Forest Enterprise
Forestry Trust for Conservation and Education, The
Forests Forever
National Small Woods Association
Northern Ireland Forest Service
Reforesting Scotland
Royal Forestry Society of England, Wales and Northern Ireland, The
Royal Scottish Forestry Society
Scottish Native Woods Campaign
Scottish Tree Trust
Silvanus Trust, The
Timber Growers UK

Tree Council
Trees for Life
Woodland Trust, The

● Forestry Authority SEE: Forestry Commission

● Forestry Commission

**231 Corstorphine Road,
Edinburgh.
EH12 7AT.**

**Tel: 0131 334 0303
Fax: 0131 334 3047**

The Forestry Commission now comprises Forestry Authority and Forest Enterprise. The Forestry Authority advises on forest practice, pays grants, carries out research and implements regulations relating to trees and woodlands. Forest Enterprise is responsible for the management of the state forests to achieve a range of objectives - as a productive timber resource, as habitats for wildlife, as landscape features and for their recreational opportunities. Both bodies have their headquarters address at Corstorphine Road, Edinburgh. In addition, Forestry Authority has three principal offices, together with a number of regional conservancies (details from the principal offices):

Forestry Authority (England): Great Eastern House, Tenison Road, Cambridge. CB1 2DU. Tel: 01223 314546; Fax: 01223 460699.

Forestry Authority (Scotland): Portcullis House, 21 India Street, Glasgow. G2 4PL. Tel: 0141 248 3931; Fax: 0141 226 5007.

Forestry Authority (Wales): North Road, Aberystwyth. Dyfed. SY23 2EF. Tel: 01970 625866; Fax: 01970 626177.

Forest Enterprise has a number of regional and forest district offices details of which are available from Commission headquarters.

● **Forest Enterprise** SEE: Forestry Commission

● Forestry Trust for Conservation and Education, The

**The Old Estate Office,
Englefield Road,
Theale,
Reading.
Berkshire.
RG7 5DZ.**

Tel: 01734 323523

The aims of the Trust are to promote a better understanding of productive forestry and show how it is compatible with wildlife conservation and enhancement of landscape. Such aims are achieved by the use of demonstration woods backed up with educational material involving both formal classroom teaching and field-based project work to demonstrate how practical forestry and nature conservation are linked. The Trust produces an annual handbook of woodlands to visit in England and Wales where provision for access or education is made.

● Forests Forever

**4th Floor,
Clareville House,
26/27 Oxendon Street,
London.
SW1Y 4EL.**

**Tel: 0171 839 1891
Fax: 0171 930 0094**

Forests Forever is an initiative of the Timber Trades Federation on behalf of all timber users and processors in the UK with the aim of helping to safeguard the world's forests, future timber supplies and to promote the cause of wood. FF is playing an active role in supporting progress towards sustainable forest management in accordance with the principles agreed at the 1992 UN Conference on Environment and Development (UNCED). FF has prepared environmental policies for the UK timber industry; is concerned about the future of all forests, both hardwood and softwood, around the globe and is now recognised as a leading voice in the continuing debate about timber, forestry and the environment. Enquiry service available.

● Fountain Society, The

**16 Gayfere Street,
Westminster,
London.
SW1P 3HP.**

**Tel: 0171 222 6037/2917
Fax: 0171 799 2900**

The Society exists to conserve Britain's heritage of fountains from the past and to develop new fountains in the present and the future. It aims to: secure the conservation and restoration of fountains of aesthetic merit for public enjoyment; promote the provision of fountains of aesthetic merit and promote the provision and restoration of cascades, waterfalls and other similar works. Referral service available.

● **Freshwater** SEE:
Freshwater Biological Association
Institute of Freshwater Ecology
National Rivers Authority

● Freshwater Biological Association

The FBA was founded to pursue fundamental research into all aspects of freshwater biology and chemistry.

**The Ferry House,
Far Sawrey,
Ambleside.
Cumbria.
LA22 0LP.**

**Tel: 015394 42468
Fax: 015394 46914**

● **Frogs** SEE: **Amphibians/Reptiles**

G

● Game Conservancy Trust

**Burgate Manor,
Fordingbridge.
Hampshire.
SP6 1EF.**

**Tel: 01425 652381
Fax: 01425 655848**

The Conservancy is a research-based organisation, run as a charitable trust, to ensure the future of game in its natural habitat. Its aim is to promote a wider understanding of game and to apply its research results by developing practical management techniques.

● Game Conservancy Trust (Scotland)

**Couston,
Newtyle.
Perthshire.
PH12 8UT.**

**Tel: 01828 650543
Fax: 01828 650568**

● Garden History Society

**5 The Knoll,
Hereford.
HR1 1RU.**

Tel: 01432 354479

The Society was founded as the central organisation for everyone interested in the history of gardens, parks and landscape architecture.

● **Gardens/Parks (Historic**) SEE:
Association of Garden Trusts, The
Centre for the Conservation of Historic Parks and Gardens
Fountain Society, The
Garden History Society
National Council for the Conservation of Plants and Gardens
National Trust for Scotland
National Trust, The
Northern Ireland Heritage Gardens Committee
Seed Bank Exchange
Welsh Historic Gardens Trust

● Geological Society

**Burlington House,
Piccadilly,
London.
W1V 0JU.**

**Tel: 0171 434 9944
Fax: 0171 439 8975**

The Society is Britain's national learned society and professional body for geology and is responsible for promoting all aspects of the geological sciences and the profession. Joint meetings are convened with specialist groups in geology, geomorphology and ecology to promote a better understanding and management of the environment.

● Geologists' Association

Burlington House,
Piccadilly,
London.
W1V 0JU.

Tel: 0171 434 9298
Fax: 0171 287 0280

The GA aims to serve anyone interested in the earth sciences, from beginner to amateurs and professionals. It takes a lead in geological conservation, through published Codes, and by funding initiatives with County Trusts, and other societies, using its Curry Fund. The GA acts as an umbrella organisation for regional geological societies with similar aims, 26 of which are affiliated to the Association. Enquiry service available.

● Geological Survey of Northern Ireland

20 College Gardens,
Belfast.
BT9 6BS.

Tel: 01232 666595
Fax: 01232 662835

The GSNI provides a source of geological expertise for Government departments, industry and the public and maintains an up to date geological map of the province. The professional staff at GSNI are officers of the British Geological Survey (see separate entry).

● **Geology** SEE:
British Geological Survey
British Geological Survey (Scotland)
Geological Society
Geologists' Association
Geological Survey of Northern Ireland
Mineralogical Society

● **Geomorphology** SEE: British Geomorphological Society

● Golf Course Wildlife Trust, The

31 Bedford Square,
London.
WC1B 3SG.

Tel: 0171 323 2722
Fax: 0171 722 0053

The aims of the Trust are to promote a positive awareness of the nature conservation value of golf courses, to contribute to the preservation and enhancement of the natural environment and to encourage greater accessibility to the countryside for public enjoyment.

● Groundwork Foundation

85/87 Cornwall Street,
Birmingham.
B3 3BY.

Tel: 0121 236 8565
Fax: 0121 236 7356

Groundwork is a national network of local initiatives committed to working with others to tackle the problems of dereliction, to restore landscapes and wildlife habitats and make positive use of wasteland in and around Britain's towns and cities. Referral service available. Consultancy through local offices.

H

● Habitat Scotland

Hazelmount,
Heron Place,
Portree.
Isle of Skye.
IV51 9EU.

Tel: 01478 612898
Fax: 01478 613254

Habitat Scotland was established as an independent environmental research charity with a special remit to investigate conservation issues arising from varied rural land and marine uses in the Highlands and Islands for which contracts may be available.

● Hawk and Owl Trust

c/o Birds of Prey Section,
Zoological Society of London,
Regent's Park,
London.
NW1 4RY.

Tel: 0158 283 2182
Fax: 0171 603 7756

The Trust is dedicated to the conservation and appreciation of all birds of prey (including owls) in the wild, especially native species. The Trust's membership is drawn from a wide spectrum including landowners, farmers, gamekeepers and ornithologists. Enquiry service, skills training and consultancy service available.

● **Hedgehogs** SEE: British Hedgehog Preservation Society

● Heritage Coast Forum

c/o Centre for Environmental
Interpretation,
Manchester Metropolitan University,
St. Augustine's,
Lower Chatham Street,
Manchester.
M15 6BY.

Tel: 0161 247 1067
Fax: 0161 236 7383

The Forum is a focus for organisations concerned with conservation, recreational use and management of Heritage Coasts in England. Its main objectives are to communicate information and advice to Heritage Coast services and other relevant organisations, and to promote the concept of Heritage Coasts. Skills training and consultancy service available.

● Herpetological Conservation Trust

655A Christchurch Road,
Boscombe,
Bournemouth.
BH1 4AP.

Tel: 01202 391319
Fax: 01202 392785

The Trust aims to improve the conservation status of Europe's threatened amphibians and reptiles. Its activities include site acquisition, habitat management, field surveys and political lobbying. The Trust works closely with the Conservation Committee of the British Herpetological Society.

● **Horse Loggers** SEE: British Horse Loggers' Association, The

● **Inland Waterways** SEE:
British Waterways
British Waterways (Scotland)
Inland Waterways Association
Inland Waterways Association (Northern Ireland)
National Rivers Authority
Scottish Inland Waterways Association

● Inland Waterways Association

114 Regent's Park Road,
London.
NW1 8UQ.

Tel: 0171 586 2510/2556
Fax: 0171 722 7213

The Association was founded to ensure the restoration, retention, conservation and development of inland waterways in the British Isles and for their fullest commercial and recreational use.

● Inland Waterways Northern Ireland

34 Ballydrain Road,
Comber.
Belfast.
BT23 5SS.

Tel: 01247 873080

● **Insects** SEE: **Invertebrates**

● Institute of Biology

20-22 Queensberry Place,
London.
SW7 2DZ.

Tel: 0171 581 8333
Fax: 0171 823 9409

The Institute represents and promotes the status of professional biologists. Activities include the formulation and submission of policy documents to Government and the maintenance of professional registers. Consultancy service available to major environmental bodies.

● Institute of Biology (Scotland)

Syntex Research Centre,
Research Avenue South,
Heriot Watt University Research Park,
Riccarton,
Edinburgh.
EH14 4AP.

Tel: 0131 451 5511 Ext. 2283
Fax: 0131 451 2067

● Institute of Ecology and Environmental Management

36 Kingfisher Court,
Hambridge Road,
Newbury.
Berkshire.
RG14 5SJ.

Tel: 01635 37715
Fax: 01635 550230

The IEEM aims to: raise the profile of the profession of ecology and environmental management; establish, maintain and enhance professional standards; promoting an ethic of environmental care within the profession and to clients and employers of the members.

• Institute of Estuarine and Coastal Studies

University of Hull,
Cottingham Road,
Hull.
North Humberside.
HU6 7RX.

Tel: 01482 465667
Fax: 01482 465001

The Institute is a commercial research organisation within the University. Its main aim is to attract contract research concerning estuaries and the coastal zone, but particularly projects requiring a multi-disciplinary approach.

• Institute of Freshwater Ecology

Windermere Laboratory,
Far Sawrey,
Ambleside.
Cumbria.
LA22 0LP.

Tel: 015394 42468
Fax: 015394 46914

The Institute is the UK's principal contractor for the study of the biology, physics and chemistry of freshwater systems.

• Institute of Terrestrial Ecology

Monks Wood,
Abbots Ripton,
Huntingdon.
Cambridgeshire.
PE17 2LS.

Tel: 0148 73381
Fax: 0148 73467

The ITE is part of the Natural Environment Research Council (NERC). It undertakes specialist ecological research in all aspects of the terrestrial environment and seeks to understand the ecology of species and of natural and human-made communities. The use of advanced computer technology enables the ITE to advise on the ecology, management and protection of the environment. Enquiry service, skills training and consultancy service available.

• International Dolphin Watch

Parklands,
North Ferriby.
Humberside.
HU14 3ET.

Tel: 01482 643403
Fax: 01482 634914

IDW is a non-profit organisation for the study and conservation of dolphins.

• International Waterfowl and Wetlands Research Bureau

Slimbridge.
Gloucestershire.
GL2 7BX.

Tel: 01453 890624/890634
Fax: 01453 890697

The Bureau was established to stimulate and co-ordinate research and conservation concerning waterfowl and their wetland habitats. IWRB co-ordinates research undertaken by national institutes and individual workers throughout the world, and alerts Government and non-Governmental bodies to threats of wetland loss through destruction, degradation or pollution. Skills training and consultancy available.

● **Invertebrates** SEE:
Amateur Entomologists' Society
British Beekeepers Association
British Dragonfly Society
Butterfly Conservation
Butterfly Conservation (Ireland)
Joint Committee for the Conservation of
British Invertebates

J

● Joint Committee for the Conservation of British Invertebrates

c/o **Royal Entomological Society,
41 Queen's Gate,
London.**

Tel: 0171 938 8905

The Joint Committee is dedicated to
promoting better conservation of
invertebrates in Britain and abroad, achieved
mainly through liaison with other bodies
and by survey of potentially threatened
species.

● Joint Nature Conservation Committee

**Monkstone House,
City Road,
Peterborough.
PE1 1JY.**

**Tel: 01733 62626
Fax: 01733 555948**

The Joint Committee is the statutory body
constituted by the *Environmental Protection
Act 1990* to be responsible for research and
advice on nature conservation at both UK
and international levels. It is established by
English Nature, Scottish Natural Heritage
and the Countryside Council for Wales,
together with independent members and
representatives from the Countryside
Commission and Northern Ireland. Enquiry
service available.

L

● Landscape Research Group

**Rolle Faculty of Arts and Education,
University of Plymouth,
Wandale House,
Douglas Avenue,
Exmouth.
Devon.
EX8 2AT.**

**Tel: 01395 255309
Fax: 01395 255303**

The Group's main aim is to advance
education and research and to encourage
interest and the exchange of information on
the subject of landscape in its widest sense.
It does this by: encouraging collaboration
and exchange between researchers and
practitioners; initiating research and seeking
out funding for projects. Referral service
available.

● **Libraries** SEE:
British Agricultural History Society
British Library Environmental Information
Service

Rural History Centre
Scottish Natural History Library
Society for the History of Natural History
(Scotland)

● **Lichens** SEE: British Lichen Society

● **Liverworts/Mosses** SEE: British
Bryological Society

● Long Distance Paths Advisory Service Limited

11 Cotswold Court,
Sandy Lane,
Chester.
CH3 5UZ.

The LDPAS provides advice to any
individual, organisation or corporate body
interested in the development or
management of new or existing long
distance paths and maintains a record of
such paths and a library of relevant
information.

M

● Mammal Society, The

15 Cloisters Business Centre,
8 Battersea Park Road,
London.
SW8 4BG.

Tel: 0171 498 4358
Fax: 0171 498 4459

The Society aims to promote interest in all
British mammals whether endangered or
common and undertakes scientific studies
and surveys. Enquiry service available.

● **Marine** SEE:
Advisory Committee on Protection of the
Sea
Aquatic Sciences and Fisheries Information
System
Association of Sea Fisheries Committees of
England
British Marine Life Study Society
Centre for Marine and Coastal Studies
Dunstaffnage Marine Laboratory
Institute of Estuarine and Coastal Studies
International Dolphin Watch
Marine Biological Association of the UK
Marine Conservation Society
Marine Forum for Environmental Issues
Marine Information and Advisory Service

Plymouth Marine Laboratory
Proudman Oceanographic Laboratory
Scottish Grey Seal Group
Sea Mammal Research Unit
Seal Preservation Group
Sir Alister Hardy Foundation for Ocean
Science
Whale and Dolphin Conservation Society

● Marine Biological Association of the UK

The Laboratory,
Citadel Hill,
Plymouth.
PL1 2PB.

Tel: 01752 222772
Fax: 01752 226865

The Association's aims are the promotion
of scientific research into all aspects of life in
the sea and the dissemination to the public
of the knowledge gained.

• Marine Conservation Society

**9 Gloucester Road,
Ross-on-Wye.
Herefordshire.
HR9 5BU.**

**Tel: 01989 566017
Fax: 01989 567815**

The main aim of the Society is to protect the marine environment for both wildlife and future generations by promoting its sustainable and environmentally sensitive management. Skills training offered to staff employed in coastal management, also consultancy service to councils and the commercial sector.

• Marine Forum for Environmental Issues

**c/o Department of Zoology,
The Natural History Museum,
Cromwell Road,
London.
SW7 5BD.**

**Tel: 0171 938 9114
Fax: 0171 938 9158**

The Forum is an umbrella organisation, one of whose main objectives is to improve communication on marine and coastal issues among all concerned with the coastal shelf seas, particularly the North Sea, Irish Sea and English Channel. It is open to all those with an interest in marine and coastal issues.

• Marine Information and Advisory Service

**Institute of Oceanographic Sciences,
Deacon Laboratory,
Wormley,
Godalming.
Surrey.
GU8 5UB.**

**Tel: 01428 684141
Fax: 01428 683066**

MIAS provides advice and data on sea waves, currents, tides, sea level and sea water characteristics. It is the point of contact for advice based on research in the fields of physical and chemical oceanography, marine geology and geophysics and deep ocean biology. Services include expert advice, provision of information drawn from a wide range of documentary and other sources for sea areas world-wide and provision of numerical data, data analyses and summaries. Enquiry and consultancy services available.

• Mineralogical Society

**41 Queen's Gate,
London.
SW7 5HR.**

**Tel: 0171 584 7516
Fax: 0171 823 8021**

The Society's aims are to advance the knowledge of mineralogy, crystallography, geochemistry and petrology. Referral service available.

● Ministry of Agriculture Fisheries and Food

**Room II,
3 Whitehall Place,
London.
SWIA 2HH.**

**Tel: 0171 270 3000
Fax: 0171 270 8125**

MAFF administers the Government's agriculture, horticulture and fisheries policies in England and has responsibilities for food, trade and animal health throughout the UK. The Ministry seeks to achieve a reasonable balance between the interests of agriculture, the economic and social interests of rural areas, the conservation of the countryside and the promotion of its enjoyment by the public. Enquiry service available (MAFF helpline - 01645 335577).

● Ministry of Defence Conservation Office

**Defence Lands Service
(Conservation),
Room B2/1,
Government Buildings,
Leatherhead Road,
Chessington.
Surrey.
KT9 2LU.**

**Tel: 0181 391 3028/9
Fax: 0181 391 3576**

The MoDCO was established with the aim of preserving and enhancing the conservation interest on the defence estate. A network of some 200 conservation groups have been established to record and monitor the distribution of species and to manage the estate, within the military framework.

● **Mosses/Liverworts** SEE: British Bryological Society

N

● National Birds of Prey Centre, The

**Newent.
Gloucestershire.
GL18 IJJ.**

Tel: 01531 820286

The Centre plays a leading role in the conservation and captive breeding of some 60 species of birds of prey. As it expands, so to does its programme of scientific research.

● National Caving Association

**Monomark House,
29 Old Gloucester Street,
London.
WCIN 3XX.**

The Association is a national federation of caving clubs, five regional caving councils and four specialist organisations. As the governing body for the sport, one of its major responsibilities is conservation through the auspices of the Conservation Officer and its Conservation and Access Committee. Activities include: the active promotion of cave conservation; production and distribution of literature; liaison with national Government and voluntary organisations, and support for the regional caving councils. Enquiry service and skills training offered.

National Council for the Conservation of Plants and Gardens

The Pines,
Wisley Garden,
Woking.
Surrey.
GU23 6QB.

Tel: 01483 211465
Fax: 01483 211750

The aims of the NCCPG are: to encourage the conservation of uncommon garden plants, valuable because of their aesthetic, historic, scientific and educational value; to list garden plants held in important collections and gardens; to encourage the widest possible cultivation of uncommon and endangered garden plants; to establish and support National Collections of specified genera, etc. Consultancy service available.

National Federation of Badger Groups

15 Cloisters Business Centre,
8 Battersea Park Road,
London.
SW8 4BG.

Tel: 0171 498 3220
Fax: 0171 498 4459

The aims of the Federation include: to promote measures which enhance the welfare, conservation and protection of badgers in the UK; help set up and support a network of local/county badger groups and provide an information and advice service for such groups (80 such groups are affiliated to the Federation). Enquiry service available.

National Rivers Authority

Rivers House,
Wareside Drive,
Aztec West,
Almondsbury,
Bristol.
BS12 4UD.

Tel: 0117 962 4400
Fax: 0117 962 4409

The NRA was established by the *Water Act 1989*, now the *Water Resources Act 1991*. The NRA's responsibilities include: the monitoring of water quality, the control of pollution and regulation of discharges; the management and safeguarding of water resources for public supply; the provision of effective flood defences; the maintenance, improvement and development of fisheries in inland waters; the continuing conservation of the water environment and its protection as an amenity and the promotion of recreational activities. The NRA has a wide ranging research and development programme to underpin all of its primary functions.

Regional headquarters:

Anglian: Kingfisher House, Goldhay Way, Orton Goldhay, Peterborough PE2 0ZR. Tel: 01733 371811.

Northumbria and Yorkshire: 21 Park Square South, Leeds. LS1 2QG. Tel: 0113 244 0191.

North West: Richard Fairclough House, Knutsford Road, Warrington. WA4 1HG. Tel: 01925 53999.

Severn Trent: Sapphire East, 550 Streetsbrook Road, Solihull. Birmingham. B91 1QT. Tel: 0121 711 2324.

Southern: Guildbourne House, Chatsworth Road, Worthing. West Sussex. BN11 1LD. Tel: 01903 820692.

South Western: Manley House, Kestrel Way, Exeter. EX2 7LQ. Tel: 01392 444000.

Thames: Kings Meadow House, Kings Meadow Road, Reading. RG1 8DQ. Tel: 01734 535000.

● National Small Woods Association

**Hall Farm House,
Preston Capes.
Northamptonshire.
NN11 3TA.**

**Tel: 01327 361387
Fax: 01327 361387**

The Association aims to promote the management, conservation and rehabilitation of small or neglected woods through: developing a network of small woodland managers and specialists, and providing a forum for the exchange of ideas; influencing policy and seeking new markets and better ways of adding value to produce from neglected woods. Enquiry service available, holds a register of practitioners.

● National Trust for Scotland

**5 Charlotte Square,
Edinburgh.
EH2 4DU.**

**Tel: 0131 226 5922
Fax: 0131 243 9501**

Owns or manages over 100 properties.

● National Trust, The

**36 Queen's Gate,
London.
SW1H 9AS.**

**Tel: 0171 222 9251
Fax: 0171 222 5097**

The National Trust is a charity, independent of Government. Since 1895 it has worked for the preservation of places of historic interest and natural beauty in England, Wales and Northern Ireland. It is Britain's biggest private landowner and the world's largest conservation organisation, with over two million members. There are sixteen regional offices - details from address above.

● Natural Environment Research Council

**Polaris House,
North Star Avenue,
Swindon.
Wiltshire.
SN2 1EU.**

**Tel: 01793 411500
Fax: 01793 411501**

NERC is a research body established by Royal Charter and is responsible for planning and encouraging research into the natural environment through its own institutes and by awarding grants and fellowships. The results of its fundamental research provide the basis for advice to Government, industry and public bodies.

● Natural History Societies

There are natural history societies working at local and county level throughout the UK. A limited information service to supply addresses and telephone numbers of societies is available from Department of

Library Services, The Natural History Museum, Cromwell Road, London. SW7 5BD. Tel: 0171 938 8743.

● **Newts** SEE: **Amphibians/Reptiles**

● Northern Ireland Biological and Earth Sciences Records Centre

**Sciences Division,
Ulster Museum,
Botanic Gardens,
Belfast.
BT9 5AB.**

**Tel: 01232 381251
Fax: 01232 665510**

The Centre maintains species' lists and other appropriate details for all sites of wildlife interest in NI.

● Northern Ireland Deer Society

**Mount Shalgus,
Randalstown.
BT41 3LE.**

Tel: 01849 472626 or 016487 63276

The aims of NIDS are: the conservation of deer and their habitat; research and education; food management and control of deer and the monitoring of legal protection for deer.

● Northern Ireland Environment Link

**47a Botanic Avenue,
Belfast.
BT7 1JL.**

**Tel: 01232 314944
Fax: 01232 311558**

NIEL acts as a forum for voluntary organisations concerned with conservation of the countryside, wildlife and the environment of NI. It acts as a link between members and the Government, provides information on environmental matters and promotes understanding through increasing public awareness.

● Northern Ireland Forest Service

**Room 38,
Dundonald House,
Upper Newtownards Road.
Belfast
BT4 3SB.**

**Tel: 01232 524471
Fax: 01232 525015**

The NIFS aims to create and manage a multiple use forest industry in NI.

● Northern Ireland Heritage Gardens Committee

**42 Osborne Park,
Belfast.
BT9 6JN.**

Tel: 01232 668817

The Committee fosters recognition and conservation of historic gardens and plant heritage in NI and promotes and facilitates research on the subject.

● Open Spaces Society

25a Bell Street,
Henley-on-Thames.
Oxfordshire.
RG9 2BA.

Tel: 01491 573535

The Society campaigns for stronger laws to protect common land, open spaces and rights of way and to secure legal access to all open country.

● Otter Trust

Earsham,
Near Bungay.
Suffolk.
NR35 2AF.

Tel: 01986 893470
Fax: 01986 893470

The Trust's aims are: to promote the conservation of otters; to maintain a collection of otters for research and education; to breed the European otter (*Lutra lutra*) for re-introduction; to promote and support field studies of otters in order to collect factual scientific data to help in their management and conservation.

P

● Plymouth Marine Laboratory

Prospect Place, West Hoe,
Plymouth.
Devon.
PL1 3DH.

Tel: 01752 222772
Fax: 01752 670637

The Laboratory is part of the Natural Environment Research Council (NERC) and studies the physics, chemistry and biology of marine and estuarine ecosystems, and the impact of human activities on them both geographically and globally.

● Prince of Wales' Committee

4th Floor,
Empire House,
Mount Stuart Square,
Cardiff.
CF1 6DN.

Tel: 01222 471121
Fax: 01222 482086

The Committee aims to encourage the development of practical projects which improve and monitor the quality of the environment, with the assistance of voluntary participation by the public, especially young people. Aims are achieved through a network of project officers working with voluntary and community groups. The Committee also runs an annual Prince of Wales' Award Scheme which recognises projects which have improved the Welsh environment or understanding of that environment.

● Proudman Oceanographic Laboratory

**Bidston Observatory,
Birkenhead.
Merseyside.
L43 7RA.**

**Tel: 0151 653 8633
Fax: 0151 653 6269**

The Laboratory mission includes strategic research in physical oceanography with special focus on shelf seas processes, global sea levels and tides. Enquiry service and consultancy available.

● Rare Breeds Survival Trust

**National Agricultural Centre,
Stoneleigh Park,
Kenilworth.
Warwickshire.
CV8 2LG.**

**Tel: 01203 696551
Fax: 01203 696706**

The Trust is a charity formed to maintain and increase populations of rare and endangered breeds of British farm livestock. Enquiry service and consultancy available.

● Red Deer Commission

**Knowsley,
82 Fairfield Road,
Inverness.
IV3 5LH.**

**Tel: 01463 231751
Fax: 01463 712931**

The Commission is a statutory body responsible for the conservation and control of red deer (Cervus elaphus) and sika deer (C. nippon) in Scotland and for monitoring populations of roe deer (Capreolus capreolous). It has a legal duty and full authority to prevent damage to agriculture and forestry interests and provides advice and information on the management of red, sika and roe deer, conducting research and publishing reports.

R

● Reforesting Scotland

**Bank Head Farm,
South Queens Ferry,
West Lothian.
EH30 9TF.**

**Tel: 0131 331 3915
Fax: 0131 331 3915**

Reforesting Scotland aims: to highlight the ecological and social consequences of deforestation in Scotland; to promote ecological restoration and rural development through reforestation; to develop and promote concepts of sustainable land-use.

● Reptile Protection Trust

**College Gates,
2 Deansway,
Worcester.
WR1 2JD.**

**Tel: 01483 417550
Fax: 01483 417550**

The Trust's prime objectives are the protection of reptiles and their natural habitats. In achievement of this the Trust conducts investigations into the problems of reptile welfare and conservation; maintains communication with influential organisations and individuals; funds non-harmful field and other research and undertakes educational activities, particularly publication. Consultancy and enquiry services available.

● **Reptiles/Amphibians** SEE:
Amphibians/Reptiles

● Royal Forestry Society of England Wales and Northern Ireland, The

102 High Street,
Tring.
Hertfordshire.
HP23 4AF.

Tel: 01442 822028
Fax: 01442 890395

The Society works to spread the knowledge of trees and forestry in this country and to encourage their positive management so that Britain's woodland and wildlife may be conserved, expanded and improved. Consultancy service available.

● Royal Scottish Forestry Society

62 Queen Street,
Edinburgh.
EH2 4NA.

Tel: 0131 225 8142
Fax: 0131 225 8142

The oldest constituted forest society in the English-speaking world. Its major aim is summed up as the advancement of forestry in all its numerous branches.

● **Royal Society for Nature Conservation** SEE: Wildlife Trusts, The

● Royal Society for the Protection of Birds

The Lodge,
Sandy.
Bedfordshire.
SG19 2DL.

Tel: 01767 680551
Fax: 01767 692365

The RSPB is the charity that takes action for wild birds and the environment. The Society: acquires land to create new nature reserves; improves land for wildlife; campaigns against adverse development and lobbies for new laws and policies to protect birds; advises landowners and planners by sharing experience and expertise; researches the needs of birds and protects breeding birds through wardening schemes and the application of wildlife law.

● Royal Society for the Protection of Birds (Scotland)

17 Regent Terrace,
Edinburgh.
EH7 5BN.

Tel: 0131 557 3136
Fax: 0131 557 6275

● Royal Society for the Protection of Birds (Wales)

Bryn Aderyn,
The Bank,
Newtown.
Powys.
SY16 2AB.

Tel: 01686 626678
Fax: 01686 626794

● Royal Society for the Protection of Birds (Northern Ireland)

**Belvoir Park Forest,
Belfast.
BT8 4QT.**

**Tel: 01232 491547
Fax: 01232 491669**

● Rural History Centre

**University of Reading,
Whiteknights,
P.O. Box 229,
Reading.
Berkshire.
RG6 2AG.**

**Tel: 01734 318660
Fax: 01734 314404**

The Centre is a national and international resource centre for research and information on the history of food, farming and the rural community from the earliest times to the present. The subject field is world-wide, but expertise is concentrated on the UK. The Centre also holds outstanding collections of archives, photographs, books and objects accumulated over forty years and representing the single largest collection of rural history material in the UK. A rural history database is under development. Enquiry service for commercial uses, also consultancy service available. Full range of reprographic services offered.

● Scottish Conservation Projects Trust, The

**Balallan House,
24 Allan Park,
Stirling.
FK8 2QG.**

**Tel: 01786 479697
Fax: 01786 465359**

The SCPT is the leading charity in Scotland involving people in improving the quality of the environment through practical conservation work. One of the most important aspects of its work is training in environmental skills and habitat management.

● Scottish Grey Seal Group

**10 Queensferry Street,
Edinburgh.
EH2 4PG.**

**Tel: 0131 225 6039
Fax: 0131 220 6377**

Established to promote the protection of the Scottish grey seal (*Halichoerus grypus*) population from culling.

R

• Scottish Inland Waterways Association

139 Old Dalkeith Road,
Edinburgh.
EH16 4SZ.

Tel: 0131 664 1070

Established like its Welsh and English counterparts to promote the restoration, use and development of inland waterways in Scotland for all commercial and recreational purposes.

• Scottish Native Woods Campaign

3 Kenmore Street,
Aberfeldy.
Perthshire.
PH15 2AW.

Tel: 01887 820392
Fax: 01887 820392

Much of Scotland was originally covered in native woodland, now reduced to 1% of land area much of which is under severe pressure. The organisation works in rural areas to conserve the many benefits of this unique resource through: establishing Local Woodland Projects with landowners to encourage appropriate management; advising on the establishment of tree nurseries; improving markets for native timber and advising Government agencies on policy in relation to native woodlands.

• Scottish Natural Heritage

12 Hope Terrace,
Edinburgh.
EH9 2AS.

Tel: 0131 447 4784
Fax: 0131 446 2477

SNH is a statutory body established by the *Natural Heritage (Scotland) Act 1991* and responsible to the Secretary of State for Scotland. It has taken over the powers and responsibilities of the Nature Conservancy Council for Scotland and the Countryside Commission for Scotland. Its statutory aims are to secure the conservation and enhancement of Scotland's natural heritage and to foster understanding and facilitate enjoyment of it. Among its specific functions are: designation and care for sites and areas for protecting habitats and wildlife (SSSIs, NNRs and National Scenic Areas); providing advice to Government and others and commissioning or supporting relevant research.

• Scottish Natural History Library

Foremount House,
Kilbarchan.
Renfrewshire.
PA10 2EZ.

Tel: 01505 702419

The SNHL was founded as an attempt to put together into one library everything which has been published on the natural history of Scotland in all its many forms - wildlife, botany, environment, geology, geography, agriculture, archaeology, etc. When complete, it will be transferred to the National Library of Scotland, where it will be maintained as the separate Natural History Section of the Scottish Science Reference Library. Items in the SNHL are for reference only.

Scottish Office Environment Department

**New St. Andrew's House,
Edinburgh.
EH1 3TG.**

**Tel: 0131 556 8400
Fax: 0131 244 4785**

The Department has environmental responsibilities which include the central administration of the town and country planning system, countryside conservation under the *Countryside (Scotland) Act 1967*, rural policy co-ordination and environmental protection and protection of ancient monuments. The Department is the parent body for Scottish Natural Heritage and Historic Scotland.

Scottish Ornithologists' Club

**21 Regent Terrace,
Edinburgh.
EH7 5BT.**

Tel: 0131 556 6042

The SOC was formed to encourage the study of ornithology in Scotland and to co-ordinate the activities of those engaged in research on Scottish birds and their conservation.

Scottish Scenic Trust

**Greenacres,
Logiealmond.
Perth.
PH1 3TQ.**

**Tel: 01738 880302
Fax: 01738 880416**

The Trust is dedicated to achieving better protection for Scotland's scenic beauty; it

acts as an independent watchdog, at the same time supporting environmentally sympathetic developments bringing jobs and income to local communities.

Scottish Tree Trust

**30 Edgemont Street,
Glasgow.
G41 3EL.**

**Tel: 0141 649 2462
Fax: 0141 884 6277**

Amongst the aims and activities of the Trust are: to raise funds to acquire land in Scotland for the purpose of creating native woodland; to involve young people in this process and to campaign for sensible policies regarding wildlife conservation.

Scottish Wild Land Group

**1/3 Kilgraston Court,
Edinburgh.
EH9 2ES.**

Tel: 0131 447 0853

The Group was set up to promote the conservation of wild land in Scotland by increasing the public's awareness of the pressures on such land and by pressing for conservation to be recognised as a worthy element in the national economy, compatible with appropriate development, long-term employment and the tourist industry.

• Scottish Wildlife and Countryside Link

P.O. Box 64,
Perth.
PH2 0TF.

Tel: 01738 630804
Fax: 01738 643290

SWCL is a forum for liaison for the wide range of voluntary nature conservation, landscape amenity and environmental protection groups in Scotland. It provides a networking opportunity for its member groups, helping them to share skills, expertise and information, improve communication with Government and play a fuller part in the debate on the future of Scotland's environment.

• Scottish Wildlife Trust

Cramond House,
Cramond Glebe Road,
Edinburgh.
EH4 6NS.

Tel: 0131 312 7765
Fax: 0131 312 8705

The Trust, which is affiliated to the RSNC Wildlife Trusts Partnership (see separate entry under Wildlife Trusts, The), acts for the RSNC in Scotland and was set up in response to an alarming decline in Scotland's wildlife and habitats. It seeks to attract the support of everyone interested in Scotland's wildlife and countryside heritage and aims to take such action as is necessary to halt the destruction of native wildlife and its habitats throughout Scotland. This it achieves through the creation and management of nature reserves; encouragement of public interest and provision of education and interpretation; advice to landowners; campaigning and conducting of survey.

• Sea Mammal Research Unit

c/o British Antarctic Survey,
High Cross,
Madingley Road,
Cambridge.
CB3 0ET.

Tel: 01223 311354
Fax: 01223 328927

SMRU is part of the Natural Environment Research Council (NERC) and provides advice to Government departments on the conservation and management of marine mammals. It has a special responsibility for seals because of the *Conservation of Seals Act 1970* which requires that NERC is consulted before licences to take these animals are granted. Referral and consultancy services available.

• Seal Preservation Group

The Green,
Scarton,
Longhope,
Stromness.
Orkney.
KW16 3PQ.

Tel: 01856 701441

The Group collects and collates information regarding all seals in British waters, and seeks to educate the general public about seals. Studies have recently started on other species of marine life and fish farms.

• **Seals** SEE:
Scottish Grey Seal Group
Sea Mammal Research Unit
Seal Preservation Group

● Seed Bank Exchange

Cowcombe Farm Herbs,
Gipsy Lane,
Chalford,
Stroud.
Gloucestershire.
GL6 8HP.

Tel: 01285 760544

The Exchange conserves and distributes British wild plants and herbs. The Exchange has built up into a thriving exchange group of people who use the Seed Bank to exchange or purchase samples of seed. A seed list is available to non-members, with a more comprehensive list to members. A consultancy and enquiry service is available.

● Silvanus Trust, The

Unit 4,
The National School,
St. Thomas Road,
Launceston.
Cornwall.
PL15 8BL.

Tel: 01566 772802
Fax: 01566 776969

The Trust, based in Cornwall and Devon, was created to halt the decline of broadleaved woodlands and to help landowners care for this rich heritage on a sustainable long-term basis. The Trust gives free advice to landowners supported financially through its trading company (Silvanus Skills Limited) which provides a full range of services and skills. Enquiry, skills training and consultancy services available.

● Sir Alister Hardy Foundation for Ocean Science

The Laboratory,
Citadel Hill,
Plymouth.
Devon.
PL1 2PB.

Tel: 01752 222772
Fax: 01752 226865

SAHFOS has been established to run the Continuous Plankton Recorder Survey, a long-term investigation (begun in 1931) of the distribution and abundance of plankton of the North Sea and North Atlantic. The Survey provides data which are used to describe and interpret geographical, seasonal and long-term changes in the plankton. Enquiry and consultancy services available.

● Society for the History of Natural History (Scotland)

Scottish Natural History Library,
Foremount House,
Kilbarchan.
Renfrewshire.
PA10 2EZ.

Tel: 015057 702419

This is the international organisation for the history and bibliography of natural history in all its forms. The national HQ is at the Natural History Museum.

• Soil Survey and Land Research Centre

**Silsoe Campus,
Silsoe.
Bedfordshire.
MK45 4DT.**

**Tel: 01525 860428
Fax: 01525 861147**

SSLRC provides a professional, high quality research, development and consultancy service in all aspects of land management, land-use planning and land policy development. Enquiry, skills training and consultancy services available. Publishes a wide range of soil maps and related or technical books.

• Speleological Union of Ireland

**c/o Drumbeggan Old School,
Monea.
BT74 8EU.**

The aims of the Union, amongst others, are: to promote and publish research in the study of caves in Ireland; to encourage co-operation amongst all cavers; to represent Irish caving interest at national and international level and to strive for the conservation of Irish caves.

T

• Timber Growers UK

**5 Dublin Street Lane South,
Edinburgh.
EH1 3PX.**

**Tel: 0131 557 0944
Fax: 0131 556 8726**

TGUK is the recognised body for Britain's private forestry owners. It works closely with the Forestry Commission and negotiates over forestry legislation and planning with central and local Government.

Toads SEE: **Amphibians/Reptiles**

• Tree Council

**35 Belgrave Square,
London.
SW1X 8QN.**

**Tel: 0171 235 8854
Fax: 0171 235 2023**

The Council promotes the improvement of the environment by the planting and conservation of trees and woods in town and country throughout the UK. It organises National Tree Week and the national Tree Warden Scheme and provides a forum for debate for organisations concerned with trees, together with advice on tree planting and management. Referral service available.

• Trees for Life

**The Park,
Findhorn Bay,
Forres.
Morayshire.
IV36 0TZ.**

**Tel: 01309 691292
Fax: 01309 691155**

Trees for Life aims to regenerate and restore the native Caledonian Forest by returning a large area of the north central Highlands to its naturally forested condition. Working primarily in the Glen Affric/Glen Cannich area TfL works in close co-operation with the Forestry Commission and other landowners, fencing areas for natural regeneration and planting native trees.

● Ulster Society for the Preservation of the Countryside

Peskett Centre,
2A Windsor Road,
Belfast.
BT9 7FQ.

Tel: 01232 381304

The USPC is a pressure group covering urban planning and countryside access and preservation, especially ASSIs and AONBs.

● Ulster Wildlife Trust

3 New Line,
Crossgar.
BT30 9EP.

Tel: 01396 830282
Fax: 01396 830888

The UWT was established to promote conservation of the wildlife and natural habitats of NI and is the largest conservation organisation based in and run solely from the province. It is part of the RSNC Wildlife Trusts Partnership (see separate entry under Wildlife Trusts, The).

U

● **Volunteers** SEE:

British Trust for Conservation Volunteers
Conservation Volunteers (Northern Ireland)
Scottish Conservation Projects Trust, The

V

● Welsh Historic Gardens Trust

Coed-y-Ffynnon,
Lampeter Velfrey.
Dyfed.
SA67 8UJ,

Tel: 01834 83396
Fax: 01834 83396

The Trust aims to encourage the appreciation of the garden heritage of Wales, including gardens, parks and designed landscapes; to develop a strategy for the identification, protection, conservation and, where practicable, restoration of threatened sites; to assist with practical and expert advice and with obtaining grant aid.

● Welsh Office

Cathays Park,
Cardiff.
CF1 3NQ.

Tel: 01222 825111
Fax: 01222 823036

The Welsh Office has overall responsibility for, amongst other things, the town and country planning system in Wales; countryside conservation and protection of the environment.

● Whale and Dolphin Conservation Society

P.O. Box 981,
Bath.
Avon.
BA1 2BT.

Tel: 01225 334511
Fax: 01225 480097

The aims of the society are to raise and maintain public awareness of the threats facing whales and dolphins throughout the world. Referral service available.

● Wild Flower Society

68 Outwoods Road,
Loughborough.
Leicestershire.
LE11 3LY.

Tel: 01509 215598

The WFS encourages a love of wildflowers among children and adults, leading them to a greater knowledge of field botany, and advances education in matters relating to the conservation of wildflowers and the countryside.

● Wildfowl and Wetlands Trust, The

Slimbridge,
Gloucestershire.
GL2 7BT.

Tel: 01453 890333
Fax: 01453 890827

The Trust works to save wetlands and conserve their wildlife through programmes of research, conservation and education. WWT has an international reputation for its research into wildfowl populations, behaviour and migration and particularly for

rearing and study of endangered species. Referral and consultancy services available.

● Wildlife and Countryside Link

246 Lavender Hill,
London.
SW11 1LJ.

The Link is the liaison body for all the major voluntary organisations in the UK concerned with the care and protection of wildlife and the countryside. Specialist working groups co-ordinate work on UK policy with respect to wildlife and habitat protection and countryside policy, particularly through meetings with Government.

● **Wildlife and Countryside Link (Northern Ireland)** SEE: Northern Ireland Environment Link

● **Wildlife and Countryside Link (Scotland)** SEE: Scottish Wildlife and Countryside Link

● Wildlife and Countryside Link (Wales)

Bryn Aderyn,
The Bank,
Newtown.
Powys.
SY16 2AB.

Tel: 01686 629194
Fax: c/o 01686 622339

● Wildlife Trusts, The

The Green,
Witham Park,
Waterside South,
Lincoln.
LN5 7JR.

Tel: 01522 544400
Fax: 01522 511616

The Wildlife Trusts exist to protect threatened wildlife. Their aim is to achieve a better future for wildlife by: protecting and enhancing wildlife and wildlife habitats; creating a greater appreciation and understanding of wildlife, wildlife habitats and their conservation; encouraging active participation by people of all ages and providing opportunities for all to enjoy wildlife. The Royal Society for Nature Conservation (RSNC) is the national association of The Wildlife Trusts - a nationwide network of local Trusts which work to protect wildlife in town and country which also incorporates the Urban Wildlife Groups. Referral service available.

wildlife value. The Trust raises money for woodland purchase, creation and management from its membership, from grant aid and from sponsorship. There are thirty regional offices - details from above address.

● Wildlife Trusts, The (Wales)

c/o Brecknock Wildlife Trust,
Lion House,
Lion Yard,
Brecon.
Powys.
LD3 7AY.

Tel: 01874 5708

Woodland SEE: **Forestry**

● Woodland Trust, The

Autumn Park,
Dysart Road,
Grantham.
Lincolnshire.
NG31 6LL.

Tel: 01476 74297
Fax: 01476 590808

The Trust is Britain's largest national conservation charity concerned solely with the conservation of Britain's native trees and woodlands. It currently owns 635 woods totalling over 8500ha in England, Scotland and Wales. Woods are acquired and then managed for their amenity, landscape and